DOG TRAINING
BY BASH

The Tried and True Techniques of
the Dog Trainer to the Stars

BASHKIM DIBRA
with Elizabeth Randolph

A SIGNET BOOK

SIGNET
Published by the Penguin Group
Penguin Books USA Inc., 375 Hudson Street,
New York, New York 10014, U.S.A.
Penguin Books Ltd, 27 Wrights Lane,
London W8 5TZ, England
Penguin Books Australia Ltd, Ringwood,
Victoria, Australia
Penguin Books Canada Ltd, 10 Alcorn Avenue,
Toronto, Ontario, Canada M4V 3B2
Penguin Books (N.Z.) Ltd, 182–190 Wairau Road,
Auckland 10, New Zealand

Penguin Books Ltd, Registered Offices:
Harmondsworth, Middlesex, England

Published by Signet, an imprint of Dutton Signet,
a division of Penguin Books USA Inc.
Previously published in a Dutton edition.

First Signet Printing, February, 1992
10   9

REGISTERED TRADEMARK—MARCA REGISTRADA

Printed in the United States of America

Bashkim Dibra is a world-famous animal trainer. His dogs have appeared in dozens of television commercials, including the classic Chuck Wagon dog food ads, and in many movies. His celebrity clients include La Toya Jackson, Mia Farrow, Martin Scorsese, Carly Simon, William Paley, Andy Warhol, and Henry Kissinger. He lives in New York City.

Elizabeth Randolph is a pet care columnist/editor for *Family Circle* magazine and has written numerous books on pet care. She makes her home in Mamaroneck, New York.

This book is dedicated to Mariah, the wolf,
who taught me so much.

CONTENTS

ACKNOWLEDGMENTS

Special thanks from Bash go to:

The many veterinarians and dog groomers, too numerous to list, who have referred clients to me over the years.

All of my wonderful clients whose dogs I have enjoyed working with.

My sister Hope for her patience and understanding.

My sister Meruet for her strength and sensitivity. She was always there when I needed her.

Thanks also to the following people:

Photographers Kitty Brown and Bruce Plotkin for the generous use of their pictures.

Mrs. Marlin Perkins for her help and support.

AKC librarians Roberta Vesley, director, and Cheryl Bailer for their time and interest.

Arthur Hettich for his patience, understanding, and editorial expertise.

And Michaela Hamilton, our editor, for all of the work she did to put this book together.

FOREWORD

WHO IS BASH DIBRA AND WHAT WILL HE TEACH YOU ABOUT TRAINING YOUR DOG?

Bash Dibra is a big, ebullient man with a warm smile, a gentle manner, and a lifelong affinity for dogs. When he was only three years old and fled with his family from Albania to a refugee camp in Yugoslavia, he made friends with the attack dogs that guarded the compound. Later, as the family traveled through Europe, Bash was able to work with master dog trainers, and he continued his work when he came to the United States. Then came the opportunity to raise and train a wolf, and through this experience Bash developed his unique methods of dog training.

Working with Bash is always an "up" experience. The core of his philosophy of training animals is always to be positive and upbeat, and it carries over into his attitude toward people. No matter how many fretful dogs or capricious owners he'd had to deal with in a week, he was always smiling and full of energy when he came to my house to work on this book. Many's the time we laughed and laughed as he bounced around my kitchen dangling a leash while he slapped his thigh and said "Heel" in loud, firm tones; or knelt on the floor, formed a hoop with his arms, and shouted "Hup" to an imaginary dog to encourage it to jump through. I often wondered what my housekeeper thought was going on!

During the course of our work, I went with Bash to a long-term-care facility for the elderly when he took his own two dogs, Goldie, a chihuahua and Kimberly, a Yorkie, for a pet-therapy visit. It was wonderful to watch him "work the room," stopping to put Goldie in one lady's lap, stooping down to listen to another person's story about her dog while he held Kimberly for her to pat, and then wheeling around to give Goldie to a white-haired man sitting in the corner in a wheelchair. Soon even the most withdrawn of the residents was smiling and talking. In the course of a half hour Bash interacted with everyone and made sure each person had the chance to pat or hold a dog. It was an unforgettable experience—I've never seen anyone have this kind of positive effect on a room full of people in such a short time.

WHAT MAKES BASH SO SPECIAL?

The majority of Bash's clients could choose any dog trainer they wished. Yet socialites, celebrities, executives, and members of the Fortune 500 all call Bash when they have a problem with their dogs. They consider him the "leader of the pack" of dog trainers.

Some of them say he has a special kinship with dogs and call him a magician. But although he likes to refer to making the "magic happen," his dog-training success entails no sleight-of-hand. His methods seem deceptively simple because they're based on an understanding of the nature of dogs, their ability to learn, the way they perceive the world around them and respond to stimuli, and their social structure. Bash translates these insights into practical applications. Much of Bash's understanding is based on his work with his wolf, Mariah.

BASH'S "SECRET" METHODS

Bash's approach to dog training contains many fresh insights and methods.

To begin with, Bash believes the key to successful dog training is to learn to think like a dog. How else can you understand what your dog is feeling, and make it clear what you want it to do? He'll tell you how to do this and soon you will realize how to make your dog understand you. He often verbalizes a dog's thoughts—"Oh, that's what he wants" or "What's he looking at me like that for?" Although this seems to smack of anthropomorphism, Bash in fact is taking the viewpoint of a *dog,* not a person. He'll tell you how to use the social pack behaviors common to wolves and dogs, such as body language and facial expressions, to communicate with your dog.

In this age of instant gratification, Bash stands out. He strongly believes there are no shortcuts in dog training. He refuses to use what he calls a "Band-Aid" approach—one that only covers a problem on the surface without getting to the root of it and solving it. Each of his carefully thought-out steps in training or problem-solving builds on the previous step. His successful results are accomplished with what Bash calls the "three P's": patience, persistence, and praise.

Bash has devised a number of special techniques to help you train your dog. For example, he'll show you how to pat your dog in a positive, meaningful way, and how to get your dog's attention and make it focus on you.

He's worked out a foolproof way to test a puppy's temperament so you can choose a dog you can live with, and he'll tell you how to form a bond with your new pet and assume a leadership role with it.

His special techniques for dealing with serious dog-behavior problems sometimes involve using what he calls a "set-up" situation that clearly shows a dog what *not* to do—deprogramming the bad behavior and re-programming a desired one. He likens this to putting data into a computer. These techniques and many more will help you deal with almost any dog behavior problem you might have, from a housebreaking lapse to an overly aggressive dog.

Once you've solved your dog's everyday problems and trained it to be in complete harmony with you, you may want to build on your success and teach your pet to become a star performer or a stellar watchdog. Bash will show you how to do these things, too.

No matter what kind of dog you have or what kind of training you want for it, Bash's techniques will show you how to "make the magic happen" with your dog.

—ELIZABETH RANDOLPH

1

WHAT MARIAH, THE WOLF, TAUGHT ME ABOUT DOGS

I had been a dog trainer for many years when I was offered a once-in-a-lifetime opportunity to raise and train a wolf. My work with this beautiful timber wolf, whom I named Mariah, helped me understand more about dogs, what makes them "tick" and how to train them, than any other experience in my life.

Although a wolf's senses and reactions are basically the same as those of a domestic dog, they're much more intense. Everything dogs do, wolves do in a more elaborate way. As I got to know her well, I realized that Mariah's physique and nature were as if all of the different kinds of dogs in the world had been rolled into one animal. Over the centuries, people have bred dogs selectively for specific purposes: for hunting by sight and scent, for guarding and protecting, for herding and strength, for speed and gentleness, and for companionship and affection. The resulting dogs have developed particular natures, temperaments, and physical characteristics to meet these purposes better. But a wolf is the essence of all of these dogs—a "dog in the raw," if you will, possessing in the highest degree each of the keen senses, instincts, and behaviors that every breed of dog has.

Because of this I had to work very hard and think through all of my actions clearly when I trained Mariah. She became my teacher as well as my pupil.

The insights I gained into dog behavior and the techniques I developed working with Mariah are the keys to my great success training the dogs of celebrities, teaching dogs to become starring performers, and in all my other work with dogs.

Mariah showed me how to understand all dogs and how to be able to speak with them in their own language. She changed my training techniques forever. What Mariah "taught" *me* will help *you* succeed in training your dog, too. I will refer to each of the following "keys," or elements, of canine behavior repeatedly throughout this book. They form the basis of my dog-training philosophy.

SEVEN KEYS TO UNDERSTANDING DOG BEHAVIOR

To work with your own dog successfully and be able to modify its behavior in a positive manner, you'll need to understand why it acts the way it does. Basic to this understanding is the fact that domestic dogs, like wolves, are pack animals by nature and all of their behavior is actually based on various aspects of pack structure and instinctive pack mentality. Even though they have been domesticated for centuries, dogs still remain wolves "under the skin."

■ PACK BEHAVIOR ■

Every dog's actions and reactions are deeply rooted in the highly social pack behavior shared with their ancestors, wolves. The relationships within a wolf pack can explain a lot of the things dogs do. Once you understand pack behavior you'll recognize the need to bond early with your dog and become its leader.

A wolf pack is a hierarchy. It's divided into layers, or levels, of dominance. At the top is the Alpha pair, the dominant male and female. Other females and sometimes young males are beneath them, and adolescents and cubs are at the bottom. All of the lesser animals are submissive to the Alpha pair; each individual in a lower level is in turn submissive to those in the levels above it.

This highly complex social order results in a strong familial sense and bonding between individuals in the pack. For protection, hunting cooperation, the raising of young, and company, wolves stick together. A wolf that is suddenly removed from its pack will suffer greatly from the separation. It will be lonely, confused, and all at sea—a condition referred to by behaviorists as "separation anxiety." Because domestic dogs are also bonding pack animals, they often suffer from separation anxiety when owners (their pack members) are away, even for a short period of time. A great deal of what is perceived as "bad" behavior can be traced to this. Once you understand the cause of your dog's destructive or otherwise antisocial behavior when it's left alone, you will be able to deal with it intelligently.

When you take a puppy or dog away from its family, or pack, to live with you, you replace that family and automatically become a member of your dog's "pack," and it is vital for you to assume the Alpha position in your dog's eyes immediately. Not only does your dog need your leadership in order to be secure and relaxed in the society of your home, but unless you seize this leadership (Alpha) role early in your relationship, you will have a constant battle with your dog for dominance.

You must also nurture your dog's trust in you at the same time you establish your authority. Just as an older wolf in the pack treats the younger, more subordinate members with firm, consistent, affectionate leadership, *you should become the kind, strong, uncompromising*

Alpha leader your dog needs to look up to and please. I like to call this combined approach "tough love."

◼ DOMINANT/SUBORDINANT BEHAVIOR ◼

This brings me to the second most important aspect of pack social structure that affects you and your dog— the constant struggle for dominance within the pack. Each of the Alpha animals can be challenged at any time by a lower-level individual; should that lower-level animal succeed in the challenge, it will then become the Alpha animal until it is successfully challenged, and so on.

Because of this constant struggle for dominance, every wolf or dog is naturally either a leader or a follower at every stage in its life. Unless you want your dog to run you and your household, this means you will have to continuously reinforce the leadership role you have established and allow no breach of your authority, or your dog will perceive that you are unsure of yourself and ripe for overthrowing. Some dogs will naturally challenge your leadership regularly. With individuals such as this, your reactions must be immediate and clear. Once you allow a dog to get away with a challenge, you'll have relinquished your leadership role and will have to go back to square one to establish your authority all over again.

Wolves and dogs use an elaborate system of body language, facial expressions, and vocalization to communicate and to indicate levels of submission and dominance within the pack. If you can learn to emulate some of these signals, you can communicate better with all dogs. For example, a submissive wolf always lowers itself in the presence of a more dominant animal. If you're aware of this you will *never crouch down when you meet a strange dog, because this lowering action will appear to the dog to be a submissive action. The dog may then try to dominate you by showing aggression.*

■ AGGRESSIVE BEHAVIOR ■

There are basically four different kinds of aggression within the structure of a wolf pack, all of which can be exhibited by domestic dogs. First of all, aggression is a natural component of the struggle for dominance in the pack. In order to overthrow a more dominant wolf, for instance, a subordinate animal must act in an aggressive way. At the same time, the dominant animal has to be aggressive to retain its position. Aggression can also stem from an animal's need to protect its territory—its family and its living area. And, it can be the result of the natural food-guarding instinct I'll discuss below. An animal can also become aggressive when it's fearful. Even a submissive dog or wolf may act aggressively when it feels cornered. In the wild, aggression is a necessary tool for survival.

But in normal human society it is not desirable or acceptable for a dog to display aggression toward either people or other animals.

Some dogs are naturally more aggressive than others, either because of their individual personalities or because of inbred characteristics. Others can be made aggressive by poor handling and training.

It is especially important to develop and retain a strong leadership position if your dog is naturally dominant, territorial, or possessive. For your own safety and that of other people you must squelch any sign of aggression in a dog immediately. As the strong leader of your dog's pack, you have to show it you will not tolerate any aggressive actions on its part.

But at the same time you have to be careful never to hit or threaten a highly dominant animal. A dominant dog will interpret this type of action as a challenge and will feel it has been given license to try to overthrow your authority. You must show your displeasure in non-challenging ways your dog can understand, just as another dog might—by scolding it firmly and using body language and vocal signals so the dog can interpret your meaning.

A strong, loving pack leader will never allow another animal to act in a way that might harm the welfare of itself or others. This is what you must bear in mind when dealing with a dog that shows signs of aggressive behavior.

That's why it's so important to retain your leadership role with your dog at all times. In your household "pack," *you must never allow your dog to get away with challenging your authority*.

■ TERRITORIAL BEHAVIOR ■

Another important aspect of pack life is the need to define and protect territory, or space for living, rearing young, and hunting. In the wild, each wolf pack must establish its own territory.

An outgrowth of this is scent marking, a device dogs share with wolves, in which a scent is left to communicate with other animals. In the wild, male wolves scent mark their territory on a regular basis with urine, feces, and the discharge from scent glands, located in various parts of the body. Anal glands, found on either side of the rectum, add to the scent when an individual defecates. Wolves, wild dogs, and feral dogs can also empty these glands at will when they are extremely frightened and want to signal complete submission. The resulting disgusting odor will usually ensure that the animal is left alone. These glands aren't needed by domestic dogs, and they sometimes become impacted and must be emptied by a veterinarian. Females also indulge in marking behavior to a lesser degree.

As wolves travel around their territory, previously laid scents provide them with a detailed set of clues. They can immediately tell which individuals have been there before and in what direction other pack members have traveled. They can also detect the presence of a stranger that may have intruded within their borders.

Male dogs do the same thing, raising their legs on every surface within reach, often to the annoyance of their owners. Females also mark their territories from time to time. This can be an especially bad problem if a dog hasn't been properly housebroken and feels the need to mark indoors.

Both males and females also scratch a surface repeatedly with their feet after they've urinated or defecated, digging up lawns and flower beds. That's because there are scent glands located between their foot pads. Understanding this won't lessen the damage, but it will at least explain the habit—dogs aren't scratching just to be perverse. It's an instinctive habit, based on the need to mark off a dog's territory.

Another instinctive habit wolves and dogs share is that of rolling in particularly smelly things—rotted carrion, dead fish, and so forth. This habit is not clearly understood, but the assumption is that the animal finds this a good way of enhancing its natural body odors in order to make its smell even more pungent and recognizable to others as it moves around its territory.

Dogs, like wolves, leave scents so other dogs will smell them and read their messages. An owner may be annoyed when his pet persists in straining at a leash in order to sniff every nook and cranny as they walk down the street. I often see someone tugging and tugging at a dog that's clearly immersed in a particularly intriguing odor. The dog will smell and smell and then leave its own mark—again a clearly instinctive territorial signal.

One more adjunct of the importance of scent in territorial marking is the need dogs have to clearly identify other animals by smell. Sometimes dogs embarrass their owners when they insist on sniffing at the crotches of human visitors. (This behavior should be corrected.) And, of course, the first greeting ritual between dogs when they meet is a thorough going-over by nose, with particular attention paid to "private parts." Dog owners should realize that this is neither perverse nor disgusting, but stems from instinctive territorial marking behavior.

Within the pack, too, each individual animal may indulge in territorial guarding behavior. A mother wolf, for instance, will protect her den from all unwelcome visitors, and a male or female will fight any other animal that pays too much attention to a mate.

Some dogs are highly territorial by nature. And, although it may be desirable for a pet dog to protect its property (your property) against strangers, care must be taken not to allow a dog to become overprotective of places or objects it perceives as its own. *A dog that's allowed to become too territorial is a dog that may resort to aggression to protect its property.*

▪ FOOD-GUARDING BEHAVIOR ▪

Food guarding is, of course, an inborn self-protective reaction of any wild animal, and especially a wolf. From a very early age, a young wolf has to guard its food from everyone, even its littermates, until it has eaten its fill—or else it will soon go hungry. In situations where there's not enough food to go around, the strongest pack members will survive and probably be able to establish a new pack eventually.

Food guarding is a strong instinctive canine behavior, and many dogs, especially highly territorial individuals, are instinctively protective of their food. It's very important for you to understand this behavior and not allow your puppy to grow up into a dog that won't allow anyone near its food or food bowl. This can be a very dangerous trait and can lead to major problems if a visitor to your home, or a child, should inadvertently approach your dog while it's eating. *You should begin to control this behavior from the very beginning of your life with your dog.*

▪ FLIGHT AND CHASE BEHAVIOR ▪

Both of these instinctive canine behaviors are necessary for survival in the wild and are triggered by a wolf's or dog's highly developed peripheral vision and perception of even the slightest motion. In each case there is an automatic, instinctive, impulsive rush either toward or away from the triggering object.

Flight behavior is the instinctive desire to get as far away as fast as possible from a threat, rather than stand and fight. A wolf that's been defeated in a dominance battle will immediately take to its heels, just as a stray dog will run from the dogcatcher, a puppy or dog will bolt at the sound of a loud, sharp noise, or a gentle dog will run from an aggressively attacking animal.

Chase behavior goes hand in hand with flight behavior. It is the instinct to rush at and chase anything that moves or runs. If it were not for this triggerlike reaction, many a wolf would go hungry in the wild. Dogs will often indulge in heedless chase behavior when they see a squirrel playing in the park, or the neighbor's cat walking in the next yard. In some breeds, such as sight hounds (greyhounds, for example), this chase behavior has become highly developed.

Once the chase has succeeded, a wolf will nip at the heels of a large prey animal in an effort to stop it or herd it away from other animals. This instinctive action has been cultivated in herding dogs. Owners of Welsh corgis and Bouviers des Flandres, for instance, are often made uncomfortably aware of this trait when their pet tries to "herd" them or their visitors with insistent, sometimes painful, heel-nipping.

A dog in the throes of either headlong flight or chase behavior is usually completely immersed in its actions to the extent that it won't even hear you if you call it to stop—a potentially very dangerous situation. You must be aware of the strength of these instinctive kinds of behavior and be prepared to anticipate your dog's actions, capture its attention immediately, and *bring it under control if it starts to bolt, either in flight or to give chase.*

■ VOCALIZING BEHAVIOR ■

When a wolf pack is scattered, individuals often call to each other to maintain contact. They communicate with a number of sounds and variations on the same sound. Their keen hearing and direction sense allow them to interpret each other's vocalizations correctly and know just where and how far away each vocalizer is.

Howling is, of course, the sound most often associated with wolves. Many domestic dogs also howl, especially huskies and malamutes—breeds that are closely related to wolves. The baying of hounds is a variation of howling. Howling is thought to communicate a wide variety of messages from loneliness to fear to just plain good spirits. It serves variously as a call to assembly, a warning, a "here I am" signal, and a greeting. When they are together, all the wolves in a pack often join in a chorus of spontaneous howling.

Wolves also whine and squeak to communicate when they are young. But, unlike dogs, adult wolves rarely whine unless they're hurt or very excited. Dogs seem to have learned that whining will often get their owners' attention, and some become annoying whiners—alternating whines with high-pitched barks when they want something.

Repeated barking is seldom indulged in by wolves. When they do bark at a stranger they usually only bark once or twice to communicate a greeting or a warning. Over the centuries, domestic dogs have been urged to bark by their owners—as a warning and protective device.

Whatever form it takes, the need to communicate vocally is an instinctive canine behavior that dog owners often must learn how to control. *Excessive barking can become a behavior problem with puppies and dogs, especially when they're left alone.*

Throughout this book, I'll tell you how to use these insights into canine behavior to communicate with and train your dog, and I'll teach you the techniques I have developed to help you work with your dog.

But first, let me tell you about my life with Mariah.

HOW I GOT MARIAH

I was hired to provide a wolf for a television show, *The Boy Who Cried Wolf*, a pilot for a funded educational children's series. The show's producers wanted a real wolf to costar in the program. They felt that not even a "wolfish" German shepherd would have the truly wolf-like look and demeanor they required.

The wolf I trained would have to be able to follow commands—enter the set on cue, stand in place, and leave at an appropriate signal, for instance. The wolf also had to be reliable and safe. This was of prime importance because it was going to work in an enclosed studio surrounded by dozens of strange people and a great deal of frightening equipment. Despite their reputation, wolves are extremely timid and instinctively avoid contact with humans, and no wolf in existence could meet these criteria. In the past, the few that had been successfully trained as pups had become nervous and unpredictable when they became adults. I had to come up with a "first." It was quite a challenge, but I was really excited at the prospect of working with a wolf.

The sponsors of the show arranged for me to go to Maine, where a group of biologists and animal trainers were breeding wolves in captivity for several purposes: Some animals were to be reintroduced into the wild to replenish depleted populations; some were going to be used for educational purposes, to restock zoos and wildlife parks; others were bred primarily for theatrical work.

Because wolves can be so difficult to work with I wanted to choose "my" wolf very carefully. The cub I chose would have to have a temperament that would allow me to train it. It had to be very young so it would imprint, or bond, with me from the very beginning of its life. Although I knew how important it is for a wolf cub (or puppy) to spend sufficient time with its mother and litter mates to develop socially and behaviorally, in this case *I* wanted to be the cub's entire family. Because of my long experience as a dog trainer, I felt I had the knowledge and ability to fulfill that role.

I knew I wanted a female cub. In my work with dogs, I'd found that males of any breed are always more aggressive and dominant than females. This is especially true of wolves because of the pack hierarchy in which a male must constantly fight in order to retain his number-one, or Alpha, position. A female cub would be easier to work with and socialize. I didn't want to have to fight a male's constant desire to dominate me.

To pick out a trainable cub, I watched the cubs interact with each other and observed each one's reactions to sudden noises and movements. Then I picked each one up and held it on its back. Finally, I chose Mariah. The behavior/temperament tests I developed to choose her can be used for any puppy or dog—I'll show you how in the next chapter.

Mariah remained with her wolf family for the first four weeks of her life and received a lot of handling and attention from her keepers—her mother was born in captivity and trusted her keepers. I visited her often.

■ EARLY DAYS WITH MARIAH ■

When I visited Mariah in Maine, I spent as much time as I could near her or with her. I bottle-fed her as she was beginning to be weaned, and once she was ready for solid food I prepared her meals and gave them to her in a bowl. Because wolves have such a deep affection and loyalty toward their families it can be extremely difficult for them to be separated from each other. I wanted her to imprint on me so she would consider me a member of her own family pack. If I could assume the role of a family member, Mariah wouldn't be traumatized when I took her away from her wolf family. She'd feel secure with me.

When she was a month old I took Mariah home with me. I kept her close to me as much as possible, and when I couldn't be with her I put her in a crate in the house so she would feel protected and safe, just as if she were in her own den.

I worked with Mariah constantly to accustom her to her new environment—to socialize her so she'd get used to normal household sights and sounds. Everything was new and potentially frightening to her—a ringing telephone or doorbell, the motor of a lawn mower or snowblower, loud footsteps. She also had to learn to negotiate stairs, doors that swung closed, and slippery floors—these were just a few of the things that startled, amazed, and confused her at first.

I developed a regular schedule for her activities—sleep, mealtimes, exercise, play, and so forth—so she would know what to expect, when. This made everyday training much easier for both of us.

At the same time I was socializing her to fit into the household and adapt to the needs of the resident humans and dogs (at the time I had ten dogs), I was careful to preserve her special, innate wolflike qualities—a certain wariness of expression, a way of walking, of observing the world, and of holding her head and body. I wanted to retain the wolf's particular behavior and manner so people would know they were looking at a wolf, not just a large dog.

But I soon found that even though I didn't want to squelch her wolflike behavior, I did have to learn how to control some of its antisocial aspects. For instance, I had to curb the extreme flight behavior that surfaced whenever she was confronted with unknown people or new experiences, and I needed to reprogram her aggression toward other animals. I wanted to allow her to remain a wolf and at the same time be able to live in our society. I was treading a very fine line!

When she'd been properly immunized and it was safe to take her out, we went for long walks to get her used to wearing a collar and leash. I also let her spend many hours outdoors in a safe, enclosed exercise pen. She loved to be outside—it was a more natural environment for her than the house.

I knew that wolf puppies were used to being with

other pups and playing with them all of their waking hours, so I gradually introduced Mariah to my dogs. It was wonderful to see her interact with them! Because wolf puppies are always subordinate to all of the adults in their pack, she immediately assumed an extreme submissive pose as soon as any of my dogs approached her, rolling over onto her back with her belly up. The dogs were all larger than she was then, but this soon changed.

My half-grown German shepherd, Orph (short for Orphan), became her special friend. He and Mariah seemed able to communicate with each other, perhaps because a shepherd's and a wolf's physique and temperament are closely related. Later on, I often took Orph with Mariah and me on training sessions because he seemed to calm her and give her confidence.

Once Mariah had been well socialized at home I needed to introduce her to the outside world. She had to get used to city sights, smells, and noises, because that's where she would be working. While we were working, people often stopped to ask what kind of dog Mariah was. I always hedged and said she was a "shepherd-mix." I was afraid if I told them she was a wolf it would create too much of a stir. I was also aware that they might become anxious around Mariah and convey their anxiety to her. I wanted her to be perfectly calm and relaxed around all people.

■ **MARIAH THE ACTRESS** ■

After many months of socialization and training outdoors, it was time to move Mariah indoors so she would be able to work in a studio. All animals, especially wild ones, are more at ease in an open area where they don't feel confined or trapped, and I knew the transition into an enclosed space would not be easy for Mariah.

I began slowly. When I was working in studios doing commercials and other jobs, I would take Mariah with me. After things were relatively calm—all set up for the shoot—I'd take Mariah out of her crate on a leash and we'd visit in the studio for a few minutes. I did this many, many times, until the sights and sounds of an indoor studio no longer fazed her at all. I also introduced her to all of the actors who were going to perform in the show. Although she would have no close physical contact with them during filming, I didn't want her to act skittish when they walked onto the set.

Finally, Mariah was ready for her debut as an actress. Her performance was wonderful. She played the role of a wolf magnificently. She came in on cue, stayed still for a while looking aloof and regal, and then moved away on signal so the cameras could record the whole thing. She amazed everyone on the set with her perfect manners and wonderfully quick responses to my every direction.

Then the film's underwriters, who actually owned Mariah, sat down with me to discuss her future. They hadn't figured out what to do with Mariah after they were finished with her. Although they meant well and wanted to do the right thing, they didn't understand the implications of taking a wild creature, taming and training it to trust people. They suggested we either turn her loose in the wild or donate her to a park or zoo.

I protested. I reminded them I'd worked with her for a full year and become very attached to her and she to me. Couldn't I keep her? They agreed.

■ MARIAH THE AMBASSADRESS ■

And so, for the next ten years, Mariah and I went on many trips around the United States to educate people about wolves. We visited malls, schools and universities, libraries, and so forth and met thousands of children and adults. Frequent appearances on the PBS television show *3-2-1 Contact* helped widen Mariah's audience.

The general public has many misconceptions about wolves and their nature that we helped to dispel. The fearful, rapacious "Big, Bad Wolf" depicted as a man-

(or pig-) eater in *Little Red Riding Hood* and *The Three Little Pigs* was seen in reality to be a beautiful, gentle, shy creature; one that is neither threatening nor dangerous unless driven to defend itself or a family member. Just one look into Mariah's lustrous amber-brown eyes convinced people that here was a wonderful creature, deserving of a peaceful place in the world.

During this time Dr. Marlin Perkins, creator and host of Mutual of Omaha's award-winning *Wild Kingdom,* the longest-running animal-related show on television, asked me to go on tour with Mariah to benefit the Wolf Canid Survival and Research Center, Wolf Sanctuary, in Eureka, Missouri, which he had founded. Because the wolves bred at the Sanctuary were slated for reentry into the wild, they couldn't be socialized with humans and weren't suitable as goodwill ambassadors for their species. So Mariah traveled around the country as their representative.

Mariah was also mascot of the 1984 Winter Olympics in Sarajevo, Yugoslavia. The Yugoslavian government had polled its citizens to find out what native animal would be the symbol for the games, and the wolf was chosen by a large majority. Wolves have always had a special place in Yugoslavian fables in which they represent courage and strength and symbolize winter.

Before her official naming as mascot, Mariah and I were invited to the Park Lane Hotel. This caused a lot of consternation among some city officials. They were afraid of what a wolf would do. But Mariah remained calm and majestic as she walked into a huge ballroom filled with representatives of the Yugoslavian government, the United States Winter Olympics Committee, the ABC Olympics broadcast team, and hundreds of TV cameras and press people with flash bulbs popping. Then and there she became the official symbol of the 1984 Winter Olympics, and we traveled to Sarajevo for the opening ceremonies.

In 1985, Marlin asked us to go to Washington, D.C., to represent the Wolf Sanctuary in the first annual Celebrity Dog Parade, given for the benefit of the Children's Museum. Dozens of members of Congress and the diplomatic corps came with their dogs. White House Press Secretary James ("The Bear") Brady was there. It was his first outing after being badly wounded in the Hinckley shooting of President Reagan. When he saw Mariah, Mr. Brady became really happy and excited. His family and doctors were so pleased with his response to Mariah that they decided on the spot that a dog would be a wonderful addition to his life, and soon after he became the owner of a Labrador retriever. What's more, his renewed interest in animals led to his ongoing participation in horseback-riding therapy, which has been very beneficial. I like to think his meeting with Mariah was instrumental in reawakening his childhood love for animals. This experience reconfirmed my life-long belief in the importance of animals to the well-being of people.

■ MARIAH IN RETIREMENT ■

Mariah was a real pro. I always felt she really enjoyed traveling and working with me. Because of her special qualities it seemed almost as if she had been born to do this work—to be a symbol of wolves in general and help contribute to the public understanding of these magnificent creatures and their place in the world. But after eleven years she was getting on in age, and I didn't want to stress her unduly. It was time for her to slow down and retire from active work.

So, reluctantly, I moved her to some property I own in upstate New York, where she lived in complete safety and comfort in a large fenced-in area. I visited her often and she was always delighted to see me.

On October 15, 1989, she died in her sleep of natural causes. I miss her. But I take comfort in knowing how much she enriched my life by teaching me about canine behavior—a lesson that I can share with other dog lovers through this book.

2

**HOW TO CHOOSE
A DOG**

One striking fact in my profession is how many of my clients, "baby boomers" who are now in their thirties, didn't grow up with dogs in their households. I'm not sure just why, but perhaps it's because both parents often worked and there was no time for a dog. Whatever the reason, many of the people I work with are first-time dog owners. Some of them are young professionals without children who want a dog in order to create an instant "family." Others, who do have children, want to provide their youngsters with the pet they themselves never had.

It's especially important for people who have no prior experience owning a dog to stop and think before they assume the responsibilities dog ownership involves.

The picture-book image of a contented, well-mannered animal stretched out at its master's feet, or the television scene of Lassie obediently fetching something for her TV owner, didn't come about overnight. That master spent many hours working with and training his dog so it became a good citizen, and Lassie's real owner/trainer, Rudd Weatherwax, spent much more time and effort training her (actually "she" was a "he") to obey his every off-camera command.

I like to compare raising a dog and making it into part of your family to raising a child, except it's much more concentrated in time. If you want your dog to be responsible and well behaved, you have to make a real commitment. I don't want to belabor the point, but if you're not willing or able to make that commitment, you should abandon the idea of dog ownership for now.

WHAT KIND OF DOG?

A majority of people choose a puppy or a dog on impulse. Of these, a few may be lucky and will end up with a dog that's just right—one that fits into their lives well, is responsive and easy to train and handle, and becomes a loving, companionable pet. The others will find out they've chosen wrong. Their dogs are either the wrong size and type for them—they're too big or too little; they shed too much; they're too noisy or not noisy enough; they're too delicate or too rough; too active or too lethargic. But, even more serious, these people often end up with a dog they aren't able to handle or train.

A person is then faced with a dilemma. If he's become fond of his pet, bad citizen that it is, he'll have to be willing to devote a great deal of time and work very hard in order to teach that dog to conform. If, on the other hand, he has neither the time nor skill to do this, he may finally have to admit defeat, get rid of the dog, and choose another kind of dog or type of pet.

This can be a very difficult decision. For most people a dog represents a considerable investment—not only in money, but in time and emotional involvement. It pays to investigate carefully before making a decision about dog ownership.

■ THE REAGANS' PROBLEM DOG ■

A good example of a dog that was unsuitable for its environment gained national attention.

When the Reagans were in the White House, they were given a Bouvier des Flandres. They named her Lucky, and Bob Maida, a Washington associate of mine, was hired to train her. Now, Bouvies are large, stubborn herding dogs that can't be trained properly unless their owners work closely with them. Right off the bat Bob realized that neither of the Reagans could do this, and they were soon having a lot of trouble with Lucky.

There was a great deal of press coverage about the Reagans' difficulty with the dog. There was even a segment on *20/20* in which Roger Caras, the dog expert, showed Lucky badgering both the President and Mrs. Reagan. She constantly jumped up on Nancy and spoiled her beautiful clothes and continuously "herded" President Reagan in a playful manner. When they were out on the lawn, she would nip at the President's heels and even draw blood.

The Reagans didn't know what to do. They loved the dog and didn't want to appear ungrateful, but they simply couldn't handle her at the White House. Moreover, she was too big and undisciplined to take along on a plane, even on short trips to Camp David.

One day Bob and I were talking about the problem, because the media seemed to be blowing it out of proportion. We agreed that the Reagans really shouldn't keep this dog in the White House. But since both of them wanted a dog with them in Washington, they needed a dog that would suit their lifestyle better. As for Lucky, they could send her to their ranch in Santa Barbara, California, where she'd have more room to roam.

In discussing what kind of dog would be suitable, Bob and I agreed that a calm, easy-to-handle lap dog would be a good choice. Of all these, a Cavalier King Charles spaniel seemed to fill the bill best. As soon as it was known the Reagans were looking for such a dog, Pat (Mrs. William F.) Buckley obtained a lovely male pup, Rex. He was easy to train and ended up traveling all over with the Reagans on Air Force One and even in the presidential helicopter, Marine One. Rex became very popular with children, and the Reagans used to send pictures of him, signed with a paw print, to young admirers. Lucky, by the way, is thriving on the ranch.

BREEDS OF DOGS

To make an intelligent choice of what kind of dog will fit into your particular lifestyle best, you need to know something about the outstanding characteristics of various breeds.

Often, a canine trait you might think is a behavior problem is, in fact, a perfectly natural action of a particular type of dog. Over the centuries, dogs have been bred selectively to perform particular tasks and to behave in special ways to meet their masters' needs. So it shouldn't surprise you when they still act in these ways. Depending on the kind of dog you get, you may have to learn to control or modify some of your dog's inbred characteristics. A retriever, for instance, that brings home all of the neighbors' newspapers is not being "bad," he is simply doing what comes naturally. Lucky, the Reagan's Bouvier, was acting in a way she had been bred to do when she "herded" the President by nipping his heels.

Some other generalizations about categories of dogs can be made. Working dogs—Akitas, malamutes, Doberman pinschers, rottweilers, to name a few—are not good pets for an inexperienced owner. Although they're calm and easygoing, they are also very stubborn and powerful. They have been bred to respect an authority figure and need a strong person to bond to or they will end up becoming dominant and pushing you around.

Terriers, too, even the smallest of them, are strong-willed and feisty and are apt to become dominant over their owners unless they're well trained early in life. Terriers, especially males, also tend to be extremely territorial, and often indulge in scent-marking and other territorially originated behavior.

Some highly active sporting dogs that can run for miles without tiring, most pointers and setters, for instance, are really not suitable for urban and/or apartment life. Others in the sporting dog category, like Clumber spaniels, do fine in a city setting with sufficient exercise.

Without getting into a discussion of every breed and category of dog, let me simply note that each differs in its behavioral characteristics and exercise and space needs. It's up to you to find out about the breed or breeds you may be considering. A general outline has been provided for you at the end of this chapter.

Physical characteristics are inbred and vary widely, too. More than just appearance—the size, the coat, and facial, tail, and ear conformation—affect the care requirements of each kind of dog. All dogs require some coat care, but those with long, fluffy coats such as collies, Shetland sheepdogs, Samoyeds, and Pekingese, for example, must be groomed on a daily basis to avoid matting and excessive shedding. Poodles and schnauzers need to be clipped or stripped regularly, while Boston terriers and whippets require little grooming.

Some very sweet dogs drool and slobber a lot—Newfoundlands and basset hounds among them. Others may snore loudly—the brachycephalic breeds (those with pushed-in faces) such as boxers and bulldogs are famous for this.

Almost more important to your future happiness as a dog owner is an awareness of hereditary, or genetic, problems that have been brought about in some breeds by close breeding. One of the saddest aspects of dog ownership is when a beloved pet suddenly develops a serious physical problem. Of course, this can't always be avoided, but if you know a certain breed has a propensity toward a particular disease or disorder, you can choose your pet more carefully. Some hereditary genes skip a generation, so it's always a good idea to ask about the medical history of a pup's grandparents as well as its parents.

For instance, because of their pushed-in faces and

protruding eyes, brachycephalic breeds are prone to nasal disease and eye problems; large-breed dogs, German shepherds and their relatives in particular, are given to congenital joint disorders, including hip dysplasia, many of which are incurable; congenital heart disease often plagues collies, poodles, and Pomeranians; toys are susceptible to tracheal collapse. This is just a small sample of the particular physical disorders some breeds are predisposed toward. Always talk to a veterinarian about possible genetic health problems before you decide on a particular breed of dog.

If you have no idea what kind of dog might be suitable for you, I suggest talking to dog owners—ask them to tell you all about their pets' characteristics and temperaments. Go to the park or local high school track—wherever dogs and their owners congregate. Talk to local veterinarians. Dog groomers are usually outspoken about their clients' temperaments. If at all possible, visit dog shows in your areas, or ask if you can sit in on an obedience class, and talk to local dog trainers. Most books about dogs, especially those about specific breeds, are apt to extol a dog's positive qualities, but sometimes you can read between the lines. I always recommend that people talk to as wide a selection of people as possible before making a decision—both professionals in the field of dog health and training, and individual dog owners. Base your choice of a particular kind of dog on knowledge, not impulse.

It's an excellent idea to make up your own checklist of the qualities you want in a dog so that you can weigh the attributes of different breeds against your "ideal" pet. I've made up a Sample Checklist for you, to be found on pages 25–26.

One further word of caution: Don't be lured into getting a currently popular breed of dog. The "dog of the year" is often overbred and undersocialized by breeders who hop onto the bandwagon and hope to make a fast buck. Even more important—just because a breed is popular doesn't make it the right kind of dog for you.

A classic example of this was a fashionable, wealthy Upper West Side New York couple I consulted with. They simply had to have an Akita because Akitas were *the* dog to own that year. This couple was childless, traveled a great deal, and left their growing Akita pup in the care of a number of different people. Akitas, though, require a strong hand and close bonding with their owners in order to become socially acceptable pets, and when the dog grew up, his owners suddenly realized he'd become stubborn and unmanageable. They expected a miracle cure from me, but they didn't have the time I told them they'd have to spend working with him to teach him to be responsive to them. In this case, I advised them to let me find the dog another home. With some relief they agreed, and I placed the dog with a man who works at home. In no time at all the dog and his new master were fast friends, and because the Akita was now bonded strongly to his owner, he soon changed his stubborn, antisocial ways and became a model pet.

If you must have that fashionable pet, be sure to research and choose wisely, or you may end up with a dog that is either temperamentally and physically unsound or one that is completely unsuitable for you and your family.

A GOOD SOURCE FOR YOUR DOG

Once you've decided on a breed or breeds of dog, you have to find a good source for your pet. There are no hard-and-fast rules about where to get a dog, and a knowledgeable person can probably select a satisfactory dog from almost anywhere. But if you're a first-time or inexperienced owner, you have to realize that all sources of your future dog are not equal.

SAMPLE CHECKLIST:
QUALITIES I WANT IN A DOG

Rate each quality on a scale of 1 to 10, 1—"not very important to me," 10—"very important to me." Once you've completed your rating you'll have a pretty clear picture of the kind of dog you want. Note: If yours is going to be a family pet, have each family member do a rating so you can reach a compromise, if necessary.

PHYSICAL APPEARANCE/QUALITIES

Size ____
    Giant ____ Large ____ Medium ____ Small ____ Tiny ____
Sex ____
    Male ____ Female ____
Color ____
Coat ____
    Thick, fluffy ____ Long, silky ____ Short, smooth ____
Ears ____
    Erect ____ Floppy ____
Tail ____
    Long ____ Short/cropped ____

PHYSICAL CARE REQUIRED

Stamina ____
    Sturdy, robust ____ Delicate, sensitive ____
    Primarily an outdoor dog ____ Primarily indoor ____
Coat care ____
    Easy/little care ____ Daily care ____ Regular professional care ____
Shedding ____
    Little, if any ____ Heavy seasonal shedding ____
    Heavy year-round shedding ____
Exercise ____
    Little ____ Moderate ____ Heavy daily ____
Space needs ____
    Little space needed/happy indoors ____
    Happy indoors with sufficient daily time outdoors ____
    Lots of space/happiest outdoors ____

BEHAVIOR/TEMPERAMENT

Activity level ____
Very calm ____ Calm indoors when properly exercised ____
Very active/lively ____
Playful ____
Vigorous, rough ____
Gentle, affectionate ____
Sociability level ____
Very good with children ____ Loves everyone ____
Reserved with strangers ____
Noise level ____
Quiet, rarely barks ____ Barks a lot ____
Good watchdog ____
Very intelligent, can learn tricks ____
Very loyal/obedient ____

OTHER QUALITIES YOU FEEL ARE IMPORTANT

∎ **PROFESSIONAL BREEDERS—GOOD MATCHMAKERS** ∎

The best source for a first dog is a reliable breeder. A
good breeder will not only provide you with the choice
of healthy, temperamentally sound puppies, but will
help you make an intelligent decision. It's in the best
interests of any professional breeder to maintain a good
reputation, and this can only be done by consistently
arranging successful pet-owner matchings.

There are good breeders of almost every kind of dog
all over the United States. The American Kennel Club
(AKC) can provide you with a list of breeders in your
area.* Often local veterinarians can be of help, or you
may be able to find a breed club in your area in the

* Write to: American Kennel Club, 51 Madison Avenue, New York,
NY 10010.

telephone book. Go to dog shows if you can. They are an excellent way to see different dog breeds in action and to contact a number of breeders. Individual owners can also be helpful. Don't be afraid to approach someone on the street or in a shopping mall if she has a dog you like. Almost any owner will be flattered and eager to tell you where she got her pet.

Once you locate a breeder or breeders, ask for references. Of course, you probably will be given the names of satisfied owners, but at least you'll be able to talk to someone who has obtained a pet from a particular breeder and will be able to find out what kind of puppies that breeder produces.

Sometimes the reverse is true. A client of mine had her heart set on a particular breed of dog. She located a nearby breeder and was given the name of an owner who lived in the same city. When she called, the dog owner proceeded to relate a long list of things that were wrong with her dog and with the breed in general. Needless to say, my client decided against that breed and chose another. In this case, checking turned out to be bad for the breeder but good for the potential dog owner.

Visit several breeders if you possibly can. This can be a problem if the breed of dog you're contemplating is rare and the only breeder, or breeders, is far away. In this case, at least try to see one or more of the breeder's dogs.

■ PRIVATE BREEDERS ■

There are essentially two types of nonprofessional, private breeders: "backyard" breeders, who have a litter of puppies either by design or by accident; and profit-motivated individuals who purposely breed a dog and have one or more litters of pups to sell. The latter are usually owners of a breed that's recently become especially fashionable. In both cases, the resulting puppies are almost always unsatisfactory.

Be very careful if you decide to adopt a free puppy from a neighborhood dog owner. Although the motives of backyard breeders are basically blameless, they often unwittingly create unsuitable puppies because they know nothing of genetics. Two German shepherds that both have recessive hip dysplasia genes, say, will probably have a litter of puppies all of which suffer from severe displaysia. In another instance, owners of a feisty little schnauzer female may decide to let their Schnapsie have a litter of puppies with the cute male schnauzer that lives down the street. They think Schnapsie is wonderful and don't mind if she barks furiously at everyone who even walks past their house. What they don't realize is that the cute male is also very territorial and somewhat aggressive. No matter how lovingly the resultant puppies are raised, they will have inherited a high level of aggression and territoriality and will never make good family pets. Be sure to follow the temperament testing steps I'll give you later in this chapter and have your new puppy checked by a veterinarian right away.

Those who breed at home for profit often have seen an easy way to make a quick buck and care nothing for either the puppies they produce or their subsequent owners. Again, a lack of knowledge about or, more likely, a disregard for, proper genetics can lead to impossible puppies.

Many years ago, a friend of mine wanted a beagle puppy. At that time beagles were all the rage and she had determined through reading that they were ideal pets for children. The family had just moved to the suburbs from the city and she was anxious to get a puppy right away for her six-year-old son. The child had never known a dog well and was somewhat fearful of all dogs—a situation my friend hoped to change by getting a puppy. She saw an ad in the paper for beagle puppies and the next Saturday the family went to a nearby town to see the pups. The puppies were adorable, and the little boy was enchanted with one in particular. The breeder assured my friend the pup's lineage was impeccable and that the "papers" would be sent along later as soon as they were processed. The family left clutching a squirming eight-week-old female puppy for which they had paid a hefty price. In the car they named her Tippy.

Their troubles began soon. The pup turned out to be very high-strung—not a typical beagle trait, they thought—and what's more she was very aggressive and territorial. Try as they might, they couldn't teach her not to steal every little thing, from a toy to a dropped earring, and carry it under the bed where she would protect "her" new possession, growling and snapping at anyone who approached. When they tried to call the breeder, they were told the telephone number was no longer in service, and, of course, no "papers" ever arrived! Being responsible people, they did their best to train the dog and teach her to respond to them, but soon they had to admit something was very wrong with her. What was worse, the child for whom they'd gotten the dog was terrified of her.

One day Tippy followed the boy to school. Shortly afterward the principal of the school called my friend. "Mrs. Jones," she said, "there's a loose dog here in the playground. Your son says she belongs to him, but I can't believe it because he seems to be afraid of her. If she's yours, please come and get her." Red-faced, she went to school and after a great deal of chasing Tippy around she finally got her into the car.

That was only the first of many embarrassing incidents in which Tippy proved to be not only disobedient and willful, but just plain obnoxious. Soon she also developed a number of serious physical problems, from severe epilepsy to kidney disease, that the veterinarian told her owners were inherited—due to bad breeding. Before she was four years old she died. Needless to say, my friend and her family were not terribly sad. Tippy was a typical example of the results of irresponsible breeding-for-profit.

Almost all of the puppies found in pet stores are also the product of profit-breeding. They begin their lives in what have been dubbed puppy mills—establishments that turn out hundreds of puppies a year as cheaply as possible. The operators of these establishments pay no attention to potential inherited physical or temperamental problems that might affect the pups, elements a responsible breeder would cull out of his stock. The puppies and their mothers are kept in the worst possible living conditions with only their most basic needs met. They are never handled or socialized—that would take too much time and be too much trouble. These places care only about making a profit selling pups to pet stores all over the country as if they were television sets. The problem is that, unlike television sets, there is no quality control or regular inspection of these animals—they bear no brand names and thus the people who produce them remain anonymous and without responsibility. The public has no redress; nor, in fact, do the pet stores.

Many infectious canine diseases have fairly long incubation periods, so the "guarantees" most pet stores offer to potential buyers may expire before a pup shows signs of illness. So you may be taking on what will prove to be a big headache with one of these puppies. Many people think that by buying a puppy from a pet store, they are rescuing the puppy. This may be true, but they are also encouraging the pet store owner to purchase more puppies from puppy mills.

One more word of caution. It's virtually impossible for even the most experienced dog handler to properly assess a puppy's temperament in a pet store setting. There's too much stimulation and confusion. A client of mine who's quite knowledgeable about dogs picked up a puppy that appealed to her in a pet store. Attempting to do a bit of Temperament Testing (page 37), she turned the pup on its back in her arms. The puppy didn't want to be held, snapped at her, and couldn't stay still, but my client thought this was just because of all the surrounding confusion, not because the puppy was aggressive. She decided to buy it. Much to her distress, when she got the puppy home it wouldn't allow anyone to touch it and turned out to be a serious biter. My client realized she didn't want to have to deal with this and, fortunately, was able to return the dog to the pet store.

If I seem to be painting too bleak a picture of pet store pups, it's because of the many, many experiences I've had with people who were conned into buying an adorable puppy from a pet store only to find they had also bought a number of problems that were very difficult to solve. Some of their stories are in this book.

A very clear example of this is another client of mine who has two chows. She bought one in a pet store and the other from a very good breeder. I was called in to help when she realized that the store-bought pup had serious problems.

There's no more adorable puppy than a fuzzy little chow, and she fell in love with a female chow pup in a pet store and bought it. Right from the beginning, the puppy was very fearful of everything. She was so intensely frightened that she was a fear-biter and was very aggressive with other dogs and even with her owners whenever they corrected her. They couldn't take her out for walks because she attacked every other dog in sight; they couldn't house-train her because she reacted so badly to discipline—in short, she was a mess. But they didn't realize just how bad she was until she was eleven months old.

At that time they thought maybe another puppy would help the first one to adjust better, and they decided to get another pup. This time they went to a good breeder. The second pup, a four-month-old male, was a complete contrast to the older animal. He exuded confidence and friendliness and loved everyone, including other dogs. When he walked into a room he seemed to be saying, "Hi, I'm cute. Want to hug me?" Even at his tender age, he was almost completely house-broken. The difference in the two pups was so striking the owners realized they needed help with the female. They were afraid her bad nature might somehow rub off on the little male.

I worked with them and showed them how to modify the female's behavior. With the use of a crate we were able to solve her housebreaking problems, and with much work the owners were finally able to assume an authority role with her. But because of her genetic aggression I made it clear to her owners that she could never be fully trusted, especially with children or strangers.

Because the two dogs were in the same household, they show clearly the difference between the kind of temperamental problems you can encounter in a badly bred puppy as opposed to one bred carefully from the best lines to have the best qualities.

▪ SHELTERS AND POUNDS ▪

I am all for rescuing unwanted animals from shelters and pounds. Many times you can get a really nice animal this way, but I must advise you to be very careful. Because you can know nothing of the animal's breeding or background you can't anticipate what you'll end up with and should be aware that you may have to work hard with your pet. If you really want to get a shelter pet, your best bet is to try to find a young puppy so you can work with it during its developmental stage.

▪ MIXED-BREED DOGS ▪

If you decide on a mixed-breed pup, it's a little bit like shooting dice—you're never quite sure what good and bad inherited qualities may surface. Many, many mixed-breed dogs are well-rounded, in good health, easygoing, and happy; able to adapt to any situation and great with children. Most will avoid the genetic health and temperament problems that can occur with too-close breeding. But if you decide on a mixed-breed pup you'll sacrifice the predictable behavior and mannerisms of a purebred dog. My strong suggestion to anyone contemplating adopting a mixed-breed pup is to be sure to begin professional training with the pup as soon as possible in order to mold it the way you want and help it learn to be a good citizen.

WHICH SEX?

I always tell people to try to choose a female puppy or dog. Females are more apt to be "homebodies"; that is, they adapt more readily to living with a family and are happy to be part of it. Although male dogs make wonderful pets, they often need more training and firmer discipline and direction than females do. Just as in a wolf pack, where the males are always more dominant than the females, many male dogs continuously battle for dominance with their owners. Even when a male dog accepts one or two adults as dominant over him, his inherent pack behavior often leads him to assume a dominance role with those he perceives as lesser pack members—the children in the family. This may not surface until a dog is four or five years old and reaches full sexual maturity. I've known several situations when this became a serious problem: a full-grown large male dog such as a Dane or Great Pyrenees decided to show his dominance over a child by mounting the youngster—a frightening experience for any child! This kind of behavior is especially common with many guarding-type dogs, working dogs, and terriers.

Not only are these male dogs more difficult to train, but because of a high hormonal level, unaltered males usually possess a strong tendency to be territorial and continuously indulge in scent-marking, both indoors and out. Roaming and aggressive behavior toward other male dogs can also become a problem with many of these males.

If you're not planning to breed your male dog, early

neutering usually offsets these problems to a large degree. It also prevents future medical problems such as testicular cancer. The operation is a simple one, and, contrary to the beliefs of some owners, a dog cannot reason and really doesn't know the difference. These days most veterinarians advise neutering all male pups that are to be household pets. However, despite all of the evidence that a neutered male is a happier, healthier, more compliant pet, there are still some owners (usually men) who refuse to have this operation performed. If you insist on having an intact (unneutered) male dog as a pet, you'll have to offset his sexual drives with a lot of work, serious training, and a great deal of exercise.

In addition to the problem of regular heat periods, unspayed female dogs also scent-mark with urine and can become territorial and snappish. But few people refuse to spay a female pup they're not going to breed. For many years this operation has been routinely performed for both health and hygiene reasons. That's one reason why females generally make better pets.

WHAT AGE TO ADOPT?

The majority of people who want a dog as a family pet choose a puppy rather than an adult animal. They feel raising a puppy is not only more fun but is educational if they have children. Most people also know that a puppy will become bonded to them more readily than an adult dog.

If you want a puppy, you should select one that's neither too young nor too old. The ideal age is somewhere between eight and twelve weeks old, after it's completely weaned and used to being away from its mother almost all the time.

A puppy that's adopted too young will miss a necessary developmental stage with its littermates. Even though a six-week-old puppy is usually weaned and can get along perfectly well without its mother from a physical standpoint, there are important elements of behavior that can be learned only through interaction with its siblings. During the period after weaning, puppies quickly become strong and physically coordinated. Through play and play-fighting with its brothers and sisters, each pup gradually develops its own personality and learns how to respond to others. Just as in a wolf pack, a hierarchy emerges within a litter of pups, and each individual eventually assumes a particular role. As I'll discuss later, in the section on Temperament Testing, the puppy that fits best into most family situations is one that evolves as a "middle-of-the-road" individual—neither too bossy nor too timid. Until a puppy is at least eight weeks old, though, it is impossible for you to assess its personality.

If, on the other hand, a pup is not adopted by the time it's three months old and is transferred to a pet shop, for example, it often develops traits that make it undesirable as a family pet. To begin with, gaining an older puppy's trust—bonding with it—is a great deal more difficult. Because it has been handled and tended to by a number of different people, it will be confused not only about bonding but also about following training directions. Dogs like this often seem to be almost retarded—unable to grasp even the rudiments of social behavior. Although it may seem timid at first, an older pup usually has already developed a strong territorial sense and often shows markedly aggressive guarding behavior toward spaces and objects. Little or no previous interaction with other living creatures naturally causes such a puppy to become unsociable. It is also quite fearful and suspicious because it hasn't become accustomed to normal household noises and activities.

An older puppy that's remained with its litter too long has many of the same problems bonding with people and may initially fight them and then identify with one person so strongly that it becomes literally a "one-man dog."

With an adult dog that's lived with another family—one that has been given to a shelter or pound, for instance—you may both be in for a difficult period of adjustment. To anyone considering ownership of an older puppy or dog, I strongly recommend that he immediately have the dog professionally trained in order to get over the rough spots as easily as possible. When an adult dog has already belonged to someone else, I feel this is a real necessity.

One final word about choosing an older dog: Sometimes a breeder may have kept a dog intending to show it. If the dog turns out not to be a suitable show dog when it reaches maturity, the breeder may be willing to sell it. This can work out very well for some people. A client of mine, a doctor who works in a home office, wanted a dog but didn't want to have to go through all of the initial training steps involved in small-puppy ownership. She contacted several good breeders and discovered one of them had just such a dog—a lovely golden retriever that had been raised in the breeder's own home and had already been socialized and obedience-trained. It turned out to be a perfect choice, and both owner and dog are extremely happy.

Beware, however, of a dog that's been sold and later returned to a breeder. Unless you really know the breeder well and are confident that she will be honest with you about the reasons for the previous owner's dissatisfaction, don't take a chance on a dog that may have been returned for serious negative reasons.

INITIAL IMPRESSIONS

When you go to select a dog, the first thing you should do is ask to see the mother of the litter you're considering. Their mother is probably the most important environmental influence pups have during their early weeks of life, and they are very sensitive to her reactions, which she communicates to them quickly and intensely. (This harks back to the wolf. A mother wolf has to be able to communicate swiftly and surely with her cubs. If there is danger, for example, they may not survive long if they can't respond fast.) If a mother dog is social and loving with people, wags joyfully when anyone approaches, and enjoys being petted, her puppies will learn to trust humans and look forward to contact with them from the very beginning. If, on the other hand, the mother of a litter is fearful of or completely indifferent to people, the puppies will learn a negative lesson about human contact from her. A friendly, wagging dam will give you pretty good assurance that her puppies will be sociable too.

Next, you'll want to look over the surroundings. Be a bit cautious if the puppies are brought out to you, away from the place where they are usually kept. Although there may be some good practical reason for not showing you their living quarters, it could be that their enclosure isn't large or clean enough. This in itself may not be a negative influence on a puppy's development, but it's sensible to be suspicious of a breeder who doesn't act responsibly when it comes to proper physical care and cleanliness—his irresponsibility may carry over into other important areas such as proper genetics and disease control.

You want to be sure the pups are outwardly in good health. Use your eyes and hands to check at least one pup's entire body. A healthy puppy should be solid and well-covered with flesh, though you should be able to feel its ribs. Its eyes, nose, ears, and anal opening should be clear and free from caked matter and any offensive odors. The inside of a healthy puppy's mouth is pink and its gums are firm. A shiny coat, firm pink skin, and foot pads with no blemishes or sores complete the picture of a healthy puppy.

Of course, a puppy can be harboring a disease or abnormal condition that cannot be detected immediately with the naked eye. A responsible breeder will always offer you the opportunity to take your new pup to your own veterinarian for a checkup—an important step that you should take right away.

TEMPERAMENT TESTING—MY SPECIAL WAY TO CHOOSE A WELL-ADJUSTED PUPPY

When you've made your decision about what kind of pup you want and have selected a breeder, then you must choose one puppy out of the litter. For those people who feel they aren't knowledgeable enough to make an intelligent decision, I have worked out several simple tests, based on my experience of choosing Mariah from a litter of wolf cubs. You can perform them yourself, and they'll immediately give you a good idea of the temperament of any puppy.

All you need is common sense when you use these techniques. As you do these tests, make a list of what's good and what's not, and weigh the pluses and minuses. If you still like a particular pup despite some minuses, then you'll have to accept the fact that you'll have to work a little harder in order to turn it into a satisfactory pet. Be aware right from the start that whatever is wrong won't get better as the pup gets older—it will only get worse unless you correct it. For example, a cowering pup won't become a confident adult just because you love it a lot—you'll have to work hard in order to gain its confidence.

If the breeder is annoyed when you ask to perform these tests, go to a different breeder. Any responsible breeder not only wants to place his dogs in the right homes but wants a new owner to be completely happy with his choice. And any good breeder knows his pups can pass a temperament test with flying colors!

▪ DOMINANT OR SUBMISSIVE? ▪

To be able to train a dog easily, you should choose a pup that's neither too dominant nor too submissive. A very dominant puppy will fight you all the way, while an extremely submissive pup is probably fearful and overly timid—a difficult combination of traits to work with. Don't fool yourself into thinking that a shy puppy is so sweet that it will be a joy to have around and a snap to train. Overly shy, fearful dogs are usually impossible to discipline at best and at worst often become fear-biters.

These simple tests will show you where a puppy falls in the "pecking order" of the litter.

First, observe the puppies as they interact within the litter (their "pack"). It will soon become apparent which pup is the dominant one and which one, if any, is submissive. Look for a puppy that holds its own in the group but doesn't bully its littermates.

An easy test to determine this is to toss something— a glove with your scent on it, for instance—into the pen with the pups. One puppy will inevitably grab it, another one may snatch it away, and the first one will growl and take it back. The puppy that finally wins the prize is the dominant animal in the litter. One puppy may be frightened of this strange object and immediately run away and cower in a corner. This pup is definitely one to avoid.

Even if you aren't able to observe a puppy interacting with its littermates, you can judge whether it is overly fearful. Take a small rubber ball and toss it. A well-balanced puppy will run after the ball, pick it up, and maybe play with it. One that runs away or shows no interest is not behaviorally sound.

Another easy, common-sense test of a puppy's stability is to make a loud noise and see how it reacts. Clap your hands loudly or throw a key ring onto the floor while the pup is doing something else, such as eating. A normal puppy will perk up its ears, look to see where the sound came from, and then go back to eating. An overly fearful animal will run away as if to say, "Oh, no, what was that? It's going to hurt me!" That pup will develop into a dog that spends most of its life crouching fearfully underneath the furniture.

Then pick up the puppy and turn it over onto its back in your arms. This is the submissive posture for canines, and you can tell a lot about a puppy by how it accepts this position. If it lies there comfortably and enjoys it when you stroke its tummy, it is an even-tempered animal that will readily accept the fact that you're dominant over it. What's more, it will like being handled and touched by family members.

As a further test, put your hand gently around its neck, just where its mother might put her mouth. If the puppy doesn't allow you to do this without growling and barking and struggling to get away, even nipping at your hand, it has a very high dominance tendency and will be difficult to work with.

If, on the other hand, the pup goes limp but acts terrified, shakes and whines, and recoils from your touch, it is probably an overly submissive, fearful puppy that will be difficult to handle because its fear of you will be so intense that it will blot out any other reactions.

A lot of experience, patience, and a great deal of time is necessary in order to train and socialize either a highly dominant or submissive puppy. If you opt to choose either kind of animal, you will have to make a commitment to seek out professional help because it will require a great deal more work than a well-adjusted puppy.

A REAL COMMITMENT TO YOUR DOG

Sometimes a person will choose a particular home in order to have a healthy and safe environment for the dogs she knows she wants to own. Other people are so committed to the well-being of dogs they already own that they are willing to adjust the environment to suit their pets.

Ana-Alicia, star of *Falcon Crest*, bought the home she now lives in partly because she knew that the surrounding property would be perfect for the pair of German shepherds she wanted. She asked me to help her choose the puppies and after a very careful search, I found two lovely, healthy eight-week-old puppies and sent them to her in Los Angeles so they could bond with her when she had time off from filming. Then, when the puppies were about six months old and Ana-Alicia had to go back to full-time work, she sent them back to New York so my sister and I could continue to work with them and give them some concentrated training. She was too busy filming *Falcon Crest* to do this.

After the dogs had finished their training my sister Meruet, who had worked with the dogs along with me so they would learn to obey a woman's commands, flew back to Los Angeles with them to help them settle in.

The dogs, a male named Helden (which means "Noble" in German) and a female, Ersehnen (which means "Longed-for" and "Dreamed-of"), soon became right at home. Ana-Alicia made them a bridge so they could reach the island in the center of the backyard pool and they learned to sunbathe on the island. She also bought a Jeep and had the back screened in just so that even with the top off she could safely take her dogs for rides to the beach and the mountains. The dogs are happy and they, in turn, fulfill Ana-Alicia's need to have two obedient, companionable, and loving dogs with her.

Another client of mine, Jack Dreyfus, of the Dreyfus Foundation, also made a real commitment to the well-being of his pets. He has a beautiful penthouse apartment in New York surrounded by a huge wraparound terrace. He also has three small dogs with which he was having a house-training problem. They didn't like pavement, and much preferred to "use" grass when the family went to the country on weekends. So when I went to the apartment, I jokingly said to Mr. Dreyfus, "Why don't you put some grass on the terrace for the dogs?"

The next week when I returned for a training session, I was amazed to see that part of the terrace was covered with new sod. Smiling at my astonishment, Mr. Dreyfus said, "If this is what the dogs really like, why shouldn't I provide them with it?" Now the animals are very happy with "their" grass and they don't need to be walked on the street anymore.

It makes much more sense, of course, to choose a breed of dog that will fit into your surroundings than to change the surroundings to suit a dog. Often, though, a minor change such as fencing in a yard or enclosing a porch may make all the difference to the contentment of a well-loved dog. That's what I mean by making a commitment to your pet—do everything in your power to help it be a good citizen and at the same time repay its devotion to you by making it as happy and comfortable as possible.

BREEDS OF DOG AND THEIR SALIENT CHARACTERISTICS, GROUPED ACCORDING TO AMERICAN KENNEL CLUB CLASSIFICATIONS

SPORTING DOGS

These are all bird dogs that hunt in different ways: by flushing birds out; finding and pointing to birds; retrieving birds. All have highly developed sight and smell, are hardy, and require a lot of daily exercise. Some are not happy kept indoors. In general, they are quiet and do not bark much.

Spaniels: Flush birds out of hiding on land.

American water spaniel

Brittany spaniel—also points—1.

Clumber spaniel—very docile and easygoing

Cocker spaniel—American—4., and English

English springer spaniel

Irish water spaniel—1.,5.

Others—

Pointer —5.

Setters:

English (Llewellin)—5.

Irish (Red)—long-lived—1.,4.,5.

Gordon—5.,6.

Retrievers: Water dogs.

Chesapeake Bay retriever—1.,2.,5.

Curly-coated retriever—1.,5.

Flat-coated retriever

Golden retriever—6.

Labrador retriever—5.,6.

Others (sometimes called European Utility Breeds): All aspects of hunting, on land and in water.

German shorthaired pointer—5.,6.

German wirehaired pointer—5.,6.

Vizsla—2.,5.

Weimaraner—1.,2.,5.

Wirehaired pointing griffon—5.,6.

Key:

1. Early socialization especially important.
2. Very easy upkeep.
3. Difficult/special coat care.
4. Often made unsound by poor breeding. Extreme care in selection recommended.
5. Requires a great deal of space/exercise.
6. Exceptionally good with children.*

* All breeds may be good with children they know or have been raised with.

HOUNDS

Hounds were bred to hunt mammals; they come in a wide range of sizes and body types, depending on the size of their intended quarry. Some breeds have exceptionally highly developed senses of sight or smell. All are hardy and have great stamina. Their space and exercise requirements are commensurate with their size. They are generally gentle and companionable. Many are noisy and may "bay."

Giant hounds: Very short-lived. Tremendous strength and stamina. Need lots of space.

Irish wolfhound—hunts by sight—5.,6.

Scottish deerhound—hunts by scent—1.,5.

Scenthounds: Both these breeds are easygoing and docile. They tend to drool a lot.

Basset hound—4.,5.

Bloodhound—1.,5.

Sighthounds: Also called gazehounds, they have a keen visual

sensitivity to movement, great speed and grace. Slim-bodied and
gentle.
Afghan—3.,4.
Borzoi (Russian wolfhound)—1.,5.
Greyhound—may be high-strung—2.,5.
Ibizan hound—shorthaired and wirehaired—2.,5.
Pharaoh hound—2.,5.
Saluki—very aloof—1.,5.
Whippet—long-lived; calm—2.,6. (gentle children)

Others:
Basenji—barkless—1.,2.
Beagle—may howl excessively—4.,6.
Black-and-tan coonhound—5.
Dachshund—1.,4.,6.—wirehaired, longhaired, smooth
Foxhound—American and English—1.,5.
Norwegian elkhound—1.
Otter hound—1.,5.
Rhodesian ridgeback—1.,5.

Key:
1. Early socialization especially important.
2. Very easy upkeep.
3. Difficult/special coat care.
4. Often made unsound by poor breeding. Extreme care in selection recommended.
5. Requires a great deal of space/exercise.
6. Exceptionally good with children.*

* All breeds may be good with children they know or have been raised with.

WORKING DOGS
A diverse group of dogs, developed as protectors of people and
property, working dogs are either large or giant in stature and are
strong and hardy. They have been bred to be territorial and aggressive with strangers, and all require a strong hand and early,
strong bonding and socialization in order to develop into the loyal
companions that they were born to be.
Draft dogs: Sled dogs, very strong and hardy. Also used for
guarding.

Alaskan malamute—heavy seasonal shedding—3.,5.

Bernese mountain dog—5.,6.

Samoyed—cheerful and easygoing—3.,6.

Siberian husky—heavy seasonal shedding—3.

Police, guard, and protection:

Boxer—short-lived; bred originally for bull-baiting—4.

Doberman pinscher—long-lived; aggressive toward other dogs—4.

Great Pyrenees—giant dog; short-lived; drools—5.

Rottweiler—5.

Schnauzers—giant—5., and standard

Rescue: Strong, very hardy, large to giant. Easygoing.

Newfoundland—short-lived; drools a lot—5.,6.

Saint Bernard—short-lived—4.,5.

Other:

Akita—1.,4.

Bullmastiff—originally bred as an attack dog—5.

Great Dane—giant; short-lived; originally bred to go to war—5.

Komondor—5.

Kuvasz—5.

Mastiff—originally bred as a fighting dog—5.

Portugese water dog—6.

Key:

1. Early socialization especially important for ALL DOGS IN THIS CLASS.
2. Very easy upkeep.
3. Difficult/special coat care.
4. Often made unsound by poor breeding. Extreme care in selection recommended.
5. Requires a great deal of space/exercise.
6. Exceptionally good with children.*

* All breeds may be good with children they know or have been raised with.

TERRIERS

All terriers, too, should be socialized early in life. Bred to be persistent, courageous, hardy, and feisty, they are territorial and aggressive by nature. Long-legged terriers were originally bred to dig for game, while the short-legged animals were trained to go into dens and burrows after small prey. Most are adaptable to city life, although all like a lot of exercise. Terriers usually don't care for other animals but are loyal and companionable with people they know. They make excellent watchdogs.

Long-legged terriers:

Airedale
American Staffordshire terrier—aggressive with other animals—4.
Bedlington terrier—aggressive with other animals
Border terrier—aggressive with other animals
Bull terrier—very active; aggressive with other animals; white and colored—4.
Fox terrier—very active; smooth, and wirehaired
Irish terrier
Kerry blue terrier—long-lived; aggressive with other animals
Lakeland terrier
Manchester terrier
Miniature schnauzer—4.
Soft-coated wheaten terrier
Staffordshire bull terrier—aggressive with other animals—4.
Welsh terrier—6.

Short-legged terriers:

Australian terrier
Cairn terrier—4.
Dandie Dinmont terrier—4.
Norwich and Norfolk terriers
Scottish terrier—very aloof
Sealyham terrier
Skye terrier
West Highland white terrier—long-lived—4.
[Not recognized by the AKC—Jack Russell terrier]

Key:

1. Early socialization especially important for ALL BREEDS IN THIS CLASS.
2. Very easy upkeep.
3. Difficult/special coat care.
4. Often made unsound by poor breeding. Extreme care in selection recommended.

5. Requires a great deal of space/exercise.
6. Exceptionally good with children.*

* All breeds may be good with children they know or have been raised with.

TOY DOGS

Toy dogs were bred as companions for people from many different antecedents, therefore they are very different in personality and temperament. The only thing that they have in common is their "portability." Contrary to popular belief, most are not particularly delicate and, in fact, tend to have longer-than-average life expectancies. Many are strong-willed, forceful, and can be headstrong and bullying if allowed to be. They usually are good watchdogs. Most are good with children they know—skittish with strangers.

Affenpinscher—1.
Brussels griffon—1.—rough, and smooth-coated
Chihuahua—longhaired, and smooth; sensitive to cold; native to North America—4.,2.
English toy spaniel—(Variation—Cavalier King Charles)—4.,6.
Italian greyhound—easygoing—2.
Japanese chin
Maltese—3.,4.
Manchester terrier (toy)
Miniature pinscher—1.
Papillon
Pekingese—originally a guard dog—1.,3.,4.
Pomeranian—1.,4.
Toy poodle—3.,4.
Pug—1.
Shih Tzu—3.,4.
Silky terrier—very active—1.,3.,4.
Yorkshire terrier—1.,3.,4.

Key:

1. Early socialization especially important.
2. Very easy upkeep.
3. Difficult/special coat care.

4. Often made unsound by poor breeding. Extreme care in selection recommended.
5. Requires a great deal of space/exercise.
6. Exceptionally good with children.*

* All breeds may be good with children they know or have been raised with.

NON-SPORTING DOGS

This group of dogs covers such a wide range of types that few generalizations can be made about it, except that most breeds were developed as companion/house pets.

Bichon frisé—good urban pet—3.,4.,6.
Boston terrier—long-lived; good urban pet; snores; aggressive with other dogs—1.,2.,4.
Bulldog—short-lived; bred to fight bulls; aggressive with other animals; docile and easygoing with people; snores—2.,4.
Chow chow—bred for hunting and guarding; aggressive with other animals—1.,3.,4.
Dalmation—all-purpose dog; good watchdog—2.,4.,6.
Finnish spitz—originally bred as a bird dog; good watchdog
French bulldog—good urban pet—1.,2.
Keeshond—1.,3.,4.
Lhasa Apso—1.,3.,4.
Poodle—3.,4.,6.
Schipperke—good watchdog; hardy
Tibetan terrier—good watchdog—1.,3.
Key:
1. Early socialization especially important.
2. Very easy upkeep.
3. Difficult/special coat care.
4. Often made unsound by poor breeding. Extreme care in selection recommended.
5. Requires a great deal of space/exercise.
6. Exceptionally good with children.*

* All breeds may be good with children they know or have been raised with.

HERDING DOGS

Once included in the Working Dogs category, herding dogs now have a group of their own because of their special talents for live-stock driving. Physically, they differ widely in size, body type, and haircoat. Easy to train, they are good watchdogs and companions. Some of the larger breeds are used in police work.

Australian cattle dogs—heelers

Bearded collie—6.

Belgians—three kinds: malinos, sheepdog, and tervuren—good watchdogs; used for police work—1.

Bouvier des Flandres—used in police and army work; good watch-dog; aggressive with other animals—1.,5.

Briard—used in police and army work; good watchdog—1.,5.

Collie—rough—3., smooth—2.—good watchdog

German shepherd—used in police work; good watchdog—1.

Old English sheepdog—1.,3.,5.

Puli—good watchdog; apt to be aggressive—1.

Shetland sheepdog—good watchdog; may bark excessively—3.

Welsh corgi—two kinds: Cardigan and Pembroke—long-lived; heeler; good watchdog—1.

Key:

1. Early socialization especially important.
2. Very easy upkeep.
3. Difficult/special coat care.
4. Often made unsound by poor breeding. Extreme care in selection recommended.
5. Requires a great deal of space/exercise.
6. Exceptionally good with children.*

* All breeds may be good with children they know or have been raised with.

3

YOUR PUPPY'S ALL-IMPORTANT EARLY MONTHS

Almost every puppy is soft, cuddly, and cute. Your new puppy is especially appealing to you because you chose it to be your companion. You may even find it difficult to think of your new pet as a dog at all. Some people anthropomorphize to the extent that they actually think of their pets as small people dressed in fur!

It's perfectly all right for you to think this way, but don't assume that a dog of any age is able to understand and reason the way a person can. When you're raising your puppy and teaching it to conform to your household you should try to think and observe the way the puppy does. If you can put yourself in your pet's place, you'll be able to make your wishes clearer to it. Sometimes, after you've learned to do this well, you'll realize that you just shouldn't ask your pet to do some things and you will discover that the best solution to a seemingly difficult problem is a compromise between your wishes and your puppy's ability to conform to them.

Although a new puppy owner naturally wants to make a pet feel at ease when it first comes home, you must start off on the right foot for both of your sakes. Dog ownership should be a relaxed, enjoyable experience—for both owner and pet. But in the long run you and your dog will have a much better relationship if you let it know what you want from the beginning.

You need to help your baby dog settle in with you when you first bring it home. It's unrealistic to expect a very young animal to understand immediately just what it's supposed to do and not do. When you adopt a puppy you're requiring it to make a big adjustment. Even though it is a domestic dog, try to think of it as a tiny wild creature that is confused and frightened. For the first few days you really can't expect much of your new puppy in the way of orderly behavior. At the very beginning, your job is to make your new puppy feel comfortable and secure. At the same time you should let it know that you are now its "mother," pack leader, and caretaker all rolled into one.

At each step in your new puppy's development and learning you need to practice the three P's—patience, persistence, and praise. As they say, "Rome wasn't built in a day," and your puppy won't become a perfectly well-behaved adult dog in a day, either. For each step forward you will probably experience two steps backward for a while. Just keep remembering that you're dealing with a young animal that needs to be shown repeatedly what you want and rewarded with lots of praise every time it does well. Patience doesn't mean, however, that you can ever afford to let a backward step go by without correction, or you will be tacitly rewarding undesirable behavior. Be consistent, clear, and loving at the same time and you'll see results. People who work with young people who have severe destructive or antisocial problems coined the phrase "tough love." Although the term has different connotations when applied to delinquents, it is an excellent description of just what I mean.

The other important thing to remember as you bring up your puppy is that in order to become a well-adjusted adult dog, it must be exposed to as many new experiences as possible. Behaviorists call this socialization, and it should begin as early as possible. I already discussed selecting a puppy that's used to people and to handling, but this process has to continue through all developmental stages if a puppy is going to grow up secure and unafraid.

Let your puppy meet new people, other animals, hear new noises, and go to new places as often as possible. Take it in the car, to the mall, and to the park, whenever you can. A puppy that grows up overly protected and underexposed will develop into a shy, nervous dog that is unable to cope when suddenly faced with a new situation.

FIRST THINGS FIRST—A VISIT TO THE VETERINARIAN

Before you arrange to pick up your new pet, locate a veterinarian and make an appointment to take your puppy in for a checkup on the way home. If you can't do it on the way home, make the appointment for the very next day.

There are several reasons why you shouldn't wait any longer than that. First of all, you want to know right away if something is seriously wrong with the puppy. If it should turn out to have a heart murmur or other congenital physical problem, for example, you will be able to make an intelligent decision about what to do before you become attached to the animal. In the case of a congenital problem, a responsible breeder will usually agree to take a puppy back and substitute another, or may offer to make some kind of financial adjustment if you opt to keep that puppy. If you do decide to keep a puppy that is not completely well, you will at least be prepared for whatever medical procedures, extra care, and costs that may ensue.

A second important reason for having your new puppy examined right away is that it might be harboring an infectious disease. The incubation periods of many common canine diseases vary in length, and even a seemingly healthy puppy may be in the process of coming down with something. A trained veterinarian can usually diagnose an illness in its incipient stages and will know whether it can be treated.

I can't emphasize the importance of this too much. A family I knew decided to get a puppy for their children. They went to a pet store and picked out a beautiful toy spaniel. They were given a forty-eight-hour return guarantee and told by the pet store to have the puppy checked out by their veterinarian. They hadn't made an appointment with any veterinarian, though, and it was late in the afternoon by the time they got home, so they decided to wait until the next day. The children immediately fell in love with the puppy and called her Baby.

The next day was a Saturday, and by the time the parents had finished with their usual chores it was four-thirty. When they called the nearest veterinarian, they were told office hours were over. The next appointment they could have was on Monday morning. The puppy seemed to be fine, so they agreed. That night Baby became very quiet, had some diarrhea, and didn't eat her dinner, but they reasoned she was just upset and tired out from all of the excitement of being in a new home. On Sunday morning she seemed better, although her nose was running and she had a slight cough—they decided she probably had gotten a cold coming home in the car that chilly Friday evening.

Late Sunday after the children had gone to bed, the parents noticed that Baby was shivering and having difficulty breathing. By Monday morning it was obvious the puppy was quite sick. The veterinarian diagnosed her illness as distemper, and because she was so young (he estimated that she was only about five weeks old) and the disease had gone undiagnosed for so long, he held out little hope for recovery. Baby died the next day. The whole family, especially the children, was devastated—they had already grown to love the little dog. What's more, the guarantee period from the pet store had long since expired. They did contact the store, showed them the veterinarian's report stating that the puppy had had the disease when they purchased her, and after much haggling were finally given a discount certificate for another puppy. Happily, their next puppy turned out to be a good, healthy pet, but I have heard many variations of this story, not all of which ended this well.

▪ **FINDING A VETERINARIAN** ▪

How do you go about finding a good veterinarian in your area? My first recommendation is to ask pet-owning friends and neighbors. If you're new in a community and don't know anyone to ask, try a local grooming establishment or even a pet-supply store. Breeders are good sources for veterinarians. Even if the breeder is in another area, he or she may have a customer who lives near you. Most shelters and pounds have an arrangement with one or more local veterinarians to perform examinations, give immunizations, and neuter animals at reduced fees. If there's a veterinary medical school or large veterinary hospital anywhere nearby, it will probably have a list of general pet practitioners in your area. The American Animal Hospital Association (AAHA) will provide you with a list of hospital members in your area if you write to them.* Failing any of these resources, you can often locate one or two veterinarians by driving around or even looking in the telephone book. Once you have names of two or more veterinarians, go to visit them. Choosing a veterinarian is very much the same as choosing any kind of doctor for yourself or your children—there's a great difference in personal preference. Some people want a doctor for their dog who has a wonderful bedside manner; others couldn't care less about charm as long as the doctor is good. You are the only one who knows what kind you want. Many veterinarians these days are in a group

---

* Write to: AAHA, Member Services, P.O. Box #150899, Denver, CO 80215.

practice; that is, two or more doctors share an office, hospital, and personnel.

Even if the doctor is busy you can usually judge a lot by the establishment itself and the personnel. Is the place clean-looking and smelling? Does it appear to be fairly up-to-date? Modern equipment and a shiny office do not mean that the doctor is a good one, of course, but do they signify that at least someone pays attention to details. Most veterinarians' offices have a brochure or handout describing their services, hours, and a schedule of fees. While you're there, find out what arrangements the particular practice has for emergencies. More and more today, veterinarians are joining together to establish central emergency clinics that are manned on a rotating basis to handle after-hours, weekend, and holiday emergencies. If you don't like the idea of a stranger taking care of your pet if it's hurt or suddenly takes ill, or the emergency center is located at the other end of the county, you may want to try to find a practice in which one or more of the regular doctors is on call all the time.

Once you've made your decision, remember that it's not etched in stone. If you decide you really don't like a particular veterinarian on your first visit, change right away while your puppy is still young. If possible, stick with the same doctor as your dog grows up. Much of veterinary medicine is based on judgment and external evidence, and a veterinarian who knows an animal can more easily spot significant changes that might signal a problem.

By the way, even though the doctor will keep a file on your pet and most send reminders when it's time to come in for booster shots or a yearly checkup, you should also keep your own records of immunizations, surgical procedures, any medications, allergies, and so forth—in case you ever do have to change veterinarians or are faced with an emergency and can't get to your pet's own doctor. Some people go to great lengths, keeping a kind of "baby book" of a pet, but a simple manila folder or loose-leaf notebook does just as well as long as it contains the relevant information.

After giving your puppy a thorough look-over to detect inherent health problems, the veterinarian will check the puppy for intestinal parasites. Many young puppies have roundworms—it used to be believed that all pups were born with them, but this is not so if the mother didn't have them. Nevertheless, any puppy that has associated with a lot of other puppies, or one from an unknown source, may very well be infested with these parasites, which cause diarrhea and eventually make the animal very sick if left unchecked. Worms are detected by stool-sample analysis and, if found, the puppy will need to be dewormed according to the veterinarian's instructions.

In addition to immediate health considerations, the veterinarian will probably also want to begin a series of immunizations. Puppies under four months of age need to be vaccinated against infectious diseases—distemper, influenza, parvovirus, and hepatitis—every few weeks in order to be fully protected. Be sure to ask the doctor whether it will be safe to take your puppy outdoors prior to the end of the immunization series. If you have an enclosed yard or patio that is not visited by other dogs, it may be all right for the puppy to go out. Some veterinarians even allow urban dwellers to take a puppy out to one spot on the street before it is fully immunized, but if there are any known cases of infectious disease in the area, she will probably advise keeping the puppy indoors until it's completely protected. Find out right away whether or not you can take your puppy outdoors safely, because it will affect the way you begin house-training.

Once you've established a schedule for immunizations, you may want to discuss other health questions such as diet (see pages 75–79) and neutering. Your veterinarian will undoubtedly stress the wisdom of early neutering for both male and female dogs that are going to be kept solely as pets. Not only is it important for both sexes for health reasons, but early neutering offsets or certainly diminishes many behavior problems that can develop when a dog of either sex matures.

Your veterinarian can also help you locate a good nearby trainer or obedience school for your puppy. Early training helps nip possible behavior problems in the bud and also helps a puppy develop good habits early on. Interestingly, two recent referrals were made to me by veterinarians who spotted potential aggression problems in tiny puppies they were examining. After a consultation, the owners of both an adorable Lhasa Apso pup and a feisty Jack Russell terrier worked successfully with me to socialize their pets before their aggressive behavior became a problem.

A word of caution here: There are no regulations governing who can advertise himself as a dog trainer. I know of one woman who went to a lot of obedience and training classes with her pet dog and trained that dog to compete successfully in obedience trials. Next thing I heard, she had cards printed up advertising her services as a "Professional Dog Trainer, $75 an hour," which she gave to her veterinarian among other people. The veterinarian was shocked when she learned that this woman had no formal training of any kind or any expertise other than less than a year of work with her own dog. So be careful when selecting a trainer for your puppy. Talk to other people who have used a trainer, because reputation and results mean more than fancy business cards or offices.

FIRST DAYS HOME

All dogs are pack animals just as wolves are. That means your puppy, no matter how young, requires order and structure in its life for it to be happy and function successfully. It needs a pack leader (you) to bond with, to give it direction and security and let it know what is expected of it, when.

From the very beginning you need to establish a schedule for your new puppy, just as I did with Mariah. At the same time you will be establishing a leadership role with your puppy. You will be defining the parameters of its life. Otherwise, confusion will reign at first and eventually a dog that grows up without leadership will take matters into its own "hands" and begin to run things its own way. Your pet will become a problem— at best an impossible, bratty animal, at worst a real menace to society. At that point, retraining or reprogramming an adult dog requires a great deal of time and work. It's far easier and more rewarding to start a new puppy off right from the beginning. From the moment you take on its care, *you* are the most important influence in your puppy's life, and although your pet has been born with certain genetic instincts that shape its general personality and behavior, it will eventually become the kind of adult animal you make it into.

If you work outside of your home, it's best to get your new puppy when you are able to take some time off. That way, just as I did when I first brought Mariah home, you can spend as much time as possible with the puppy in its first days in your home so it will bond with you and learn to become responsive to you. Another key time when you either need to be around yourself or arrange for someone else to be is when you are teaching your puppy to go to the bathroom outdoors instead of on paper in the house.

If you aren't able to take time off, perhaps you can arrange to come home at lunch time every day until the puppy settles in. If this sounds excessive to you, think of those first few weeks of time spent as a positive investment toward a successful long-term relationship with your pet. Quality time spent with your puppy at the very beginning of your lives together really pays off in the long run.

ESTABLISHING A SCHEDULE

Your first priority with your new pet is establishing a schedule, or timetable, for meeting the puppy's essential needs—feeding, outdoor or paper training, sleep, play, and affection. This may sound rigid and not much fun, but it's very important for a new puppy. If a puppy has no order and structure in its life, nothing will make sense to it.

According to their nature, some puppies require a tighter schedule than others in the beginning. Some remain "babies" for a long time, while others seem to have been born grown up. You will soon be able to tell how well your own puppy is reacting. For instance, if it's very regular in its bathroom habits and understands right from the start where it is supposed to "go," you can probably afford to allow it more freedom and wait longer between walks or trips to the paper.

Some puppies leave you little choice about certain aspects of their care. As Mariah did with me, your puppy may tell you in no uncertain terms that it wants to get up at five in the morning to have breakfast, go to the bathroom, or have its paper changed. If you don't respond, it will usually continue to bark or whine until you do.

To a certain extent, of course, whatever schedule you develop depends on your own lifestyle. If you're able to be home all day or have someone who can take over for you when you're out, you can immediately establish an all-day schedule of meals, exercise, and so forth. If, on the other hand, you're going to be leaving your new puppy alone for more than several hours each day, you have to adjust its schedule to fit in with yours.

However you work out your puppy's timetable, stick to it in the beginning. A puppy needs to know it will be fed, watered, walked, and given attention on a regular basis. As it gets older and begins to have more control over its bodily functions and learns to understand your desires and requirements, the schedule can gradually become less rigid. But until you're sure that you and your puppy have really reached an understanding, keep it on a regular timetable. See the sample schedules I've worked out on pages 60–62.

SAMPLE SCHEDULES FOR PUPPIES

Notes: Schedules will work better if the puppy sleeps in a crate (see "A Crate" in the following section, and other references).

Times of day for each activity can be adjusted according to your own timetable (e.g., get up later), but the lapses of time between each activity should remain the same.

■ SCHEDULE FOR A PUPPY UP TO FOUR MONTHS OLD ■

6 A.M. You and the puppy wake up.
Immediately put it on paper or take it outdoors.
Give it food and water.
Put it on paper or take it outdoors.
Socialize/play with it for as long as possible.
Put it back into the crate.

7–7:30 A.M. Go to work, etc.

10 A.M. Wake puppy up if necessary.
Put on paper or take out.
Give water.
Put on paper or take out.
Socialize/play.
Put it back into the crate.

1 P.M. Wake puppy up.
Put on paper or take out.
Give food and water.
Put on paper or take out.
Socialize/play.
Put it back into the crate.

4 P.M. Same as 10 A.M.

7 P.M. Same as 1 P.M.

10–11 P.M. Wake puppy up.
Put on paper or take out.
Socialize/play.
Give biscuit/snack and an ice cube.
Put on paper or take out.
Put to bed in crate.

■ SCHEDULE FOR A PUPPY
BETWEEN SIX AND NINE MONTHS OLD ■

Note: At this age a puppy can be fed two meals a day as long as it is eating a highly nutritious diet. If it is eating a less densely nutritious, commercial diet it will probably still require three meals a day. Check with your veterinarian.

6 A.M. Wake up.
Take or let puppy outdoors.
Give food and water.
Take or let puppy outdoors.
Socialize/play.
Put back into crate.

11–12 A.M. Wake up.
Give water.
Take or let outdoors.
Socialize/play.
Put back in crate.

4–5 P.M. Same as 6 A.M.

8 P.M. Give water.
Take or let outdoors.

10–11 P.M. Give snack/biscuit and an ice cube.
Take or let outdoors.
Put to bed in crate.

Under ideal circumstances, at about nine months of age, your puppy should be able to last without needing to go out for up to five or more hours during the day, depending on its size, breed, and degree of maturity. Puppies from shelters or pet shops may need longer because of a lack of early socialization. They are often confused because they have been confined in a small enclosure where there was no other place to go. A key aspect of their schedules, house-training, is discussed in the next chapter.

A SAFE PLACE—WHERE TO KEEP A PUPPY

A primary component of order in a young dog's life is the need for physical boundaries. This is very important—not only to keep both your new pet and your home from harm, but because even if you live in a small apartment, it will be a very confusing place for a young puppy. A puppy needs a den—a small, safe space it can become familiar with and feel secure in. It needs to be able to find its food and water, its toys, its bed, and its bathroom area easily.

A space for your puppy can be created in several different ways. The easiest method, used by most people, is to fence off a small room or a small part of a room with a pressure gate. A gate works better than a closed door because it allows you and your pet to see each other. A bathroom or part of a kitchen is usually best because of the tiled floor and the ease with which these rooms can be "puppy-proofed." This is an important step and one that first-time puppy owners often overlook. Here's your first opportunity to look at an environment from a puppy's point of view. Sit or kneel on the floor and look around for things that might intrigue you if you were a little puppy: dangling electric wires waiting to be chewed, lamps to be knocked over, edges of tablecloths and plant fronds to pull on, wastebaskets or garbage cans to dump over and so forth. In short, anything within a puppy's reach (and don't forget, your puppy will grow quickly) that you don't want your puppy to chew on or play with should be removed.

Don't make the mistake of closing off too large an area in the beginning. If you watch your puppy exploring, it will go all around the perimeters of the area, sniffing and sniffing; then it will crisscross from side to side (this is called zigzag behavior). It is imprinting the area onto its senses so that it will quickly learn just where things are—its bed, dishes, and so forth. If you make the area too large, the puppy will be confused. As your puppy grows and feels more at home, you can gradually enlarge its area if you wish, each time making sure that the animal feels secure in the larger space and remembering to "puppy-proof" the enlarged area.

A method of space management that works well for small-breed dogs is to use a child's playpen as a puppy's "room." Again, one section should be designated for sleeping, one for eating, and another for the bathroom. If you decide to use a playpen, make sure ahead of time that your pup won't outgrow the pen before it's ready to be allowed the run of the house.

■ A CAGE/CRATE ■

For some puppies, a crate or portable cage is an excellent tool to use as part of space management. Many breeders raise their puppies to sleep in a crate, and, if your puppy has become accustomed to this, it's a very good idea to continue to use it. Just as I trained Mariah to feel at home and safe in her crate so that she would be comfortable and calm when traveling, early crate training stands a dog in good stead. Many owners I know keep a crate with its door open, and their adult dogs sleep in the crate by choice. In any case, when you first bring your puppy home, you can make a crate into its bed. Be sure that the crate is not big enough to allow the puppy to establish one section for a bathroom area and another for lying down to sleep. This defeats the whole idea of the crate. It should be just large enough for the puppy to be able to lie down comfortably. Does this mean that you'll have to keep buying new crates as the puppy grows? No. A simple way of adjusting the size of a large crate is to purchase a wire divider and attach it in the crate to form a temporary wall. As the puppy grows, the divider can be adjusted to accommodate it, until the entire crate is used.

This works especially well for an owner who wants to have his pet sleep in the bedroom with him at night. One of the first questions that I ask a new puppy owner is if he is going to want his pet to sleep with him. If so, he needs a crate because he undoubtedly doesn't want to have an unhousebroken puppy in bed with him. My advice is to put the crate right next to the bed where you can see the puppy and it can see you. You can even put the crate up—securely—on a nearby chair or table so that it's on your eye level if you want (this is what I did with Mariah when I first brought her home). Once the puppy is able to make it through the night in the crate without wetting, then it will be relatively safe to allow it in the bed with you.

Please note, when properly used, a crate does not represent a punishment or cruel confinement for a puppy. Rather, it is a safe haven—a space that the puppy can call its own and feel secure in. However, you cannot confine a puppy in a crate unless you are able to follow a schedule and let it out on a regular basis during the day.

For those who still cringe at the idea of confining a puppy or dog to a crate, I say this: I agree that it is not ideal, but it is sometimes necessary. I like to make the following analogy. Our forefathers lived in the open without shelter, just as Mariah and all animals did. However, they soon found that this way of living wasn't comfortable or safe, so they took to living in caves. I like to ask clients who are opposed to putting a dog in a crate, "In a dog's view, what's the difference between a crate (which can be compared to a little room), and a room such as a kitchen or bathroom, or even an entire apartment or house? A room or even a large house are simply different levels of a crate for a dog." I don't ever want a crate to become something that's needed for the entire life of a dog, but at the same time I never feel bad about the use of a crate as a safe training tool. The aim is to gradually transform the crate into a bigger room, and eventually to the whole house or apartment. We have to continue to look at things from a dog's point of view and keep everything simple and clear.

■ WHEN TO ALLOW MORE FREEDOM ■

As your puppy grows and gains an understanding of what you want it to do, is able to find the paper or wait until it goes outdoors on a pretty regular basis, you can allow it a bit more freedom. If you want to take your puppy into the den with you while you're watching television, for instance, that's fine. Just be sure it's recently had a chance to go to the bathroom, and keep it in the room with you all of the time. If you don't want to close the door, use a pressure gate to keep the puppy from roaming around the house unattended, or keep it in its crate while it's with you. It's especially important to remind children not to leave a puppy alone in a room other than its own, even for a minute. The brief time that it may take a person to go to the bathroom or answer the telephone is enough time for a puppy to get into trouble.

Left unattended, a curious puppy can chew an electric wire or swallow a chicken bone, for instance, in seconds. Always stay with your puppy when it's out of its room, or put it back into its safe enclosure if you have to leave.

A SENSE OF TOUCH

One sense that is rarely talked about when it comes to dogs is the importance of the sense of touch.

Touch contact was especially important to Mariah. She loved to be stroked, rubbed, and petted. Friendly wolves continuously engage in a great deal of physical contact, nuzzling, licking, and wrestling to show their approval of one another. Wolf cubs get a lot of affection and attention from all of the adult pack members all day long. Touch is also important to most dogs, and praise in the form of a pat means more to almost every animal than a food treat does.

When you praise a dog, or are trying to calm it down, a gentle rubbing will convey your message. Dog handlers and veterinarians know the value of gentle, all-over massage to calm and relax an animal. Never pat a dog on the top of its head—that only serves to seem to push it down. Instead, rub it gently under the chin. The dog will immediately raise its head.

From the beginning of a wolf cub's life, its mother licks its belly continuously. In the very beginning, this is to stimulate elimination, but the behavior doesn't stop when the cub is old enough to urinate and defecate by itself. When a grown submissive wolf turns belly-up it is usually belly-licked by the dominant, Alpha, animal as a form of reassurance. Dogs also present their bellies as a sign of submission.

I often use this important touch language to make an aggressive or hyperactive dog relax and become submissive to me. Holding it upside-down in my arms, I stroke its neck, stomach, and perianal region. When a dog is too big to pick up, I turn it onto its side to stroke it. If you watch the handlers in a dog show, you'll notice that they often stroke their dogs on the undersides before judging to relax them and make them more responsive to being touched by the judges.

Newborn wolf cubs and dog pups are born with the instinct to nuzzle and probe with their mouths and noses in order to find a nipple to nurse on. As they grow, puppies naturally explore the world with their soft mouths and, later on, their sharp teeth. Although this is a perfectly normal behavior it is one that owners must learn to control early on to avoid damage to themselves and their belongings.

Another aspect of the touch sensation is the ability of wolves and dogs alike to feel vibrations in the ground. Along with hearing and smell, this keen sense allows wolves to actually feel the tiny motions of small animals underneath the ground and the faraway footsteps of a deer or other large prey. Dog owners are often surprised when a pet seems to "sense" a coming electrical storm or earthquake. This cannot be attributed to some mystical power, but merely to the fact that the dog is able to feel the vibrations of faraway booms of thunder or rumbles of an earthquake long before humans can.

Familiar footsteps can also be identified by a dog long before the person walking comes into view. This ability survives a hearing loss and owners are often not immediately aware that a dog has become deaf because it still seems to be able to "hear" their approach when it is sleeping on the floor.

■ LOVE AND AFFECTION—TOUCH CONTACT ■

Puppies crave and need a lot of physical contact with other living creatures. When a puppy is living with its mother and littermates, it is constantly being nuzzled, mouthed, and licked, wrestling and curling up to sleep in a tight ball. A puppy that is suddenly deprived of close physical contact and touching will be most unhappy.

In addition to being an enjoyable experience, touching and loving a puppy and playing with it serves another very important purpose. In order to bond with a puppy and assure it that it's a member of your pack and deserving of your protection—to assume the Alpha role, in other words—you have to give it a lot of touching and loving.

Frequent handling and touching of every part of a puppy's body is also an important aspect of socialization. A well-mannered adult dog should not be afraid to stand still and allow anyone—a veterinarian, handler, groomer, for instance—to touch and manipulate its body. At times you, too, will want to be able to groom your pet, examine its body, and so forth. Begin early to accustom your puppy to simple routines, paying special attention to areas that many dogs don't like to have touched. Clean its ears gently with a soft cotton ball. Touch its feet and manipulate its pads and toes. Play with its nails and grasp them between your fingers as if you were going to clip them. All of these actions should be enjoyable for both your puppy and you, and will get it used to having all parts of its body touched and manipulated. A dog that's used to having its body touched as a puppy is usually an easy dog to handle.

This is also a good time to accustom your puppy to the upside-down, submissive position. When you pick up your puppy, turn it upside-down and cradle it in one arm while you stroke its throat, belly, and groin area gently. By rubbing your puppy on its underside, you are not only calming and reassuring it, you are communicating that you are its leader—dominant over it. This is an especially good tool to relax an overactive puppy. If your puppy refuses to allow you to turn it over onto its back, it is an aggressive animal and you will have to take steps to modify its aggressiveness immediately.

Sometimes owners are afraid they will spoil a puppy if they are too affectionate. Just the reverse is true—a puppy that is not handled, loved, and socialized all the time will in fact be "spoiled" as a pet. It will develop into an unresponsive adult dog that is difficult to handle.

During the time you're touching and petting your pup you should also begin to get it used to wearing a collar and leash.

PLAYTIME: LEARNING THROUGH FUN AND GAMES

"All work and no play" is just as applicable to puppies as to people. In the wild, wolves romp and play to relieve tension, let off steam, and just for the sheer pleasure of it. Wolf cubs' play also serves to hone their physical abilities and hunting skills. Puppies and dogs, too, need the stimulation and release of "silly" behavior and play, plus the opportunity to develop both their mental and physical abilities that play provides.

Mariah used to indulge in a low, nonthreatening growl when she wanted to play or during a play session. These play-growls were short and contained no threat. Puppies and dogs also use this kind of growling.

Play-growling is often accompanied by excited panting, which is also usually a play signal. This differs from panting caused by overheating or pain in that it is accompanied by a "play bow."

That is, an animal that wants to encourage play begins by lowering the entire front end of its body, front legs extended, rear end up. This play bow is usually accompanied by excited panting, possibly barking or growling, and often rear-end and tail waggling. If there is no immediate response, the wolf or dog will then jump up and bounce around vigorously, apparently in an effort to attract attention. Owners of dogs that like to play ball or other retrieving games are familiar with this play signal—as the dog drops the retrieved object at the owner's feet it bows down, panting rapidly and sometimes making little throat noises as if saying, "Throw it again, I want to play more." A clear signal that the dog is tired and the game is over occurs when the animal stops its panting and bowing. A large animal, or one that is older than its potential playmate, may lie down in a semisubmissive pose after it makes the first play ovations in order to encourage a play response from a smaller or younger animal and reassure it there is no threat. A dog owner can usually solicit play from even the most staid animal if he or she is willing to imitate this play-encouraging activity.

When I had Mariah with me in a school, for instance, I often demonstrated her playfulness by bending low and growling and panting rapidly at her. She would respond with a play bow and her own excited panting, and we would then wrestle and play.

Play can take two forms with a puppy. You can play with your pet by creating games such as fetch, catch the Frisbee, rolling a ball back and forth between you, chase, and so forth. "Scent finding" is an excellent game to play with your dog that will provide endless hours of entertainment and reinforce your puppy's natural instincts to explore and chew on whatever it finds. Take a hollow burlap toy or well-boiled knuckle bone with a hole in the middle and put a piece of cheese or a liver treat inside it. (*Caution:* Be sure to check with your veterinarian before you give your dog any kind of bone. Some dogs have sensitive stomachs and a bone might cause a gastrointestinal upset. Be sure to get a large beef knuckle bone that won't splinter—any other kind of animal bone can cause severe problems.) Let the puppy smell it; then hide it somewhere and say "Find it." The puppy will go all around the room, sniffing to find the toy and get the reward. Once the toy is found, the puppy will chew on it. In addition to entertaining your puppy, you have provided it with an acceptable item to chew on, and every time the puppy begins to sniff around and explore, you can hide the toy again.

Play together will make your relationship more stimulating. Not only will it help you and your puppy bond together as pack members who share a common pleasure, but it also helps your puppy recognize you as its leader and learn limitations in its behavior. Just like young children, young animals sometimes get carried away when they play. If a wolf cub forgets itself and bites too hard when playing, its mother or another adult immediately stops it with a growl. If a human child suddenly hits a parent too hard during a game of tag, the game stops with a reprimand. In the same way, if your puppy becomes so excited playing fetch with you that it nips you, immediately stop it with a sharp "No!" and the pup will learn that you control the limits of how far it can go.

You can also show your puppy how to entertain itself by playing alone. This helps to divert a puppy from developing undesirable behaviors out of sheer boredom. A good example of this is a Jack Russell terrier whose owner called me for help. It seems she had wanted to allow the pup some playtime outside his crate, but didn't have time to play with him the entire time, so she left him alone in the room with a few toys lying around. After a week or two, the puppy became very sick, and when the veterinarian diagnosed lead poisoning, she realized that the pup had been picking chips of paint off the wall and chewing them. The owner needed help to devise some kind of plaything for the puppy that would keep him stimulated and entertained by himself (and distracted from wall-chewing).

After some thought, I took a simple child's spring toy and attached it firmly to the top of the crate with a piece of rope. On the bottom of it I tied the pup's favorite squeaky toy and showed him that every time the toy was pulled out and let go, it would retract by itself. After a few tries the terrier learned how to work the toy by himself. He was fascinated, and the owner reports that he now spends hours playing alone with the toy and gets enough exercise and stimulation so he never resorts to wall-chewing.

This particular toy won't work for all dogs, but a variation of self-play games and devices can be worked out for most. A favorite toy hung off the ground on a doorknob, for instance, can provide a puppy with endless activity running back and forth to grab the toy. So can rolling a ball against a wall so that it comes back. Things to climb on and run through, such as tunnels and hurdles, can be very entertaining. Of course, you again have to put yourself in your pup's place and be sure that whatever self-play toy you rig up is safe. A lot depends on the size and strength of the puppy—the squeaks can be chewed out of toys and swallowed by a large puppy, and strings or ropes can become caught around a puppy's neck, for instance. But with a little imagination you should be able to develop a safe self-play toy for your puppy.

Some puppies even create their own games to play by themselves. With a little encouragement from their owners in the form of approbation and the proper equipment, they can entertain themselves for hours. One Labrador retriever I knew loved to play catch with a tennis ball, especially if it was thrown into the water so that he had to swim to get it. But in the absence of someone to throw the ball, he invented a game to play by himself. He would go to the top of a gangplank that led to a dock with a tennis ball in his mouth. He'd let go of the ball and as it rolled down the gangplank, he'd chase it. If he caught it before it bounced into the water, he'd go back up and release it again. If it did go in the water, he'd jump in, retrieve it, swim to shore, go back up to the top of the gangplank, and release the ball again. He could do that all afternoon as long as he had a supply of tennis balls in case one or two got lost.

Although self-play doesn't take the place of playful interaction with you and other family members, it goes a long way toward providing an active puppy with enough activity and stimulation when you can't be around.

COMMUNICATING WITH YOUR PUPPY

Touch is, of course, a way to communicate love, affection, and a feeling of security to your puppy. But there are other ways of letting your new pet know how you feel about it and transmitting your wishes to it.

Your puppy is naturally sensitive to the signals that you convey by your facial expressions, body movements, stance, and the position of your body. By using your face and body in different ways you can signal approval or disapproval, threat or friendliness. Hand and arm motions are easily perceived by dogs—I will talk more about how to use them as training tools later in this book. For now I just want you to be aware that you give messages to your puppy with your entire body, no matter what you do. If you learn to communicate with your puppy through body language and at the same time interpret its physical messages to you, you will be well on the way toward establishing an understanding.

■ USING YOUR VOICE ■

The other important communication tool you have is your voice. From the start you should decide on a name for your new pet and use it often so that the puppy learns to understand that you are addressing it when you use the name. The actual name makes no difference, since the sound of it is what the puppy learns to recognize. Thus it's best to keep the name short and uncomplicated.

Although your puppy cannot understand what you say to it, it certainly interprets your messages by the tone of your voice. Because of their keen hearing, puppies are particularly sensitive to nuances in tone and pitch. If you say "Bad boy" in a soft, soothing tone, your puppy will think that you're praising it.

Soon, however, it learns what you mean when you use certain key words or phrases in a particular tone of voice. Some animal trainers insist that a low-pitched, sharply enunciated command that sounds like a growl is a good attention-getter. Certainly a command spoken in a loud, firm tone stops a puppy in its tracks faster than one that's softly given. A mother wolf or dog that needs to alert her pups to danger, for instance, always gives a sharp command.

People often think that a new puppy is too young to benefit from training. This is simply not true. Puppies are eager to learn from the time they are born. Your most important tools in teaching your pet what you want are your body and your voice.

CONTROLLING YOUR PUPPY'S WATER INTAKE

We all know how important water is to all living beings in maintaining their bodies' balance and ridding their systems of unwanted wastes. Like many animals, dogs do not store a lot of water in their bodies, do not obtain enough water from their food, and therefore require a source of fresh water in order to survive.

Why, then, would I ever advocate withholding water from a young puppy? Am I being cruel and capricious, as some people might say? No, not at all. I am not suggesting that you deprive your pet of water, but that you limit its water intake to certain times in order to help it gain bladder control.

If you think about it, wolves and other wild animals do not have fresh water available to them all day long. They go to a water hole or stream one or two times daily in order to drink. The National Academy of Sciences, in its *Nutrient Requirements of Dogs* (1985), says that dogs' need for water "can be met by permitting free access to water at all times *or* by offering water at least three times a day." Of course, this is based on the assumption that the pup or dog is in good health. Certain medical problems, such as diabetes mellitus, for instance, preclude limiting water in any way. Be sure to check with your veterinarian before you ration your puppy's water intake.

This is what I suggest for puppies under six months of age in order to program their systems and bladders to work in unison and control the need to urinate. If you look at my schedules on pages 60–62, you'll notice that I suggest that you withhold water after a certain time of night (during most of this time the puppy will be asleep). Although drinking water (unless it's very cold) does not trigger urination as rapidly as eating does defecation, it creates a need to urinate in about fifteen minutes in young puppies.

Thus, if you allow a young puppy free access to water all day and night, you are obligated to either walk that puppy every three hours or so or resign yourself to having a lot of wet papers to clean up.

Once a puppy grows up, however, you should allow it to have free access to water at all times. As its body grows, it requires more water at the same time that it gains more control, and drinking no longer stimulates urination as quickly.

FEEDING YOUR PUPPY

Your veterinarian may have specific suggestions as to the proper diet for your puppy. In recent years veterinarians have become increasingly aware of the importance of proper nutrition in maintaining good health and extending life expectancy. The old philosophy of "If a dog likes it and will eat it, the food's fine" has been replaced by a closer look at just what constitutes optimum nutrition. Veterinarians know that if you feed a puppy correctly from the start, many of the health problems formerly considered inevitable in older dogs, such as obesity and heart, kidney, and liver disease, can either be avoided completely or at least delayed.

■ KINDS OF FOOD ■

Because dogs, like wolves, are remarkably adaptable in their ability to obtain nourishment from a variety of foods, historically people have fed them a wide gamut of diets, from catch-as-catch-can table scraps to nothing but the highest-quality meats. Just like wolves, dogs are carnivores, or meat eaters. But wolves do usually consume some vegetable matter, including grass, and they eat whole field mice and the organ meat of the animals they kill. They also eat the bones of their prey, which provide a valuable source of calcium.

When commercial dog foods were developed, they usually contained a mixture of meat and vegetable/grain ingredients. They differed a great deal, however, in the proportions of these nutrients: dry dog foods are usually made up primarily of grains; semimoist diets contain equal amounts of meat and soybean products (and sorbates in order to keep them moist); while canned, or moist, foods are usually based on meat and meat by-products alone and contain little vegetable matter. In each form, good-quality commercial dog foods can be nutritionally complete when fed according to the manufacturer's instructions.

Recently, several brands of "natural" dog foods have been developed. They are usually sold through veterinarians and/or specialty pet-supply stores, and are generally more expensive than the grocery store brands. More and more veterinarians recommend feeding these diets, not to make more money, as some cynical pet owners might think, but because they really are better for your dog.

This is because they contain higher-quality ingredients and are therefore more concentrated nutritionally. Rather than being based on grain and meat by-product fillers, they have a high meat content. An important direct consequence of this high nutritional content is that a smaller amount of food is needed in order to meet a dog's daily nutritional needs. What's especially good for you, the owner, is that because your pet is eating less food, it defecates less often and its stools are smaller and better-formed than if it were eating commercial-grade food. This can be an especially important consideration if you have a large-breed dog, and it is a plus in house-training any size puppy.

The point is, be an educated consumer when you purchase food for your puppy. Your veterinarian may say that it's perfectly all right to feed your puppy a commercial diet. If this is more convenient for you, that's fine—just be aware that you will probably need to feed your pet more food in order to meet its nutritional needs than if you feed it a special diet.

I am very much against feeding a puppy table scraps, because it creates problems later on. A puppy that becomes used to expecting a treat from your plate will probably become a table-beggar and a food-stealer. Although a dog can be trained out of these bad habits, why create the potential for them at all? A puppy should expect to be fed at a different time than human mealtime and should not learn to associate its eating with yours.

Dog biscuits, on the other hand, are excellent for an adult dog, not as training tools but as a regular, expected part of its diet. They can be used as breakfast instead of a full meal, or as a bedtime snack. However you feed biscuits, they are good for a dog's teeth and gums and provide a good source of roughage in the diet, which is especially important if you do not feed your pet any dry food.

■ CHANGING A PUPPY'S DIET ■

If you decide to feed your puppy a different diet from the one that it's been used to eating, go easy.

A sudden change in food usually upsets a puppy's digestion and may cause it to have diarrhea. Don't wait until the old food runs out, but introduce the new food by mixing a little bit in with the old for a few days. If your puppy assimilates the small amount of new food well, you can go ahead and mix a little more in with the old. Stop and go back a step if the mixture disagrees with the puppy. Continue with this process until the puppy is eating nothing but the new food.

Sometimes a particular food or food in a particular form does not agree with a puppy. If your puppy's insides continue to be upset when you are trying to introduce a new food, don't force it. Go back to the old diet and begin again with a different new food if you still want to.

■ WHEN AND HOW MUCH TO FEED A PUPPY ■

Because their stomachs are small and they require a lot of food energy to grow and develop, young puppies need to eat frequently. According to *Nutrient Requirements of Dogs,* previously mentioned on page 74, a puppy between two and six months of age requires approximately two and a half times the number of calories per pound of body weight that an adult dog does. Between six months and a year, a puppy still needs twice the number of calories that it will when it reaches adulthood. In order to meet the need for high nutrition, special puppy foods have been developed.

Because of the wide variation in caloric content between different kinds of food (dry food, for instance, has more calories per ounce than canned food, which contains more moisture), it is impossible to give you specific amounts of food to give your puppy. Check with your veterinarian.

If you are feeding your puppy moist, canned food and do not use up an entire can at a feeding, the leftover amount has to be refrigerated to avoid spoiling. But don't give your puppy the leftovers directly from the refrigerator. Ice-cold food loses a lot of its taste and "smell-appeal" and will be rejected by many puppies. You can enhance the food's aroma and palatability if you warm it up in a microwave oven (be sure to put it in a microwave-safe container first). Microwaves vary, of course, so you'll have to experiment on the timing, but about a half-minute is usually enough. If you don't have a microwave, you can warm the food by placing the can directly into a pan of boiling water on top of the stove (just as you'd warm a baby's bottle). Whichever method you use, stir the food well to avoid hot spots, and test it with your fingertip before you give it to your puppy.

Don't allow your puppy to eat a bit, go away and play, and then eat a bit more. You can prevent this habit from developing if you pick up the puppy's plate after about ten minutes whether or not the meal is finished. Why do this? Because when it comes time to train your puppy to eliminate outdoors, you want to be able to stick to a timetable: The puppy eats its meal, goes out, and eliminates. If the meal is half-eaten and the puppy goes back indoors and finishes it up, the urge to defecate will probably occur again. You want to create a schedule in which mistakes are not encouraged. As a dog gets older and is in more control of its body ʔou can allow it to eat its meal more slowly if it wants. for now you should be sure that your puppy un- ʔs that it should eat each meal up right away.

A problem arises if someone is not going to be at home all day to do this. Puppies under four months of age need to eat three times a day, and very small-breed puppies continue to require frequent meals until they are fully grown. If you cannot arrange for someone to feed and exercise your young puppy during the day, the only solution is to leave some dry food for it to snack on and give it regular meals in the morning and evening. Obviously, during the time that a puppy is left unattended, you have no control over when, or where, it goes to the bathroom. You have to trust that it will go on the paper, and you must not scold it if it doesn't, because *you* have created the opportunity for it to "misbehave."

FOOD-GUARDING BEHAVIOR

Food guarding is a strong instinctive canine behavior. However, *you must not allow your puppy to grow up into a dog that won't allow anyone near its food or food bowl*. This can be a dangerous trait leading to major problems if a visitor to your home, or a child, inadvertently approaches your dog while it's eating. Even if your puppy shows no signs of food guarding now, the arrival of a new baby, adult, or pet in the household later on may trigger the behavior.

I recommend that you automatically follow steps to prevent it from occurring at a later date. Get your puppy used to having you nearby when it is eating. Sit on the floor next to the bowl. Reach out and move the bowl. Pick the bowl up and hold it for a moment before putting it down again. Stroke the puppy gently while it eats. If your puppy tolerates all of these actions you know that it does not have a strong food-guarding instinct. Nonetheless, you must continue to accustom it to having you handle its food, bowl, and body while it is eating so that it will never perceive you or anyone else as a threat. If you wish to carry this a step further, ask a good friend to come in and pick up the food bowl from time to time.

If your puppy growls or snaps when you touch it or its food bowl, you have to take stronger steps right away to nip this behavior in the bud before it becomes ingrained. Feed your puppy all of its food from your hand at first, gradually putting a piece or two of food in the bowl as you sit nearby. Do this for several weeks, or as long as it takes until your puppy tolerates your presence nearby while it eats and allows you to touch and move its bowl at will.

OTHER INSTINCTIVE FOOD-RELATED BEHAVIORS

Puppies may instinctively indulge in a number of other food-related behavior traits that are not as potentially serious as food guarding but that owners may nevertheless find puzzling and/or upsetting. In no case do they constitute "bad" behavior, but they may be traits you will want to control.

■ CARRYING FOOD AWAY FROM THE BOWL ■

When there is plenty of food, or too much to consume in one meal, a wolf often takes some leftovers and stashes them, burying them for future use. A domestic dog that buries a bone in the yard is indulging in the same kind of behavior. Even when there is enough food to go around, an individual wolf may take its share off a small distance in order to be able to eat at its leisure.

You may observe your puppy doing somewhat the same thing. It may take a piece of food from the bowl and carry it in its mouth to another location, where it will then eat. This can be annoying when your puppy grows up and is allowed more freedom. A client of mine complained that her little Yorkie always took juicy, meaty morsels of her dinner out of her bowl in the kitchen and carried them into the dining room, where she carefully placed them on an Oriental rug before eating them. My solution was quite simple. I told my client to close the swinging door between the kitchen and dining room before she fed her dog so that the animal couldn't get into the dining room with her food.

■ BEGGING ■

Begging for food is a perfectly natural canine behavior that owners often unwittingly encourage. Both wolves and dogs often watch another friendly animal eating or chewing on a bone, waiting for an opportunity to get a bite or even to steal the whole treasure away.

When people eat, a puppy often stares fixedly at them, hoping for a dropped morsel or a handout. Many people cave in to this emotional blackmail and toss the puppy a tidbit. Once you begin this insidious habit, the puppy will never give up and will become a really bothersome beggar.

There are several steps you can take to prevent your puppy from begging for your food. First, feed your pet just before you eat so that it will (hopefully) be sated. Second, you can teach your puppy to stay out of the dining area when people are sitting down to eat. If you do not allow your puppy to get the idea that human mealtimes are an automatic signal for handouts, you can usually offset begging behavior.

■ STEALING FOOD AND GARBAGE ■

The concept of stealing is not one any dog understands. In a dog's wild heritage, food that is available is for the taking and eating. Your puppy has no way of knowing that the chicken that you put on the kitchen table to defrost or the wonderful-smelling steak bone in the garbage can on the kitchen floor is not for it.

Again, think like a dog. If you are new to puppy

ownership, you must realize that you cannot put temptation literally in front of your pet's nose and expect it not to react. You have to think for your puppy and, to a certain extent, protect it from itself. Put food and garbage well out of the puppy's reach. As your puppy gets older you will be able to teach it that there are places that it can't go to get food, but in the beginning the best defense against food or garbage stealing is prevention.

■ GRASS EATING ■

People are often curious as to why a puppy or dog will nibble on grass and eat it, only to usually throw it up later on or pass it, undigested, in its feces. (Because grass is made up mostly of cellulose, it is undigestible for all but herbivores.) Wolves also eat grass regularly, especially in the spring when the first fresh shoots appear, usually to rid their digestive tracts of parasites.

There are many theories as to why dogs do this, but my opinion is that dogs, like wolves, also eat grass *because* they cannot digest it. It acts as an emetic, purging unwanted bodily fluids, and the chlorophyll it contains makes their mouths feel fresh.

■ COPROPHAGIA ■

A balanced nutritional diet will prevent your puppy from developing the all too common, unpleasant habit of stool eating, or coprophagia. Although some behaviorists and veterinarians treat this as a behaviorally originated habit, it is nutritionally related. Seen in wolves as well as dogs, it stems from a need to ingest certain minerals and other nutrients that have not been absorbed in the animal's digestive system and are passed out in the stool. If a puppy is fed a complete diet from which the nutrients can be readily absorbed into its system, it has no need to resort to coprophagia.

Sometimes a puppy that is left alone a great deal plays with and even eats its own stools. This, of course, is not a nutritionally related problem but is a direct outgrowth of severe boredom and a lack of cleanliness on the owner's part.

DESTRUCTIVE BEHAVIOR—
CHEWING AND MOUTHING

Biting, chewing, and mouthing of objects might seem to be related to eating, but they are actually instinctive exploratory behaviors. They can become highly destructive, however, if they are not brought under control early in your puppy's life.

When wolf cubs are young, they explore their world by all of their senses, especially using their mouths, lips, tongues, and teeth to gain the feel of objects around them. Puppies instinctively do the same thing. At the same time, when a young puppy is cutting its teeth, the sensation of biting down on something hard helps relieve teething discomfort.

Although this is a perfectly natural thing for your puppy to do and is an important part of its development, it doesn't mean that you have to put up with painful nipping or the ripping apart of your favorite possessions. The behavior can and should be controlled.

First things first. In the normal course of puppy-proofing your puppy's living quarters you should remove any objects that you don't want your pet to chew. The problem of chewing toys, books, clothes, and other household objects usually surfaces for the first time when you allow your puppy more freedom in the house. Unfortunately, this often coincides with serious teething, which goes on for months.

So, the most sensible first step is to police the area before you allow your puppy into it. If there are small toys on the floor, pick them up. Shoes and pocketbooks are always attractive to a puppy, especially if they're made of leather. By making sure that your puppy won't have objects that are desirable to chew right in front of its nose, you can avoid many problems. Again, while your puppy is young, always be sure that it is supervised at all times when it is outside its usual living area.

At the same time you can redirect the normal chewing behavior with an appropriate toy that will entertain the puppy and distract it from unsuitable objects, just as I did with the Jack Russell terrier mentioned earlier.

If the puppy picks up any object that is not its own toy, immediately take it away. If you have been handling its food bowl, this should present no problem. Don't let the puppy run away with the object, because this may provoke territorial guarding of the possession, which the puppy now considers its own.

As you take the object out of the puppy's mouth, accompany it with a verbal command such as "Drop it" or "Baby, let go." If your puppy refuses to drop an object, you must insist by prying its mouth open if necessary and forcefully removing whatever it is. Immediately praise your pet when it gives up whatever it has in its mouth. The "Drop it" command will serve you and your puppy well in the future and can help to protect it from eating something poisonous or harmful that it may find on a walk, for instance.

Needle-sharp puppy teeth can hurt and do a lot of damage to you and your possessions. You should not allow your puppy to bite or chew on you or anything else that is not a toy that you have given to it. To stop this behavior, do as a mother wolf or dog does if her puppy is biting on her nose or ear. She puts her mouth around the pup's muzzle and holds it closed. Put your hand around the puppy's muzzle and gently but firmly squeeze it shut at the same time that you say "No bite" or just plain "No." Hold on until the puppy calms down, and immediately give it something suitable to chew as soon as you let go. If the puppy persists, continue with the action and the verbal command. Do this every time the puppy begins to chew on you or anything else that it shouldn't. The "punishment" of having its mouth held closed is a message the puppy will understand clearly—but it must be repeated every time the puppy even begins to chew in order to be effective. While the puppy is in its enclosure alone, be sure it has plenty of safe chew-toys.

MY BASIC TRAINING MANUAL FOR ALL DOGS

4

MY DOG-TRAINING TECHNIQUES

Once I clearly understood the framework within which Mariah and all wolves and dogs operate—the social structure of the pack and all of its ramifications—I was able to develop training techniques to work within that framework. These techniques will help you train your dog in a positive way, a way your dog will understand. Ideally, you and your dog will eventually be able to communicate and act in harmony instead of indulging in a clash of wills.

The three chapters that follow consist of a basic training manual. These are the tools and techniques I've developed for you to use when you train your dog.

TRY TO PUT YOURSELF IN YOUR DOG'S PLACE AND SEE THE WORLD THE WAY YOUR DOG DOES

One of the first things I tell my clients is: Try to figure out what your dog is perceiving and feeling. This is the beginning of being able to reach an understanding with your pet and learning how to communicate with it.

Dogs, like wolves, have acute, highly developed sensory perceptions through which they observe the world around them. To be a successful dog owner/trainer, you need to work with these perceptions and use your dog's keen senses to help you train it.

When you work with your dog, you need to communicate with it in a language it can understand. Wolves and dogs use an elaborate system of body language and facial expressions to communicate with each other. If you can teach yourself to read this language you'll know what your dog is trying to tell you. At the same time, if you can emulate this language, your dog will understand what you're trying to tell it.

Throughout the following chapters I'll suggest ways you can use your voice and your body to help your dog understand how you want it to behave.

ESTABLISH A SCHEDULE

It is very important to develop a schedule in the beginning of your relationship with a dog or puppy. Life within a wolf pack is highly structured and ordered— each individual member of the pack knows its role and what is expected of it. Domestic dogs share this need for order.

For a dog to understand what you want it to do, it has to know what's going to happen, when. It should be fed, played with, exercised, and allowed to sleep on a regular basis. Then your requirements will seem logical—the time for elimination, for example, will follow the time for eating, or sleeping, and so forth.

Scheduling is probably the most important tool you can use with a dog while you're training it. I'll explain more about this as we go along. I'll also tell you how to use a crate to help develop a schedule. When used properly, a crate will provide a puppy or new dog with security and keep it out of trouble when you're not around.

USE WHAT I CALL THE "THREE P'S": PATIENCE, PERSISTENCE, AND PRAISE

Physical force will only seem like a challenge to most dogs, and you never want to indulge in a clash of wills with your dog. But at the same time, you must develop a foolproof way to let your pet know what you want. If you can stay calm and patient at the same time you insist, or persist, in making your wishes clear, and then praise your dog lavishly when it does what you want, you can teach it without ever having to resort to anger. If you use the three P's you'll be successful in teaching your dog.

USE REINFORCEMENT AND REWARD

Hand in hand with the three P's, you need to continuously reinforce every lesson you give your dog. In order for a dog really to learn a command, you have to repeat it for reinforcement many, many times.

Every time your dog performs correctly, reward it with praise, which will further reinforce the lesson. Constant reinforcement accompanied by rewards for good behavior will make any training lesson stick.

DEVELOP A SENSE OF TIMING

Correction and praise mean nothing to a dog unless they're timed to occur at the exact moment of a transgression or a proper action. Teach yourself to read your pet's body language and anticipate its actions. Then you can correct your dog *as* it reacts to stimuli. Otherwise, it will be too late. If you do this with your dog, you'll soon develop a wonderful rapport.

MAKE YOUR DOG FOCUS ON YOU

This is a great tool to use at times when your dog becomes distracted, upset, or wild. When Mariah was frightened or her strong instincts made her aggressive, for instance, I found that if I immediately forced her to look at me—focus on me—I could calm her down and then make her listen to me. If you plan to go on to off-leash work with your dog you must learn how to do this to avoid potentially dangerous situations. I'll tell you how to use a number of different sound stimuli to help you make your dog focus on you when it's necessary.

These are the basic techniques and tools I've developed to train all dogs. In the following chapters I'll teach you how to use these methods to train your dog.

5

EARLY PUPPY TRAINING

For the first week or two that you have your puppy home, you will both be busy getting to know each other, and you'll be learning how to take care of your new pet's physical needs. But very soon it will be time to begin some training. Once a puppy is settled into the household comfortably and has begun to trust you, you should start what many people call "kindergarten" training and I prefer to call early basic puppy training.

Whatever you call it, these early weeks of training are extremely important if you want your puppy to grow up to be a well-mannered dog. Just as it is never too early to socialize a puppy to handling and touching, it is never too early to begin to teach it some elementary social skills such as going to the bathroom in the right place, wearing a collar and walking on a leash, and learning its name.

Many people still hold the theory that young puppies aren't ready to learn anything until they reach a certain age and that they should be allowed to simply grow up with no rules or parameters. In my experience, this is not true. Because they are pack animals by nature, all canines, no matter how young, are happier and more secure when they know what is expected of them. Young wolf cubs are not allowed simply to run wild until they reach a certain age. Their mothers and the other adult pack members keep careful watch on the cubs and clearly show them exactly what they are allowed to do, where they should eliminate, and so forth. In other words, wolf cubs are given rules to live by from the moment they leave the den, for their own safety and for the good of the entire pack. Puppies need this kind of direction, too.

This is not to say that a very young puppy is ready for rigid, sophisticated training. But it is receptive to you, eager to please, and will be happier and less confused if it gets clear signals from you, its combination mother and pack leader.

One good example of early puppy training that was very successful is that of Mr. and Mrs. Ed Finkelstein (he's CEO of Macy's), and their golden retriever, Candy. Candy was three months old when the Finkelsteins got her from a very good breeder, and they immediately hired me to help them to start her off on the right foot. I worked together with them and Candy all the way from beginning housebreaking through advanced off-leash training. I'm pleased to say that she turned out wonderfully. Her owners are delighted with her good behavior and take her everywhere, from their townhouse in New York to their estate in Connecticut. What's more, all their friends are impressed with how well behaved and responsive Candy is to them. Her good behavior is a testimony to what time, energy, and the proper training methods can accomplish.

When their friends the Henry Kissingers got a Labrador retriever puppy, Amelia, the Finkelsteins referred them to me for the puppy's early training. The Kissingers, however, decided not to begin to teach Amelia right away.

Then, last summer, when Amelia was four months old, a picture appeared in the New York *Daily News* of Dr. Kissinger holding Amelia on a leash with the large headline "Heel, Amelia! Please," and a caption that read, "As Secretary of State, Henry Kissinger had little trouble making nations listen, but he isn't getting any attention from his 4-month-old Labrador, Amelia. The puppy has a mind of her own about taking orders." The next day I received a call from the Kissingers' secretary. The media attention had convinced them that Amelia needed some early basic puppy training. I gave her some lessons and she responded very well.

The advantage of early training is now recognized by many people. Under various names, there are now group classes for puppies to help them learn basic skills. These are excellent for puppies and owners to participate in, because they help socialize the animal to other dogs and people and at the same time provide an owner with professional help and guidelines that make training a puppy easier and more successful. However, you can't take your puppy to a group class until it has been fully protected against infectious diseases, and this usually isn't until it is at least four months old. So, there is a great deal that you will want to begin teaching your dog yourself.

CORRECTION AND DISCIPLINE

Before I begin to discuss the basics of training a young puppy, you first must understand the proper use of correction and discipline. If you establish a rapport with your puppy early on, you may very well arrive at a point when you will be able to convey your approval or disapproval with a simple word or look alone. At the beginning, however, you have to be more explicit so that your puppy understands what you want.

The first and most important rule to follow when training a puppy is to be sure that the punishment fits the crime. If you react the same way to a puppy's inadvertent mistake as you do to a serious infraction, you will confuse the animal. For instance, if your puppy knocks over an ashtray on the table out of sheer exuberance, you shouldn't react the same way as if it had purposely raised its leg and urinated on a table leg. If you scream "No, bad dog" at your puppy instead of reprimanding it calmly every time it does some "childish" thing, the poor animal not only won't know what you want from it, but may become stressful, nervous, and fearful of you. What's more, it will soon become so inured to your yelling at it for every little thing that it will tune you out, and after a while you'll have to resort to harsher and harsher methods in order to make your pet listen to you at all.

Another important rule when dealing with a puppy is to avoid giving it mixed messages. For this you need the cooperation of all the other members of the household. Once a particular rule is established, such as no getting up on the sofa, everyone in the household must agree not to let the puppy get up on the sofa, even for a moment, and must follow through on correction every time the rule is broken. If teenaged Susie is going out the door, notices that the puppy is on the sofa but is in too much of a hurry to bother making it get down, or ten-year-old Jim invites the pup to sit on the sofa with him while he's watching TV, that puppy is going to get the message that "It's all right to get on the sofa." Then, when Mother walks into the room, scolds the puppy severely, and makes it get right off the sofa, the poor animal will be really confused. Many puppies and adult dogs take advantage of a lack of consistency or follow-through on the part of one or more members of the household and soon learn that with some people they can get away with things. They will make something of a game of this, constantly testing to see just how far they can go before being reprimanded. This is particularly true of strong-willed dogs that have grown up without a clear sense that all the humans in the house are its pack leaders. Consistency and follow-through by all the people in a household are very important if you want your puppy to understand the rules of the house. Remember, if you have a hit-or-miss attitude about mistakes, the end result will be a dog that's more-or-less trained.

The third rule concerns timing of punishment. Although most people understand the importance of catching a puppy in the act, emotions can get in the way of common sense. If you come home and find that your puppy has soiled all over the rug or chewed up your favorite book, it's natural to react angrily. Unfortunately, discipline that takes place after an event will have no good effect on a puppy, but will simply confuse and frighten it. Even if the undesired activity took place as recently as ten minutes ago, a puppy has no way of connecting *that* activity with your anger or displeasure. If a puppy greets you happily at the door when you come home and you immediately begin to scream at it, its logical conclusion is that it shouldn't greet you at the door. No matter how upset you may be at a puppy's past activities, you must remember that animals live in the present; they do not have the reasoning powers that you do. In order for discipline and correction to work at all, they must occur *at the exact moment of the transgression.*

This brings me to another key element in successful puppy training—praise. At the same time that you consistently let your puppy know when an action displeases you, you must also reward it with praise when it pleases you. But be careful not to give a puppy a double message. Don't say "Stop barking," for instance, and then praise the dog the moment that it stops. If you do that, the dog will think, "She praised me when I barked," and go right on barking in order to gain your approval. You are saying one thing and doing another, conveying an undecipherable double message to your pet. Praise should be used in training when the puppy does something right, such as coming when called or walking well on a leash, *not* as a reward when it stops doing something wrong. Also on this subject, I am usually not in favor of using food as a reward in training most animals. Praise from you in the form of a "Good dog," and a pat under the chin should usually be the only reward that your pet receives.

So, keep it appropriate, keep it consistent, keep it

straightforward and simple, and the puppy will connect your reaction with its action. At the same time that you let your puppy know what you *don't* want it to do, you must show it what you *want* it to do instead (e.g., urinate on the papers instead of the floor; or chew on a toy, not the table leg).

Don't forget your puppy's limitations when you are beginning to train it. Continuously bear in mind that puppies are baby animals. For each step forward you take, be realistic and expect that you and your puppy will probably take a couple of steps backward from time to time. Only by showing your puppy over and over again with calm, consistent repetition will you achieve your goal. Don't despair if your puppy seems slow to understand. If you're patient, one day you'll suddenly be able to say, "At last. I think he's got it!"

■ **WAYS TO CORRECT A PUPPY** ■

Puppies vary considerably in their reaction to discipline, and what works for one individual may roll off the back of another. You want to avoid overdoing it with a sensitive animal. On the other hand, correction will do no good at all if the puppy hardly notices it.

In order to get any kind of message at all through to your puppy, however, you have to make it look at you, *focus* on you and what you are saying or doing. There are several ways to do this. Your voice is the most common training tool. A sharp "No!" will cause most pups to stop what they're doing and look at you.

Some puppies, however, will glance up at the sound of your voice and then go right back to whatever they were doing. For them, a loud clap of hands along with the verbal command may work. Or a harshly jangling object such as a large key ring thrown on the ground often works well to make a puppy stop short and look at you.

With a very strong-willed, determined individual, harsher methods may be needed in order to startle it into attention. Of course, you should never actually hit an animal. Not only can this lead to hand shyness and fear-induced aggression on the dog's part, but it puts you into an adversarial position with your pet when you should be striving for partnership and understanding. But sometimes the threat of physical action is necessary with a particularly stubborn animal. If a wolf cub is being particularly obnoxious and ignoring its mother's attempts at discipline, the parent may grab it by the back of the neck and shake it firmly. Likewise, you may have to grab a strong-willed puppy on either side of the neck and shake it in order to make it focus on you.

Only when you have gotten a puppy to pay attention to you can you then tell it "No" and proceed to show it what you want it to do. You must establish a role of authority before you can *be* an authoritative figure.

Please note that threats of isolation or punishment mean nothing to a puppy. Owners sometimes use the same reasoning with a puppy as they might with a child. Statements like "Go to your room and think over your behavior" or "If you don't stop right now, no TV tonight" may work with children, but they mean absolutely nothing to a puppy that cannot reason and has no concept of the future in terms of its current actions and the consequences thereof. Don't ever lose sight of the fact that you are dealing with a dog when you are training your pet. No matter how intelligent it may seem, remember that it cannot understand what you want unless you show it in the simplest, most direct terms.

HOUSEBREAKING

Most new puppy owners are anxious to housebreak a puppy right away so that it can safely be allowed more freedom to be with them around the house. But, along with the notion that a young puppy can't learn any rules until a certain age, there is also a theory that is still held by some that a puppy under three-to-four months of age is not sufficiently developed physically to begin house-training. Although it may take some time for a puppy to become completely housebroken to the extent that it can be trusted to have a complete run of the house unattended, it is never too early for a puppy to start to learn the basics of where and when you want it to go.

Any nonarboreal animal instinctively deposits its wastes a distance from where it lives so that its enemies won't be able to find it by scent and attack it when it's sleeping. As soon as a wolf's cubs are able to leave the den, she shows them an appropriate spot to eliminate in. Except in situations when a puppy has been continuously confined since birth in a small space such as a cage or kennel, its normal instincts make it seek an area away from its bed when it wants to urinate or defecate. If you do have a puppy that has been caged all its life, you will have to train it in a special way—see the section on Special Situations on page 113.

Thus, you already have the basis for teaching a puppy where you want it to "go," no matter how young it is. All you need to do is to provide it with an appropriate area, show it where you want it to go, arrange a schedule so that you are always there to take it to the appropriate spot at the right moment, and lavish it with praise when it does the right thing at the right time. Simple? Yes, in theory, but unfortunately, except with unusual dogs, there's usually a bit more to it than that. Essentially, a puppy needs to be programmed to go to the bathroom where you want and at a time that fits into a schedule that you can both accept. If you can do this right in the beginning, your pet will never develop a housebreaking problem later on in its life, no matter how circumstances change.

Before you begin on a housebreaking program, you should be sure that your puppy doesn't have any physical problems. Intestinal parasites, urinary tract infections, and certain systemic illnesses make it impossible for an animal to control its elimination. If you haven't already done so, have your pet checked over by a vet-

erinarian. If you encounter any problems along the way
that might signal a previously undetected physical ail-
ment, be sure to insist on further tests, because not only
is it impossible to house-train a dog that has an intestinal
or urinary tract disease, but it will cause both of you a
great deal of unhappiness and tension if you try.

Now is the time to decide exactly how you want your
puppy to be trained. As an adult dog, will you want
your pet to go only when it is outdoors in the backyard
or a run? Will you want it to go only when being walked
on a leash? Will you perhaps want it to use papers or
a "bathroom station" in the house exclusively? Or, as
is often the case, will you expect your dog to be able
to use a variety of spots, depending on whether you're
in your city or country house, or if you're delayed getting home on occasion? Look at your lifestyle and decide how you want to handle this important aspect of
your puppy's training now when it's young. Although
it is possible to reprogram an adult dog to different
"bathroom" arrangements, it's much easier if you can
anticipate your needs and start right from the beginning.

No matter what area you select for your puppy's elimination, the first few weeks of house-training should
establish certain things. The puppy will gradually learn
to recognize the sensation of needing to urinate or defecate, and with this awareness it will begin to develop
the physical ability to retain it for a short time. It will
simultaneously begin to understand that there is a place
in which you want it to eliminate.

■ FOOD, WATER, AND A SCHEDULE ■

A large part of early house-training depends on being
able to follow a schedule. It is very difficult to house-
train a puppy if you are not around to show it what you
want of it, although it can be done.

If you have followed a schedule from the start, you'll
soon notice that your puppy eliminates at certain times.
Eating and defecating are directly related in a young

animal. Usually a puppy needs to defecate about fifteen minutes after eating. If you observe this in your puppy, take it to the spot that you want it to use a few minutes after each meal. The pup will almost always defecate in that spot, you will praise it, and it will get the idea that you are pleased with it when it goes there. Soon it will begin to go to the spot by itself as soon as it becomes aware of the sensation of wanting to have a bowel movement.

If you are feeding your puppy one of the special nutritious foods mentioned in Chapter 3, your job will be much easier than if it is consuming a diet that creates a large volume of stools.

The relationship between drinking water and urinating is not as clear-cut as eating and defecating are, but in my experience, puppies usually urinate about fifteen minutes after drinking (adult dogs four hours later). Therefore, I use water-drinking as a trigger to help me teach a puppy when and where to urinate. After I give a puppy a drink (cold water works best), I take it to the spot I want it to urinate. Soon the puppy is able to recognize the sensation of a full bladder just as readily as the need to defecate, and it automatically eliminates in both ways when it's taken to the spot.

A CRATE/CAGE FOR HOUSE-TRAINING

If you are going to paper-train your puppy initially, a crate is probably not necessary, because the paper will always be accessible to the puppy when it's in its area. But if you want your puppy to learn to go outdoors in the yard from the beginning, or if you decide that you want to train your puppy to use a bathroom station that's in another room, a crate is a necessary house-training tool.

Even a young puppy will try very hard not to soil its sleeping area unless it's ill (pet store and shelter puppies are an exception).

If you are able to follow an appropriate schedule of

feeding and watering, take the puppy out of the crate and immediately to the spot where you want it to go, and give it a verbal command. The dog will eliminate, and you will praise it. Soon the puppy will understand that it doesn't need to eliminate the moment that it feels the urge, but can wait a few minutes until you come to take it out of the crate, and the first step in housebreaking will be accomplished. A crate is also a very good tool to use when you are retraining an adult dog to use a new, or different, location for elimination.

You must never use a crate with a puppy, however, if you cannot be absolutely certain that you or someone else will take the puppy out to eliminate at the appropriate time (every three hours during the day when it's under four months). Otherwise, the puppy will have no recourse other than soiling its crate and you'll end up with a difficult house-training problem to solve.

PAPER-TRAINING

Your puppy will undoubtedly first learn to eliminate on paper. This is by far the easiest way to begin housetraining, especially if you aren't able to be at home all the time. When you first get your puppy, begin by papering the entire floor of its enclosure so that the puppy will have no choice but to eliminate on it. As I discussed in the previous chapter, the area in which the puppy is confined should be small at first.

After three or four days, you'll probably notice that the puppy uses a general area that's as far away from its sleeping area as possible. Once this pattern is consistent, you can take away the few pieces of paper immediately adjacent to its bed. If the puppy soils or wets on the bare floor, put the paper back and try again a few days later.

Gradually reduce the area covered by paper, a few pieces at a time, and praise your puppy lavishly whenever you actually see it going on the paper. To help make your message clear, tear off a small piece of paper that has been soiled and put it in the area that you want your pet to use. You'll be reinforcing your lessons by utilizing the puppy's strong sense of smell. Do not make the mistake of leaving heavily soiled paper down, though, because after a while most puppies won't go back to a really dirty, smelly area. Also, you have to adjust the size of the final papered area to the size of your dog and also to its particular habits. A large puppy obviously needs room to circle and squat and still make the paper, but even some small dogs prefer large areas to eliminate in or won't urinate and defecate in the same spot. A client of mine had a Maltese that consistently urinated on the paper but defecated off it. I suggested that she put two pieces of paper down side by side, and the problem was solved.

Some puppies are quicker to catch on than others. If your puppy should regress at any time during the simultaneous reduction of the paper-covered area and enlargement of the area in which it's confined, you'll have to go back a step and recondition the puppy to living in a smaller area at the same time that you cover a larger percentage of space with papers. After several days of success you can begin to reduce the papered area again, and so forth. Regression of this sort is very common and has no particular significance—the puppy may have simply lost its concentration or have been distracted—but you can't ignore it and must be sure that the area for elimination is clearly defined each time before creating a smaller area. Remember, sometimes you have to go back a few steps in puppy training in order to achieve your goal.

In this case, your goal is for the puppy to use a clearly defined paper-covered spot for elimination. Now, some owners ask, "Why bother with this? Why not just leave paper all over the floor?" My answer is: Do you want your puppy to go into the den with you and proceed to tinkle on a section of today's *New York Times* you left on the rug by your chair? Or poop on a school report that your son has spread out on the dining room floor? No, of course not. But how do you expect your puppy to differentiate between these papers and the paper that's all over the floor in its room? Obviously it can't. To a puppy like this every piece of paper is a potential toilet. That's why it's so important to teach your puppy to eliminate on a particular *spot* that is covered with paper, rather than teaching it to simply use paper that's all over the floor.

What about taking a piece of paper with you and putting it on the floor of the den when you have your puppy in the room with you? Same problem. You simply confuse the animal, which then assumes that it's OK to use any piece of paper it finds on the floor.

Once your puppy is really paper-trained—that is it regularly goes directly to the paper from whatever area of its own room that it happens to be—you can begin to allow it some household freedom, under supervision. Wait until it has just eliminated and then take it and keep it with you. The minute it seems restless or edgy, immediately take it back to the paper and show it where it is. If it uses the paper, praise it lavishly. After a while the puppy may be able to find its paper by itself when it's in a different part of the house. But this may take a while for some puppies, and it's best not to push it too fast because if a mistake is once made, you'll have to go back several steps to reinforce and be sure that the puppy understands.

If you catch your puppy in the act of making a mistake, stop it immediately with a strong "No," and take it to its paper. But if you haven't seen the mistake made, it's too late for reprimands. Simply clean up thoroughly so that no odor remains to tempt the puppy to go in the same place again.

AN INDOOR BATHROOM STATION

An indoor bathroom station is a device that a dog can use to eliminate in. It should be easy to keep clean and odor-free and large enough for the dog to use comfortably. There are commercially available tray-type devices that can be lined with disposable absorbent material. Some have posts for males to lift their legs on. They come in various sizes and are usually made of nonporous plastic or some other easily washed material. For travel, there are even folding bathroom stations, or some owners choose to purchase simple absorbent paper "wee-wee pads" that can be easily discarded when necessary (these are made out of the same kind of material as disposable diapers). But any other device that suits you and your dog is fine—a cat-litter tray, for instance.

Owners opt to train their puppies to use an indoor bathroom station for many reasons. Especially for a small dog, it is very easy to use and does away with the need to take the dog outdoors. This works out very well for elderly or infirm owners and is especially useful for people who travel a lot with their pets and stay in hotels or motels, for instance.

The actress Kaye Ballard is a client of mine who uses a bathroom station for her little Shih Tzu, Sally, with great success. Because she has to travel all the time and wanted to be able to take Sally with her, she asked me to help her train Sally to use a bathroom station. Now she takes Sally everywhere with her, and the little dog is conditioned to use her portable toilet wherever she is. No matter how many different places they go, Sally always knows her very own bathroom station is nearby.

Sometimes an owner may want a dog that normally goes outdoors to use a bathroom station in emergencies—when she is unavoidably delayed getting home, for instance. If you want to do this, now is the time to accustom your puppy to using both a comfort station *and* the outdoors. If you wait until later to introduce this kind of dual approach, you may run into difficulty because some dogs, large ones in particular, simply refuse to go indoors no matter what once they're programmed to the outdoors. The best way to teach both systems to a puppy is to train it to the bathroom station first, and then the outdoors.

Most people place a bathroom station in an out-of-the-way location such as a stall shower or basement room. The area shouldn't be so out of the way, though, that the puppy has difficulty getting to it. Recently a client of mine with a very large apartment was having difficulty teaching her little dachshund to use a bathroom station. The moment I saw that the poor little dog had to go to one end of the apartment and through at least ten doors to find the station, I suggested that the owner get another one so that the dog could go at either end of the apartment. It solved the problem immediately.

The basics of teaching a puppy to use a bathroom station are the same as those of teaching it to use a paper-covered spot. If you begin with the station in the puppy's enclosure, you'll probably want to move it later on. In my experience, most people start their puppies out in the kitchen, and no one wants an adult dog's bathroom station in the kitchen. So you will have to go through the same steps outlined in the next section when it's time to make the change.

GOING OUTDOORS

Once your puppy is completely paper-trained and has been immunized against infectious disease, you can begin to teach it to go outdoors if you wish. At the same time you are house-training your pup, you should have been accustoming it to wearing a collar and leash so by the time it's ready to go out, it will be comfortable with them.

Those people who have a private patio or fenced-in yard where no other dogs can enter may be able to take their puppies outdoors right from the beginning. Others may have permission from the veterinarian to take a pup out to one specific safe spot in a nearby park. For these people, outdoor training can take place right from the start. This is really the best system if possible because it avoids the confusing transition period later on.

Whenever you begin outdoor house-training, you

should continue to keep your puppy confined. If it has been paper-trained initially, its papered spot should still be available. The puppy may need some time to understand that outdoors is now the place to use, and while it's in this transition stage it must have an acceptable place to go. Although you shouldn't scold your puppy if it does go on the papers, you now shouldn't praise it either. Reserve your praise for outdoor elimination—don't give mixed messages!

If you are going to train your puppy outdoors from the beginning, a crate should be used for confinement.

This is a time when it's very important for you, or a surrogate, to be able to follow a rigid schedule until the puppy understands what you want. Unless it has the opportunity to eliminate regularly, according to its feeding and watering schedule, the trips outdoors won't be successful: the pup won't get the message that's where you want it to go. The more often the puppy goes outdoors and is praised lavishly by you, the sooner it will learn.

Choose your spot carefully. Find a quiet area somewhat free of distractions from other dogs, children playing, or continual traffic. You want your puppy to be able to concentrate on the job at hand. If it clearly doesn't like a particular spot and strains at the leash to leave, don't push it or punish the pup. This will defeat your purpose and make going outdoors into an unpleasant experience for the animal. Move on and find an area you and your pet agree on. Don't forget you'll have to be able to clean up whatever area you both choose, so aim to find an easily accessible spot—you don't want to have to climb under a bush or down an embankment every time you take your dog out.

But what if you take your puppy outdoors (or to its bathroom station), wait and wait, nothing happens and, as soon as you get indoors, it eliminates on its paper? This is a common situation. The puppy may be so well paper-trained that it can't make the transition to the outdoors. Some people suggest taking a piece of soiled paper outdoors and placing it on the chosen spot. But a puppy that is really well trained to use a certain spot won't use that paper any more than it will use a piece of paper in the den.

What you have to do is encourage your puppy to eliminate when and where you want it to.

ENCOURAGING ELIMINATION AT THE RIGHT TIME

It should be fairly obvious that if you take a puppy out when it doesn't need to eliminate, nothing will happen. Be sure to time your outings so that they coincide with your pet's own elimination schedule. Although most dogs need to defecate about fifteen minutes after a meal, some may not need to go for, say, half an hour after eating. If yours is one of the latter it will serve no purpose to take it out for a ten-minute walk fifteen minutes after supper because the urge to defecate won't come over it until after you've both returned home. Use your common sense and gear your walks to coincide with your own puppy's natural timing.

If you have gotten in the habit of using a command such as "Hurry up" or "Go, Fred" each time you see your puppy beginning to eliminate, it may be trigger enough for you to use this phrase when you reach the desired spot outdoors. Establishing this kind of verbal inducement can be very helpful, especially if you plan to travel with your pet. A dog that is particularly devoted to one particular spot may have great difficulty eliminating in a strange place. Your spoken command can stimulate the required urge in your pet.

■ PHYSICAL INDUCEMENTS ■

You can also encourage the need to eliminate in a puppy by gently stroking its tummy and groin area, just as a mother dog stimulates newborns to evacuate by licking. Holding the puppy cradled in your arms, rub it repeatedly on its underside and then place it on the ground. The puppy will usually eliminate right away. At the same time, give a verbal command so the pup will connect it with elimination. Of course, once the puppy goes, praise it. After a few times, the puppy usually outgrows the need for physical encouragement.

Quite often, however, no matter what method you use, your puppy simply doesn't understand that you want it to eliminate outdoors. I can't tell you the number of times owners have called me in complete frustration. A puppy happily goes out for a walk, comes home, and goes on the paper. No matter how long they stay outside—sometimes for hours—the puppy waits until they get back indoors and it can go on its regular spot. What should they do?

The first thing to try is to keep the puppy on the leash when you enter the house and restrain it from going to the paper. It will probably struggle to get to the paper because it really needs to go by now, but pick it up and take it right back outdoors again. If it has to go badly enough, this may work; as soon as it does, be sure to let the puppy know how pleased you are.

If even this doesn't work, the urge to defecate must be programmed to occur at the same time that the puppy is outdoors in a chosen spot. The way to do this is to induce the urge with a suppository. Choose a time when the puppy would normally defecate and insert an infant-size glycerine suppository into the puppy's rectum. To avoid an accident, pick the puppy up and hold it in your arms, its tail tightly against its body, until you reach the desired spot. The reflex to defecate will be induced by the suppository, and the puppy will immediately go. Of course, then reward it with praise and playtime. If you remember to use command words at the same time the puppy is having a bowel movement, the words alone may serve as a sufficient inducement the next time. Some puppies only require one or two times with this kind of an inducement to get the idea. Others may need more repetitions, but this is a surefire way to program a puppy that is having trouble adjusting to eliminating outdoors.

TEACHING A PUPPY TO SIGNAL WHEN IT NEEDS TO GO OUT

Of course, if your puppy uses an indoor comfort station, it doesn't need to learn to let you know when it needs to relieve itself—it can simply walk to its station and go. The same holds true if you live in a house in the country or suburbs where you can provide your pet with some kind of door it can go in and out of at will.

For puppies that need to either be taken out or let out, you should teach them how to signal you or whatever caretaker is around when they need to go out. When your puppy is first being trained to use the outdoors, you are the one who must be "trained" to pay attention to the time and take it out on a regular basis. As the puppy matures and is able to wait longer between outings, though, you want it to be able to let you know when it wants out.

It will take a while before your puppy is sophisticated enough to learn to signal you all the time, but you can encourage this behavior. Whining, barking, scratching at the door, and running back and forth "Lassie fashion" are some of the more common signals dogs use, and if they meet with success each time, they become a habit.

In some instances, though, when owners or pet caretakers are preoccupied, these signals are too subtle, and more noticeable signals are called for. Some owners, for instance, teach their pets to fetch their leads when it's time for a walk. A dog that has been taught to do this will often go and get the leash and present its owner with it if it needs to go out. This is a signal that's hard to ignore.

One owner with whom I work was at her wits' end. She worked at home and had recently moved from a city apartment to a suburban home with a fenced-in yard for her small terrier. When they had lived in the city, the dog had scheduled walks and was fine. But in the suburbs she found she would become preoccupied with her work and forget to let the little dog outdoors. Although he whined and barked at the door, her office was upstairs and she often didn't hear him until it was too late. I thought about it and worked out a signaling system that worked perfectly.

First, I hung a string of carriage bells right beside the door. Then I sat in the next room and every time the little dog barked or whined to go out, I rang the bells loudly before opening the door. After doing this several times, I showed the dog how he could make the bells ring by pulling on a string. Each time he asked to go out by barking or whining, I went over and made him ring the bells before I'd open the door. Soon he got the idea, and now his mistress can clearly hear the bells ringing from her upstairs office and let him out when he asks.

URINE LEAKING

Urine dribbling, or leaking, is a very common submissive action on the part of young puppies, and stems from pack behavior. A wolf, such as a cub, that is not dominant in the pack and doesn't want to challenge a more dominant animal will always adopt a submissive pose when approached. It will lower itself to the ground and present its belly in an "I give up. I'm helpless" gesture. It will often lick the dominant wolf's face at the same time it dribbles urine. A puppy or young dog that's otherwise well house-trained, often dribbles or squirts urine as it greets its owner (the more dominant animal) as he arrives home.

I'm currently working with two sweet female golden retrievers that have this problem. Sally is under a year old and as soon as her owners come in the door, she rushes to greet them, then squats and urinates. Six-month-old Sasha's reaction is even more elaborate. When she sees a familiar human, she grovels on the ground in ecstasy, rolls over onto her back, and lets go with a puddle of urine.

In either case, this is not a "bad" or conscious action on the part of the dog, and it should not be punished. Punishment will teach it nothing and will only serve to make the dog more anxious and worried and will add to the problem.

Most puppies outgrow urine leaking as they get older and gain better control of their bladders. However, there are things you can do to prevent and control this behavior in the meantime. Bear in mind that, in addition to the instinctive submissive behavior I described, your puppy has usually been asleep when you come home and hasn't been out for a while. It has a full bladder, and most animals urinate as soon as they wake up. Add this to the excitement of your arrival, and boom, an accident is in the making.

If you live in a house with an enclosed yard, put your dog out the minute you come in, before you even say "Hello" to it. Once it's had a chance to relieve itself, then you can indulge in an elaborate greeting without risk of a leak.

If you live in an apartment and can't let your dog outdoors alone, keep a leash right by the door. Again, before you greet the dog, make a loose loop of the leash, like a lasso, and put it around the dog's neck. Immediately make the dog focus on you and have it Heel with you for a minute or two. This will calm it down and get it out of the greeting mode until you can take it out for a walk.

Most important, don't encourage your dog to become all excited when you come home. Curb your enthusiasm and try not to even look at your pet until it's had a chance to relieve itself. Then you can play with it and tell it how happy you are to see it with impunity.

SPECIAL HOUSEBREAKING SITUATIONS

So far, the housebreaking situations I've described have been based on the assumption that a puppy has normal elimination instincts, and that you or someone else will be around during the time it takes to house-train the pup. But in some instances, these basics don't hold true.

First, let's take the case of a puppy that has spent its entire life up until the time you get it confined in a small cage. A puppy from a pet store or animal shelter has often lived this way. Because it has had nowhere else to go, it has had to eliminate in the same area in which it sleeps and eats, and its natural instinct to leave its wastes some distance from its sleeping and eating areas have been programmed out. In a case such as this, the animal needs to be completely deprogrammed out of its inappropriate behavior before it can be programmed in appropriate behavior.

This will take an enormous amount of dedication, time, and patience on your part. The use of a crate and a very rigid schedule is necessary. The crate must be only large enough for the pup to lie down and stand up, with no room for it to squat and eliminate at all. You must take the pup out of the crate and to the papers on a religious basis every few hours and praise it lavishly every time it goes on the paper. If you leave this puppy alone in an enclosed room to go on the papers by itself, it will never be properly programmed because it will still be able to go whenever it needs to instead of learning to wait for an appropriate time and place. These puppies sometimes take a long time to be finally housebroken.

Another special situation arises if you are unable to be at home or are too busy to follow a schedule during the time your puppy is growing up. If this happens, you have to face the fact that it will take a great deal longer for it to become properly programmed, even if you are able to devote full time to it on weekends and evenings. If, for instance, you can't follow a regular feeding or watering program during the day, you have to leave dry food and water out for the puppy to eat and drink at will. If you leave papers on the floor and aren't there to correct or praise your puppy when it eliminates, the chances are it will go on the paper about half of the time. Some fastidious animals learn to eliminate in one spot all by themselves as they mature, but most puppies are unable to figure this out without help from you. If you have to be away from home for even one full day during the training period, you realistically have to expect your puppy to backslide.

The best solution in this type of situation is to hire someone who can take over for you during the critical house-training period. Sometimes a veterinarian's or groomer's assistant will be able to come to your home and perform this service. In every big city, there are also people who are in the business of dog-walking. But whoever you get must be able to follow an appropriate schedule for your pet.

An example of how this kind of arrangement may have its pitfalls is a six-month-old Norfolk terrier I recently worked with named Daisy, who was paper-trained and ready to be transferred to eliminating outdoors. In her busy household it was difficult for the owners to adhere to a schedule for Daisy during the important transition period, so they hired a dog walker for her. The dog walker, who regularly exercised about a dozen dogs, came to the apartment and picked Daisy up three or four times a day. Daisy would be walked for about an hour, and when she got home, she'd run in happily and immediately urinate and defecate right on the rug! She obviously enjoyed her walks, but didn't understand that this was the time to eliminate. All the walks did was stimulate her so she was really ready to eliminate when she arrived home. I suggested that she was too young for group walks. She hadn't yet been sufficiently well programmed to eliminate outdoors, and needed the individualized attention of one person during this learning stage. The walker had to act as a surrogate owner and stick to Daisy's schedule. After a period of time in which the walker followed all the steps that I outlined above, Daisy became perfectly trained to go outdoors.

Whatever investment you make at this time in hiring a reliable assistant will pay off in the end. Otherwise you may end up with an adult dog that will never be reliably house-trained and will always have to be confined when you're not home.

HOW TO TEACH YOUR PUPPY TO RECOGNIZE ITS NAME

One of the first things you want to teach your puppy is to recognize its name and to respond to it. The puppy couldn't care less what you call it, but for your own sake, choose a name, or nickname, that isn't a tongue twister. A simple one-syllable word is easier to say and also easier for your dog to recognize immediately. Thus, you may want to name your dog Mr. Bojangles, but you'll probably call him Bo, and Rebecca of Sunnybrook Farm will undoubtedly become Becky. Don't confuse your puppy by calling it Bo one day, and Bojangles the next. Be consistent and it will learn its name much faster.

A young puppy will naturally want to be with you and will follow you around eagerly at every opportunity. When it does, say its name to it repeatedly so that it becomes used to the sound. Crouch down and pat the ground in front of you, saying "Come, Bo" or "Here, Becky." As soon as the puppy runs to you, pet it and praise it. Make sure you have your puppy's full attention when teaching it its name. Clap your hands, wiggle an intriguing new toy, make a kissing or clicking mouth noise, or slap your thigh sharply at the same time that you say its name.

As you play with it, feed it, and brush it, always speak to your puppy by name so it learns to associate hearing its name with pleasant things. Every time you use the puppy's name, say it in a bright, upbeat tone of voice that conveys approval. Soon your puppy will learn to look up at you when you say its name. When it does, pet it under the chin and tell it what a good puppy it is.

HOW TO TEACH A PUPPY TO WEAR A COLLAR AND LEASH

As soon as your puppy settles down in the household, you want to teach it to become accustomed to wearing a collar. This is the first step toward learning to walk on a leash.

Sometimes a new puppy owner will say to me, "Bash, I don't see any need to teach Poopsie to wear a collar. I'm going to teach her to use an indoor bathroom station and I never intend to walk her." My response is that every dog needs to be able to wear a collar and walk on a leash. What about trips to the veterinarian? What if you want to visit a friend who has several cats? What if there's a fire or other emergency, and you have to go out to the sidewalk? What if you should become ill and a friend has to take Poopsie to her house? Unexpected things do come up in everyone's life, and for the sake of your dog and its safety, it should be able to wear a collar and leash without panicking. The only way for that to happen is if it learns when it's still young.

A tiny puppy should begin with a soft rolled leather or nylon collar that buckles around its neck. The collar should be long enough so the puppy can grow a bit, but not so long that it trips over the end at first. The rule of thumb when fitting a collar is to allow enough space so you can fit three fingers underneath, between the collar and the puppy's neck.

Sit the puppy in your lap, put the collar on, and pat the puppy soothingly. Then set the puppy down on the floor. Most puppies don't pay much attention to the collar, but some shake their heads, run around in circles, and try to rub the collar off. If the puppy does become frantic, take the collar off immediately and try again the next day. After a few tries the puppy usually realizes it's not going to be able to shake or rub the collar off. It helps if you can distract the puppy with a favorite toy or game so it will soon forget all about the collar. Don't leave a puppy alone with a collar on—it can easily become caught on something and hurt itself.

Once the puppy is comfortable wearing a collar, snap a lightweight leash on and let the puppy drag it around to get the feel of it. After a couple of days of this, hook the leash to a doorknob or place it under a chair leg while you sit in the room. You want the puppy to become used to being restrained a bit. You're saying to it, "I like to have you in the same room with me, but I don't want you all over me. I want to sit quietly and read." After struggling to get away for a while, the puppy will usually give up and lie down at the end of the leash. Then you can give it a favorite chew-toy to play with. This is an important lesson in restraint for a puppy to learn. For safety's sake, never leave a puppy alone with a leash on, even for a minute.

As the puppy gets older and is perfectly comfortable wearing a soft collar, it's time to graduate to a training, or correction, collar for more control. A training collar is what some people refer to as a choke collar, but this is a misleading name for it. If put on and used correctly, a training collar will *never* choke a dog! Now's the time to begin to teach your puppy to walk properly on a leash. There's more about how to do this in the next chapter.

HOW TO TEACH YOUR PUPPY TO RIDE IN A CAR

At about the same time that your puppy is learning to walk on a leash and beginning to learn about the environment outside your home, it's time to introduce it to car travel. There are many occasions when you may want to take your dog in the car with you, and the earlier it learns proper car manners, the better. If you wait until your pet is grown up before socializing it to car travel, you may find it becomes a major production.

I'm reminded of a shaggy, mixed-breed dog named Hampton with whom I've been working. Hampton grew up at his family's home on Long Island. It never occurred to his owners that he would need to learn about car travel. But when he was about two years old, the family decided to move back into New York City for the winter, and keep their home in the Hamptons for weekends. Naturally, they wanted to bring Hampton back and forth with them in the car. But much to their distress, Hampton, who had never ridden in a car before, reacted with hysteria. He became so upset that he drooled all over himself—the entire backseat of the car was wet. They couldn't seem to reassure him that everything was all right, and finally their veterinarian had to prescribe a tranquilizer for Hampton so that he could ride in the car without making a complete mess of himself and all of the car's other occupants.

If only Hampton had been accustomed to car riding when he was a puppy, this would not have happened. Even if you don't think you will ever take your dog on car trips, you can't always anticipate what you may do in the future, and this is an important part of its early socialization. Take your puppy on short trips in the car, get out and take a walk, and then go home again so the dog learns what it's all about.

One of the biggest problems with puppies is that they often become sick to their stomachs in a car. Car motion sickness may be related to nervousness, so one way to prevent this is to accustom your puppy to riding in a car early in life so it doesn't feel threatened or insecure. If you're going on a ride of any length, remember not to give the puppy anything to eat or drink for an hour or more before your departure. A puppy with an empty stomach generally does not become carsick.

If car sickness persists, I recommend putting the puppy in a carrying case or travel crate with closed sides. It's well known that children who are regularly car sick during the day can usually ride comfortably at night. This is because motion sickness is thought to be closely related to vision. Thus, when a puppy is in a case or crate with closed sides, it can't perceive the landscape whisking by and won't become nauseated. A crate or carrying case also protects the car's upholstery and other occupants in case mistakes do occur.

Two things you have to consider when you travel with

a dog in the car are its safety and comfort and yours. The animal should be secure so it doesn't fall or get thrown into the windows in case of a sudden stop. At the same time, it needs to be taught not to interfere with the driver in any way. An overexuberant dog who jumps all over the driver can become a serious hazard.

Some people choose to have a dog sit in the front passenger seat, while others put a dog in the back, either on the seat or the floor. If a dog is going to ride on a car seat, many owners protect the upholstery with a cover. It's a good idea to crack the window open if a dog is riding in the back, but don't ever allow a dog to ride with its head out the window. This can cause serious eye and ear problems—infections from the wind and lacerations from bits of soot and other debris.

There are several ways to travel with a dog in the car. If the puppy is comfortable and secure in a crate at home, have a small crate in the car as I did with Mariah. After one or two trips, the dog will jump happily into its crate and look out of the window while you travel. On long trips a dog will often go peacefully to sleep.

If you have a station wagon, another way to confine a dog in the car and keep it safe from harm is to have a car barrier—a wire mesh gate-type device that keeps a dog confined to the back of the wagon.

There are now seat-belt systems for dogs on the market. They consist of a harness with a clip to attach to the car's seat belt and allow the dog freedom to move around and lie down, at the same time keeping it safely in place. They cost around twenty-five dollars and are available at pet-supply stores and through mail order.

However your dog rides, a favorite chew-toy can help keep your puppy happy and content while you drive.

Don't forget the most important rule of all if you take your dog with you in the car. *Never leave your dog alone in a parked car.* Not only do you risk the possibility of theft—over a million pets are stolen every year for sale to research laboratories—but you also risk your dog's life from heat prostration. Even in relatively cool weather (seventy degrees, for example) it takes only a few minutes of bright sunshine to raise the temperature of the interior of a car to well over one hundred degrees. A dog in a car this hot can die from heatstroke or suffer from permanent brain damage in ten minutes. So on warm days, confine your car riding to short trips, or go out in the evening when the sun is down.

NIP ANNOYING HABITS IN THE BUD

The time to prevent annoying habits from developing is when a puppy is young and malleable. Don't forget that what seems cute in a puppy may become an obnoxious habit in an adult dog. Think ahead. Anticipate what kind of an adult you want your puppy to become.

■ JUMPING UP ON PEOPLE ■

"Oh, how cute, he's so happy to see me!" This may be your reaction when your puppy exuberantly jumps up on you when you walk into the room. But five months later, it's not so cute when your almost-grown dog snags your stockings, tears your sweater, or almost knocks you over. Jumping up on people is a habit that should be discouraged early on.

You have to teach your puppy that jumping up is not acceptable at any time, with anyone. There are several ways to do this, and which way is effective depends in part on the dog's temperament. For some puppies you merely need to show them that this is not acceptable behavior. As soon as the puppy begins to jump, open both of your hands in front of its face, palms down, and say "No" firmly. If you need to make the message clearer, push the puppy down, or pull it down by grabbing the collar on either side with both hands; if the puppy isn't wearing a collar, grab it by the loose skin on either side of its neck. Do this every single time the puppy begins to jump up.

Visitors may prove to be a problem when you're trying to teach this lesson because some may encourage your puppy to jump up on them. I recommend that you put a leash on your puppy whenever visitors come to call. Then if the puppy begins to jump up when they come in, you can immediately correct it with a snap of the leash while you say "No." This programs the puppy not to jump. Then drop the leash and watch the puppy. If it looks as if it's going to jump again, step on the leash just before it begins and say "No" again. This reinforces the programming in the puppy's early stages.

If your puppy is really exuberant you may need stronger measures to make it realize that jumping up is never acceptable. If the dog jumps up even after you say "No," raise your knee in a reflex action so it goes right into the dog's chest and say "No" simultaneously. Then set the dog up—encourage it to jump just as a visitor might do, and immediately hit it with your knee. After a few times the dog will realize that no matter what the encouragement, it should never jump up.

Later on, what if you want to be able to hug your dog, or train it to stand up against you? If you want, you can crouch down to the dog's level and begin to hug it there. Then you can put your hand beneath your dog's paws and lift as you stand up. This way you are the one who is doing the lifting—the dog is not jumping up on you. The other method I use when training a dog to stand up and hug me as a stunt is to put my right arm out at an angle from my body and encourage the dog to put its paws on my arm. Then I can bring my arm over to my body to hug the dog. Again, this action is one initiated by me, not by the dog.

■ **WHINING AND BARKING** ■

The need for companionship and communication in dogs is directly related to pack behavior. Many puppies will bark and whine and cry the first time they're left alone at night. If you come back and cuddle and comfort the puppy as soon as it cries, its natural reaction will be to begin to cry again as soon as you leave to get you to come back. Each time you come back and leave you will be creating more anxiety and the puppy will soon learn that all it has to do to get you to come back is to cry some more—you'll inadvertently be reinforcing its behavior.

If you can stand it, the best thing to do is to ignore the puppy's cries as long as you know its physical needs are taken care of. Before long the puppy will tire itself out and go to sleep and after a few nights the crying will cease.

If you can't do this, or if the puppy seems to be working itself into a frenzy you may feel you have to do something to help it stop. Go into the room and clap your hands sharply and say "No." This should startle it into quiet. If it starts to call again after a few minutes, repeat these actions. It will also help to take the puppy's muzzle firmly in your hand and squeeze it gently together as you say "No." This is the action a mother wolf or dog takes if a pup becomes hysterical and can't stop crying and a puppy will usually understand it right away. Always walk away immediately after taking this action to signify "Incident over. Settle down now."

Sometimes excessive barking behavior doesn't surface until a dog is older. Usually it occurs when owners who have been around with an animal all of the time suddenly leave it to go back to work. This is a symptom of separation anxiety, and ignoring the behavior at this point will usually cause a dog to become more and more hysterical. You will have to stop the barking. See Chapter 9 for more about how to do this.

6

BASIC ON-LEAD OBEDIENCE TRAINING FOR DOGS OF ALL AGES

Owners whose dogs are going to be family pets often ask me why they should bother with obedience training. They say, "All I really care about is that Alice is housebroken and able to walk pretty well on a leash. She doesn't need to learn all that other stuff." Others worry about the old-fashioned theory that obedience training will "break a dog's spirit."

Let me explain why I think obedience training is so important for *every* dog, regardless of its role in life. First of all, you can never predict what may occur in the future. In the course of the twenty or so years your dog lives with you, your family situation might change or you may have to move to a different location, and your dog may be required to adapt to a whole new set of circumstances. If your dog is well trained it will be a relaxed, secure animal—never "spooked" or skittish. It won't matter where it goes or what unusual situation occurs, because it will trust you. It will be able to tolerate strange places and people, boisterous children, unusual circumstances, and even loud, frightening noises because it will know what to do around them. Just as I was able to safely take Mariah (a wolf!) onto a chaotic TV set amid a horde of people she'd never seen before, you will be able to take your well-trained dog anywhere, secure in the knowledge that it will behave well.

The structure and security of obedience training provide a dog with "rules to live by." Part of every dog's natural pack mentality includes the need for order, to know what is expected of it and when. Your aim is to establish this structure so that your pet knows how to act in any situation. Even if you don't want to have a movie dog, like Lassie or Benji, you do want your dog to be responsive to your wishes no matter what comes up. I sometimes tell my clients that a dog needs a "dogma" to live by and that they must be somewhat "dogmatic" in order to teach this to it.

At the same time you give your dog guidelines for behavior, you automatically develop a rapport with the animal and reinforce the bonding you began to establish when it was a puppy. You also firmly establish the pack leadership position that's so important for a successful ongoing relationship with your pet. By constantly reminding your dog you are its Alpha person, you give it the security it needs in order to function well in society.

Let's look at an analogy. An untrained dog is like a teenager who's never been taken to a restaurant by his parents. When he finally does go out to dinner, he has no idea how to act or what to do and is embarrassed and uncomfortable. Just as a thoughtful, responsible parent teaches a child how to behave in public, a responsible dog owner does the same for a puppy. An untrained dog wants to please and do the right thing, but doesn't know how.

If you're an owner who still questions the need for obedience training, I urge you to try once more to take your dog's point of view. If you do, you'll realize your pet will be happy and secure only when it knows how it's supposed to react in order to gain your approval. Far from breaking a dog's spirit, obedience training frees your dog from anxiety.

▪ AN OBVIOUS NEED FOR TRAINING ▪

Sometimes it's obvious from the beginning that a dog will require serious training.

J. P. Molyneux, the Park Avenue decorator, called me the minute he brought home two little Neapolitan mastiff pups. He wanted them to be able to run loose on his Vermont estate and act as watchdogs.

The five-month-old "boys," Tiziano and Palladio, were adorable, but I knew they would grow to be powerful, aggressively territorial, and potentially dangerous adult dogs—mastiffs have traditionally been bred to protect estates in Europe against poachers. What's more, we had to establish dominance roles between them early on. Otherwise, the two males would continuously battle for leadership.

We worked together with the dogs and first taught them basic obedience. After they'd mastered that, we moved on to off-lead training. When Tiziano and Palladio were perfectly reliable off-lead, Mr. Molyneux asked the caretaker of his estate to come to New York to learn how to control the dogs properly. That done, the dogs moved from the city to Vermont. There they roam the estate in complete security and harmony.

Recently Mr. Molyneux called to see if I could go to Vermont with him. It seems he's now gotten two new dogs—Scotties this time—and wants me to come up and help Tiziano and Palladio learn to accept the newcomers.

WHERE TO GO FOR OBEDIENCE TRAINING

Whether a puppy or dog goes with you to obedience school or you hire a trainer to come into your home, basic on-lead obedience training usually follows either a puppy or beginner class. In this case, a puppy is around six to eight months of age, but basic on-lead obedience can be successfully taught to a dog at any age. It's a necessary first step if you anticipate going on to any other type of obedience work with your pet, and serves as a foundation for all other kinds of training.

Several types of obedience instruction are available. There are individual, nonaffiliated trainers who either serve as personal instructors or who run dog schools and conduct group training classes. Often park and/or recreation departments of municipalities hire dog trainers to conduct group dog-training classes for their residents at a nominal fee. Humane societies also sponsor group dog-training classes for adoptive owners and others.

The American Kennel Club (AKC) sanctions obedience trial competitions all over the country. These are open to the public. If you visit a local AKC-sponsored dog show, you will be able to see well-trained dogs in action and may even be able to make contact with a local dog trainer. AKC-sanctioned obedience clubs usually hold dog-training classes throughout the year. To find out about an obedience club in your area, ask your breeder, veterinarian, or dog groomer, or contact the AKC directly.*

SHOULD YOU SEND YOUR DOG SOMEWHERE TO BE TRAINED?

Many clients come to me after they've spent a lot of money sending their dogs to be "trained" by someone else only to find that once the dog got home, it forgot all of its expensive training. If you believe in the advertisements that say things such as "Give me your dog for two weeks [or a month], and he'll return home perfectly trained," then you believe in fairy tales.

Nothing is that easy when you're dealing with a complex animal like a dog. I won't take on the training of any dog unless the owner is willing to make a commitment to the training process. After all, it's the owner who will be the constant in a dog's life, no matter how

* American Kennel Club, 51 Madison Avenue, New York, NY 10010.

many other caretakers take over from time to time. In addition to the all-important bonding of owner to dog and vice versa, an owner must establish a proper leadership role, providing consistent signals and rules. Otherwise the dog just becomes confused.

I insist that the owner work with a dog at least in the beginning. Then, as is the case of many of my celebrity clients, if the owner is really too busy or travels too much to continue with all of the dog's training, I sometimes take the dog to stay with me and fine-tune its training.

Appropriate substitutes can also step in for the owner, but they must learn how to communicate with the dog and be willing and able to follow the proper training steps and routines. What's more, the owner still has to remain the overseer to make sure the dog doesn't get mixed messages. The housekeeper, dog walker, and so forth needs to be taught how to proceed or chaos will reign. Many's the time I've been called in to solve a behavior problem only to discover that the problem isn't with the dog but with its caretakers, who have, say, failed to take it out according to its schedule but invented a schedule of their own.

Occasionally, circumstances are such that I will take on the training of a dog away from home. But again, the owner must be willing to make a commitment. He has to agree to take the time to work with me afterward to learn how to communicate with his dog and follow through on its training.

A dog is not a car or TV that you can take to the shop to have fine-tuned. To be sure a dog "works well" and is responsive to you, you must be willing to make a commitment of time and affection.

MAKE THE MAGIC HAPPEN

Obedience training serves a very positive purpose, and in order for it to really succeed, you should approach it with the attitude that you and your dog are going to have fun while you both learn. Only then can you really succeed. If you go about training your dog as if it were an unpleasant necessity, the animal will soon sense your mood and become bored and inattentive. As they always say, "You'll attract more bees with honey than with vinegar."

If you could be a fly on the wall during one of my group classes or individual lessons, you'd see that I always combine a firm, businesslike attitude with an upbeat, positive manner. Although I insist that a dog focus on me and pay attention, I am never grim or cross. And I always praise a dog when it does well.

Key to success is to develop a sense of timing and rhythm. I like to think of the steps in dog training as an elaborate choreography that combines body language with verbal commands to form a foundation for communication between dog and owner. You and your dog will work and move together as one, in tandem, just as Randy Gardner and Tai Babalonia did when they skated. After a while you should try to create a pace comprised of the various steps in the training routine—your action/the dog's reaction/action/reaction, and so forth. At the same time, move in rhythm. Many of my clients count to themselves as they go through the steps with their dogs. Others find it helpful to put marching music on the stereo. Do whatever works for you to help you and your dog to move in rhythm.

Sometimes you may have to manipulate your dog a bit in order to modify its mood and make it receptive to training. For instance, if your dog clearly doesn't feel like going through the paces one day, you can do what I do with my bulldog, Zack, who often seems bored and too tired to bother with a training session. I sneak into training with him. First we play and I let him get silly. Then, after we've played for a while and Zack's no longer bored, I slip on his leash and off we go into our training routine!

What if it's the other way around—your puppy is full of beans and driving you crazy when you want to relax? Then it's time to say, "OK, you want my attention.

Well, it's training time." After a ten-minute workout, the puppy will be all tired out—the mental exhaustion of a training session does the trick faster than a half-hour of mindless play. You will have turned a "misguided missile" into a calm, relaxed animal.

An important point: *Always stop a session on a successful note.* Even if your dog has gone through its paces well ten previous times, if the last exercise isn't correct, you must repeat it until it is right. You always want to end a training session positively. Otherwise, if you break for play or food after a mistake, you have allowed the *dog* to take the initiative. This kind of misplaced kindness makes training your dog very difficult. If you allow your dog to quit when it wants to, you're giving it the message that the entire training process is unimportant to you. Be consistent. If you're not, your dog won't respect you and take you seriously.

HOW TO COMMUNICATE WITH YOUR DOG:
SIGNALS AND COMMANDS

I have developed a starter system of training that uses a combination of signals, both body language and verbal commands. You use your entire body, in rhythm, to communicate your wishes to your pet. Both verbal and physical signals are important during the initial learning period because they work directly with a dog's enhanced senses and help it to focus on you and respond to your wishes. Later on, if you decide to go into obedience competition with your dog, you will only be allowed to use one form of communication—either verbal commands or physical signals. If you anticipate going this route, now is the time to figure out which form of communication your dog is most comfortable with so you can concentrate on it later on. If, like my Muffin, your dog ends up performing in movies and commercials, you will eventually have to graduate to the sole use of off-camera physical signals.

There are four main reasons to communicate with

your dog when you're training it. First, you want to make your dog *focus* on you and give you its undivided attention. Then you need to *show* it what you want it to do with a clear set of commands and signals that always remain the same. If your dog doesn't react correctly, you have to communicate your displeasure and immediately *make a correction*. And, last, you want to convey your approval and *praise* at the end of the exercise when your dog responds right.

Body language is usually easier for dogs to understand than vocal commands. Because of the social structure of the pack, canines instinctively look for physical signals conveying messages such as aggression, submission, and so forth. Even so, the signals you give your dog during training may be hard for it to interpret at first.

Dog owners often unwittingly convey contradictory messages to their pets with their body language and facial expressions. Sometimes people forget that a dog doesn't understand the exact meaning of their words. If they're scowling or making an impatient hand gesture at the same time they are saying "Good dog," the dog will interpret the message as a negative one. On the other hand, a naughty puppy won't take your scolding seriously if you're also chuckling at its antics. The old saying "Actions speak louder than words" has a special application when you're beginning to train a dog.

Your body motions must be exaggerated in order to convey your messages clearly to your dog. I tell people to pretend they're on the stage and need to communicate with someone who's sitting at the top of the highest balcony. The more you ham it up, the more easily your dog is able to avoid distractions, focus on you as a point of reference, and clearly understand your meaning. This is all part of the tandem approach I talked about earlier—your aim is total communication. Some people find it hard to loosen up enough to do this well, but you should really try—sometimes practicing in front of a mirror helps.

I want you to use your entire body when you train

your dog. Use your hands and arms to give signals. At the same time you'll also give messages with the position and motion of your feet and legs. To get your dog's attention, call on its keen hearing and slap your thigh sharply. Communicate disapproval and correction with a snap of the leash, often accompanied by a critical facial expression. Approval and praise are conveyed with a pat under the chin and perhaps a smile.

At the same time, use your voice to give commands and to convey both disapproval and praise. Each physical action (use of body language) will be reinforced by words at first.

In beginning training, you shouldn't address your dog by name during any of the exercises except Heel and Come. I'm often asked why. This is so you can emphasize the words of your commands. If you say, "Sam, sit," "Sam, stay," "Sam, heel," after a while the dog's name itself becomes a nagging word and the dog ceases to listen. Commands should be short, positive, and easy to focus on, and most owners tend to use a dog's name too much. Never use a dog's name in training except where I've indicated in the following steps.

TECHNIQUES OF PRAISE AND CORRECTION DURING TRAINING

Praise and correction in every form ought to be exaggerated at first, just as your body language is. You want to convey your approval or disapproval in no uncertain terms. In each case, an immediate response is called for—your reaction must directly follow the dog's action or it will have no effect at all.

■ PUNISHMENT ■

Some people confuse punishment and correction. Punishment occurs when you react in an angry, impulsive, illogical way and strike out at your dog by yelling at it or striking it. Punishment of this sort does not result in a learning experience for a dog. All it accomplishes is to let the dog know it's been bad; it doesn't show it how to be good. From a dog's point of view, this means nothing at all. A dog cannot think in human terms and has no way of knowing what "bad" and "good" actions consist of—it must be shown.

Properly applied correction, on the other hand, does become a learning experience for a dog.

■ CORRECTION ■

Each time you correct a dog you are saying, in effect, "No! Action wrong. Stop what you're doing. Focus on me and follow my directions." The dog must stop in its tracks and pay attention right away. This means the correction must be quick and sharp. Always accompany whatever physical correction that you make with a loud, sharp "No!"

It is extremely important for every dog to be programmed to respond immediately to a verbal "No." Many times this automatic response could save a dog's life or prevent a serious situation from occurring. For instance, say you open the door of your apartment with your dog by your side and see a little old lady walking down the hall with a cane. Your big, gallumpy, half-grown dog starts to bolt out of the door after the lady and will surely knock her over! You say "No" sharply, and the dog stops in its tracks. You grab its collar, say "Good dog," and lead it back inside. Crisis over. Or, imagine your terrier is playing with you in the backyard and somehow the gate has been left ajar. The dog sees a neighbor's cat across the road and starts to run out the gate just as a car comes along. Your "No" will stop the dog in its tracks. Then you can either tell it to "Come" or "Sit/Stay" and the dog is safe.

In order to reinforce a verbal command in the beginning, you usually need to accompany it with a physical action. A quick, sharp pull and release on the training collar serves to emphasize the command. After a few times your dog will associate the word "No" with a tug on its collar, and in order to avoid the tug it will respond immediately to the verbal command alone. You have taught your dog to heed the "No" command and no longer have to reinforce it with a physical action.

To backtrack a minute, I want to amplify on the right way to apply correction to a training collar. The object is not to hurt the dog, but to make the dog stop and pay attention—focus on you. You want to shape the dog's behavior to suit your wishes, and in this respect you must always come out ahead. If the collar is put on the dog correctly (see below), the pressure on the dog's neck will release the minute you release your pull on the leash. The object is to give a quick snap, then release, to startle the dog into paying attention. Although the snap needn't be hard, you may want to turn or twist your body slightly to the right, against the leash, to emphasize the snap. This is especially helpful if you aren't very big, and your dog is. Never apply sustained pressure to a training collar. This will only defeat the whole purpose—you won't be able to startle the dog into paying attention when you want. What's more, a dog that has continuous pressure on its neck will soon develop strong neck and shoulder muscles and you won't be able to correct it at all.

In some situations, however, you may have to enlist the help of the force of gravity to correct a dog and make it comply with a command. If your dog is powerful or aggressive and simply refuses to perform a certain action (this often happens when you want a big dog to go Down), you may have to exert pressure on the leash with your foot in order to pull the animal down—more about this when we get to the basic training routine.

Timing is extremely important when you make a correction. Don't wait for your dog to decide to comply with a command. I always tell owners to count to three and then correct the dog. Three seconds is all the time the dog should wait before it obeys you. Watch your dog and anticipate it if it's not about to obey. This three-second margin is important at first—time your dog's response and correct the dog if it doesn't respond in this time. You will have programmed the dog to respond on time. Often, for instance, a dog will begin to come when called, but will then have to make a last run around before actually coming—the dog seems to feel it has to say good-bye to everything and everyone before it finally comes to its owner. It's just like the little child who has to say good night to all of the guests and family members one more time before going up to bed. This may seem cute to you at first, but it won't be when you're really in a hurry one day.

An extreme example of this is a client who has a Rhodesian ridgeback puppy. Every day when she took the dog out in the park, she would have to give him a half-hour "warning" before he would come to her to go home. It went like this: "OK, come now. I'm leaving." Five minutes later, "I'm leaving," and so on. Finally, she'd have to ask all of the people nearby to help her catch the dog so she could go home. With concentrated on-leash training in which we corrected the dog when it didn't respond to the Come command in three seconds, he's now perfectly trained to come as soon as he's called.

Remember, correction must always be immediate in order to be effective. Don't go on to the next step until a correction has been fully made. That is, the dog has stopped its incorrect behavior, focused on you, and then performed the action correctly. Otherwise, you have taught your dog it can get away with mistakes with impunity.

■ **PRAISE** ■

Applied correctly, praise is a more valuable training tool than correction. Most dogs are anxious to please their owners, and once they know an action will gain approval it will become a well-programmed action. Patience, persistence, and *praise*—remember, these are my key words for successful dog training.

Be careful not to give your dog mixed messages with praise, however. Don't praise your dog lavishly when it stops doing an incorrect action. Reserve your praise for the times when it does something correctly. In my training program I often see an owner make the mistake of praising his dog in the middle of an exercise. It goes like this: The dog sits nicely at the other end of the leash during the Sit/Stay, and before the owner comes back to the dog's side at the end of the routine he says "Good dog" enthusiastically. The dog naturally jumps right up excitedly and runs to the owner before finishing the exercise. From the dog's point of view, praise means "Well done, I'm pleased with you," and signals the job is over. Reserve your lavish praise until an exercise is finished.

Having said this, I have to add there are times during an exercise when you may want to encourage your pet and let it know it's doing well. When your dog is performing perfectly in the midst of a long, difficult exercise, or if it suddenly masters something you've been working on for a long time, a gentle tap or a murmured "Good dog" will reassure a dog that you're pleased with it. Just don't gush too enthusiastically or your pet's concentration will be broken.

Nothing reassures a dog better than a gentle, approving touch or pat. A pat can also help you communicate with your dog if it's given in the right way. One of my pet peeves is that most people pat a dog incorrectly, on the top of the head, probably because it's the part of the body nearest their hand. This is a mistake, because when you do this you force the dog to look down toward the ground as you tap on the top of its head—each tap drives it further down. Naturally, the dog can't understand why you're doing this and thinks, "If I'm being good, why does this person keep hitting me on the top of the head?" It's uncomfortable and unpleasant. You want your dog to look up at you, to focus on you and see your face, especially when you're training it. The correct way to praise a dog is to pet it underneath the chin. Starting from the tip of the chin, stroke gently and smoothly in the direction of the hair growth, down to the dog's breastbone, in a soothing, calm way. This forces the dog to look up at you so you can continue to communicate with it. If you wish, you can reinforce your praise by moving your hand around to the back of the dog's neck and scratching there.

In general, I am against using food rewards as a training tool with dogs. To me, it smacks of bribery—"If you do what I want, I'll give you a food treat." You want your dog to do what you want because you are its pack leader and authority figure, not because you're going to give it a piece of cheese. I always wonder what happens when a dog that's been trained solely by the use of food rewards is too distracted to pay attention to food or decides that it isn't hungry. What's more, food treats are not allowed in obedience competitions or field trials, and they certainly make no sense for training either retrievers or guard dogs—they would defeat the entire purpose of the training. (A retriever might eat the game it was supposed to bring back, while a guard dog could be distracted from doing its job if an intruder gave it food.)

As with all other rules, though, this one, too, has certain exceptions. Very young puppies are hungry all the time, and sometimes when you're working with one a dog biscuit or other food treat serves to capture its attention better than words or actions can and will make it associate coming to you with a pleasurable experience. It helps teach the puppy to respond at an early age.

In the ring in dog shows, for conformation, handlers often hold a food treat in one hand. It serves as a focus point so the dog will appear alert and calm as it looks at the hand that's holding the treat.

I also have used food rewards in certain circumstances when working with professional dogs and in teaching some tricks. For instance, on one occasion Muffin was taping a TV commercial and had done a scene ten times. He had performed perfectly, but each time something had gone wrong—the lighting was off, a camera broke, an actor missed his cue, and so forth. At this point the director said, "OK, I need two more takes." Muffin was worn out, and his attention span had been exhausted. The only way to perk him up for two more takes was to give him a nice food treat, which brought his energy level back up. In this case the food was clearly a bribe, but at least the scene was completed.

Another time food is used in show business is when we want a dog to act as if he belongs to an actor and really loves him. The dog may never have seen the actor before, but if he has an especially wonderful food treat in his pocket, the animal will look up at him expectantly and lovingly as if he were his best friend. Although this may be cheating in the strictest sense, it works.

These are some examples of the appropriate use of food rewards—but they should never be used in obedience training to signal approval or praise.

THE RIGHT TRAINING EQUIPMENT AND HOW TO USE IT

There are two pieces of equipment you will need in order to train your dog—a collar and a leash. Just like the tools of any trade, these accessories have become standardized over the years so they are now easy to use and do the job well. They can be purchased in any pet-supply store and are not expensive.

■ THE COLLAR ■

When your puppy's ready to graduate to basic on-leash training, it is time to switch from its closed puppy collar to a training, or correction, collar, incorrectly called a "choke collar."

Training collars come in many forms. Those most

frequently used are made of woven nylon, rolled leather, or flat metal chain links. Each type comes in varying widths and strengths for dogs of different sizes. Chain-link collars provide very good control. They are strong and the links make a distinctive metallic "chunking" sound as they move together when the collar is tightened. This sound can be an additional training aid for some dogs and serve as a reinforcement for a command. But they can rub the fur off a long-haired dog's neck due to friction. In this case, or in the case of an extremely sensitive dog, a nylon collar works well. However, if it doesn't give enough control, an owner will have to resign himself to temporary hair loss with a chain collar or perhaps switch to a rolled leather type. If you're unsure of what kind of collar to get for your dog, talk to a breeder, groomer, veterinarian, trainer, or pet shop proprietor before you make a purchase.

There are also collars on the market with studs and prongs that restrain a dog with pressure on its neck. These should only be used in special circumstances and are not recommended for the average dog. Collars that give electric shocks to a dog are sometimes used for training. These devices should be used only under the direct supervision of a veterinarian or a certified animal behaviorist. Otherwise they could do a great deal of irreversible damage to a dog.

Sometimes you'll hear that a harness should be used instead of a collar. This is nonsense. You cannot give a dog directions with a harness—it's useless as a training device. A harness can be used once a dog has been trained, or if it develops tracheal problems later on. An exception to this is with a tracking dog, which must wear a harness instead of a collar. This is because a tracking dog can't have any restriction on its neck. It needs to be able to put its head down to sniff the ground and pull its handler along with it as it follows a trail. In this case, the *dog* pulls the owner, not vice versa. Sled dogs also wear harnesses, because the team works in unison to pull the sled. But the lead dog is always trained initially with a closed (not training) collar so it will respond to a driver's commands.

Whichever kind of collar you choose must fit correctly. If it has too much slack, the dangling end can catch on things and be a hazard. If it's too tight, there'll be no give to work with. To determine the right size, measure your dog's neck about halfway between its head and its shoulders and add two to three inches (or the width of three fingers). Dog collars usually come in even-numbered sizes, so if you have to err, do so on the large side—your dog's neck will grow as the animal matures.

How to Put on a Training Collar

The proper way to put a training collar around a dog's neck is so it will never choke but will automatically loosen as soon as you let go after a correction has been made, because of gravity.

This is how I teach my clients to put on a training collar:

1. Form a loop by passing one end of the collar through the ring at the other end (either end will do).
2. Hold the collar in front of you with the long (running) end hanging down, so it looks like a *P*. As I like to say, the way to remember this is that *P* stands for my three key words—Patience, Persistence, and Praise.
3. With the dog standing or sitting in front of you, facing you, put the loop of the *P* over its head, with the free end on the dog's right side, and attach the leash to the dangling end—the *P*'s tail.
4. Now, when you pull on the leash to make a correction, the collar will tighten, but the moment you let go, the force of gravity will cause the collar to loosen—the loop of the *P* will simply slide down.

If instead you put the collar onto the dog backward, in a *Q* position (*Q* for Quit it! You're choking me!), the collar will still tighten when you make a correction, but it won't release when you ease up and will continue to choke your dog. The force of gravity will drag down on the tail of the Q and put continuous pressure on the dog's neck. This will negate any corrective action you might want to take later on, and will also cause a dog to develop overstrong neck muscles.

Another common mistake people make is to attach the leash to the wrong ring. This creates what is called a "dead collar" that won't slide closed when it's pulled or snapped. Sometimes a dead collar is used on purpose when a dog is very well trained and the owner doesn't want to put pressure on its neck but still needs to retain some control. I often use this technique when I work with a young puppy that's just getting used to walking on a leash and hasn't yet been obedience-trained.

If you practice with a collar and your dog a couple of times, you'll see exactly what I mean. The purpose of the collar is to allow you to exert a single, strong snap on the dog's neck to make it pay attention to you. The moment the dog pays attention, you allow the pressure to release. If you put the collar on incorrectly, it will choke the dog all of the time and you won't be able to snap it.

■ THE LEASH ■

Although you may have to replace a training collar occasionally as your puppy grows up, a training leash should last for a long time. Therefore, purchase a good quality leash of the proper length. No matter how small your dog is, get a six-foot leash, because you'll eventually need six feet of slack in order to teach it to Stay, and also to allow it some freedom when you walk it. When your puppy's little, you can always shorten the leash by looping it up in your hand, but you can't do anything to lengthen a too-short leash later on.

Training leashes are usually made of either webbed cotton, nylon, or leather. For most dogs, a good-

BRUCE PLOTKIN

Otter hound Clancy and Yellow Labrador retriever puppy Betty model the correct way to put a training collar on a dog. Note the collar forms a P for Patience, Persistence and Praise.

BRUCE PLOTKIN

BRUCE PLOTKIN

quality, heavy webbed cotton leash works well. Leather is stronger, but it can be hard on your hands unless it is well worked with softening agents or you expect to wear gloves all the time. Chain-link leashes are impossible to handle, with or without gloves, and should be avoided. A good training leash has a strong snap-type spring-action clasp and a loop at the other end to put your hand through if you wish. Several different kinds of clasps are used for leashes, so be sure the type you choose can't open accidentally if you grasp it while training your dog.

Later on, as your dog progresses in its training, you'll need an even longer lead to use as a check-cord while you give your dog signals from farther and farther away in preparation for off-lead work. You can either extend your existing training leash with a piece of nylon rope or clothesline or purchase a retractable leash. The latter will work well as you gradually move away from your dog. When you finally achieve control at a distance of twenty-six feet, your dog will be ready for off-lead work.

How to Hold a Training Leash

Just as there are standard pieces of equipment to use in training and a correct way to put a training collar on a dog, there is a correct way to hold a training lead so that you can communicate well with your dog and achieve proper control.

With the dog on your left side, bring the leash across in front of your body and hold it in your right hand, either grasped in your palm between your thumb and hand or with the loop around your wrist (this works best for children). Then bring your hand across your body to your right side—that's the correct distance between your hand and the dog's collar when the leash is held taut. Take up any slack in your right hand for now. Your left hand is free, or can hold the leash lightly, ready to assist the right hand in correction if necessary.

When you work with your dog you always want to allow some slack in the leash, not only so that the dog doesn't feel any pull when it is performing correctly, but also so it learns to walk without any tension on the leash. The correct amount of slack will fall naturally when you extend your hand down into a comfortable position. Then if you have to make a correction you have some slack with which to make a snap.

People often ask me why the dog must always be on the trainer's left side. This is simply part of the standardized structure of training and communication, just as mounting a horse from the left-hand side is. I have a theory that this practice stems originally from hunting. When the first dogs hunted at the side of early man, the man held his spear in his right hand. When game was spotted, the dog would circle around to the left and drive the quarry toward the hunter's upraised spear. Later, when guns were developed, they were always held in a hunter's right hand while the bird dog walked on the left—same results when the dog flushed out game. So when police and military canine work came along, the same way of handling dogs was adopted. Weapons are carried on the right-hand side, and dogs walk on their handlers' left. Seeing-eye dogs also always work on the left, leaving their owners' right hands free.

This way of working can be adapted easily by a left-handed person, by the way. With the dog on his left and holding the leash in his right hand, he can readily use his left hand for correction and his right hand for assistance.

■ **A CRATE/CAGE AS A TRAINING TOOL** ■

Some trainers advocate using a crate for training to give a dog an extra incentive to work. The theory is that if a dog is confined to a crate before it is taken out to be trained, it is more eager to pay attention when it is let out and will learn faster and better.

I don't recommend this method for training the average puppy or dog, although it is useful in certain circumstances. For example, it works well for advanced training, and for dogs that are adopted later in life and need structure before they can begin to learn.

THE BASIC ON-LEAD TRAINING ROUTINE

The basic training routine has a very structured form. Each lesson, or exercise, is designed to build on the former one. Each has a logical beginning and end, and every time an exercise is performed, it must be in the same order at first in order to imprint the entire routine on a dog's mind. You should not go on to the next exercise until you have pretty much mastered the one before. Each time you add something new to the repertoire, though, you must repeat the previously learned lessons first, and eventually you will be running through the entire routine each time you have a training session. In this way you program the dog to a certain set of actions.

If you read other dog-training books, you'll notice I've added signals that don't appear in most of them. I believe that the only way to train any dog is to make your wishes as clear as possible. Again, put yourself in your dog's place and imagine what it must be like to suddenly have all of these new procedures thrown at you. To help the dog understand what's wanted, I always combine body language and vocal commands instead of using one or the other. I also exaggerate all of the signals at first so they can be easily understood by any dog. Don't worry, you may look unprofessional to a purist, but what do you care as long as your dog is learning? Later on, you can always tone down your gestures.

Remember, your job is to make your wishes clear to your dog in a calm, patient way. Don't be tentative— capture your dog's attention and give each command firmly, only once. Praise your dog at the end of an exercise every time it does well.

Each time you give a command, remember to count

off three seconds. If the dog has not complied with the command by then, correct it.

■ **STEP ONE: HEEL, STAY, SIT (HEEL, AUTOMATIC SIT)** ■

If your dog learns nothing else, it will at least be easier to live with if it masters this simple exercise. No matter how big a dog is, it should be able to walk along on a leash without pulling. I can't count the times I see some poor person being jerked around in every direction by the dog on the other end of the leash, or standing on the sidewalk trying to have a conversation with a friend while the dog wraps its leash around their legs. No wonder so many city people hire dog walkers! A dog like this is no fun to take out.

A dog that has learned to Heel well is a joy to take a walk with. It will never pull you in any direction, but will walk at your side, at your pace, without any tension on the leash. What's more, it will stop when you do, and sit until you give it a signal to move again.

What in fact is Heeling? A funny story will help illustrate.

Before I begin a new group obedience class, I always take time to talk to each owner and dog. I want the people and dogs to know me, and I also want to see just what kind of previous training and/or behavior problems each dog may have.

Recently, at the start of a new outdoor group class, a family arrived with their wheaten terrier, Max. When I introduced myself to them, the young son told me, "Well, one thing Max does very well is Heel."

"Great," I said, "let's see him do it."

What came next reminded me of something out of a Robin Williams movie. The boy and dog began to walk, but not in normal Heel position. Instead the boy walked along behind his dog, meticulously following Max at the same distance wherever he went. He was Heeling behind his dog—chasing the animal wherever it went! I really cracked up—I couldn't believe it!

BRUCE PLOTKIN

My Doberman, Pinka, demonstrates the correct Starting and Finishing position. *Note slack in leash.*

When I asked him what he would do if he wanted to go somewhere the dog didn't, he answered with a straight face, "Well, that's a problem." Needless to say, I then explained the principle of Heeling and we went on with the class.

Starting Position

You will use this basic position for almost every other exercise as well. Your dog should sit at your left side, facing front, in alignment with your left leg, while you hold the leash in the proper position across your body. You may have to put your dog into position the first few times you do this, but soon it will learn to assume the proper position as soon as you stand by its side.

Heel

To start, have your dog in position. To get its attention, use body language and slap your thigh sharply against

Beau, a Golden retriever, just before starting to Heel. *Note that I am about to slap my left thigh and step onto my left ("Follow me") foot.*

Betty, a yellow Labrador retriever puppy, begins to Heel *while I step out with my left foot.*

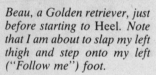

your left thigh. When the dog looks up, praise it. Pet it underneath the chin and say "Good dog." Immediately begin to walk with your left foot—the foot nearest to the dog. This is important body language, because as the dog sees you move your left foot forward its natural instinct will be to go with you. At the same time, continue to slap your thigh while you say "Muffin, Heel." Don't look at your dog and don't tug it at all— simply start off and keep on walking.

Some dogs heel correctly right away, but in my experience, many are overeager and will run ahead. Still others are laggers. For each there are specific corrections.

If your dog suddenly runs ahead of you, allow it to get to the end of the leash, then quickly turn and walk the opposite way while you give the leash a snap. This is the purpose of the slackness of the leash. It allows the dog the leeway to make a mistake if it's not paying

BRUCE PLOTKIN

I use the Pause/Stay *hand signal to stop Ben, a Dalmation, from moving.*

attention. As soon as the dog reaches the end of the leash, slap your thigh and say "Heel." You will have startled the dog back into attention and it will come back to your side.

If, instead, the dog hangs back, snap the leash at the same time you slap your thigh and say "Muffin, Heel." As soon as the dog is back in position, start off again. Whatever you do, never get into a tugging match with your dog. Use a quick, sharp, properly timed correction and then combine body language and verbal commands so you *show* your dog what you want it to do. That is, slap your thigh at the same time you tell it with the words "Muffin, Heel." Praise the dog when it does well.

A dog is in proper Heel position when its front foot is in alignment with yours when you both take a step.

Stay

Once the dog is Heeling well, come to a halt and grab the leash close to the collar while you put your open

BRUCE PLOTKIN

BRUCE PLOTKIN

I use the Sit *hand motion for Max, a Maltese. This also shows how a table or platform can help save your back when you're training a very small dog.*

Sometimes it's necessary to push down on a dog's back to make it Sit, as I'm doing with Clancy, an Otter-hound.

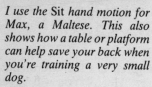

right hand, palm facing the dog's face, right in front of its nose, and say "Stay!" The dog will naturally be startled by your hand into stopping, but if reinforcement is needed, tug up on the leash. "Stay" alone can be useful if you just want to pause before crossing the street, for instance. But you may want your dog to sit quietly for a while to wait for traffic, or you may need to make it focus on you because of a distraction ahead such as a large group of children or a noisy construction site. So at this learning stage, the "Sit" command should always come immediately after the dog stops.

Sit

The "Sit" command consists of an upward scoop of your right hand. Initially a dog will probably need a little help from you in order to interpret this command. While you give the motion and say "Sit," pull upward sharply on the leash with your left hand. This causes the dog's head to go up and force it to sit. In order to give a puppy the idea, you may have to switch the leash to your right hand and push down on its rear end with your left hand at the same time that you pull up on the leash and give the command. Praise the dog as soon as it sits properly (timing!). It may stand right back up, but this is all right for now because all you want it to do at first is sit on command. After a while the dog will learn to sit automatically as soon as you stop walking. This is called the Automatic Sit.

Don't give more than one command and nag the dog if it doesn't sit at first. Simply start again with Heeling and go through the whole routine again until the dog understands what you want.

That's the end of the first lesson, but even if your dog did wonderfully, you will have to practice every day in order for the routine really to become programmed into the dog's memory.

■ STEP TWO: HEEL, TURN (FIGURE 8), AUTOMATIC SIT ■

Now you can take your dog out for a walk without having your arms pulled out of their sockets. But what happens when a youngster comes barreling toward you on a skateboard, or four people are walking along side by side, taking up the whole sidewalk? As you dodge to avoid these obstacles, your dog's leash will invariably get all tangled up, or the animal will end up under your feet. To avoid this, the next step in your training is to teach your dog how to stay by your side while you turn corners or walk around things in any direction.

Note: This exercise should be performed around two objects placed about six feet apart. Chairs will do, but if you are planning to go on to serious competition with your dog, you may want to purchase a couple of traffic cones to work around so the dog becomes used to them.

I'm bringing my right knee into Hud, a Great Pyrennees, to help move the dog around when making a Left About Turn.

Right About Turn

As your dog is Heeling nicely by your side, take up the slack on the leash and turn toward your right, around an object. Lead with your left foot, while you slap your left thigh and say "Heel." Your dog will have to hurry up a bit to make the wider turn and stay in proper heeling position as you turn. To help, hold it on a close lead. Walk halfway around the object so you end up facing in the opposite direction, and immediately begin to walk forward again with the dog Heeling. Encourage the dog with soft praise when it does well during this exercise, but reserve enthusiastic praise until the end of the entire exercise.

Left About Turn

After you master this, turn left around an object. This is a bit trickier because the dog has to understand the need to stay out from under your feet as you both turn.

Hold the leash tight, step on your left foot, and pivot into the dog while you slap your thigh and say "Heel." Bring your right knee around and into the dog's shoulder or head (depending on how big it is) and push it around as you turn your own body. You want to end up facing in the opposite direction with your dog in proper Heel position so you can continue walking. Again, encourage the dog with gentle praise.

Now you're ready to combine the two turns. Walk from one object to the other in a Figure 8 formation.

Always remember to lead with your left foot as you round a corner in either direction, so the dog understands that you want it to come along with you.

These turns are now a part of your routine, and are always followed by a Sit, which by now should be an Automatic Sit. Praise the dog.

■ STEP THREE: SIT/STAY ■

Now your dog has learned to walk along with you, even around obstacles, and to sit at your side when you stop. But what if you want to leave the dog's side when it's sitting to make a phone call, for instance, or you want it to stay quietly in the car when you get out? Once your dog learns Sit/Stay it won't move until you tell it to. It will also learn to trust and obey you, because its natural instincts are to follow you.

Sit/Stay

Begin with the Heel, Stay, Sit routine. With your dog in the proper sitting position, flash your left hand in front of its eyes and say "Stay." Start to move away with your *right* foot (the foot farthest from the dog, not the "follow me" foot). As soon as you begin to move, the dog will probably want to come and will rise from its sitting position. Immediately snap the leash and say "No!" You're letting it know, "I don't want you to follow me now. I used a different foot. Stay where you

I signal Clancy to Sit/Stay as I move away on my right foot.

are. I'll be back.'' When the dog sits again, signal once more, step onto your right foot, and turn counterclockwise so you end up directly in front of the dog, facing it. Still holding the leash, back up six feet and pause for a few moments before you return to your starting position. If the dog breaks and begins to come toward you, immediately grab the leash with your hand, say "No!" Jerk upward, snap the leash, and give the command "Stay." Go back and stand next to the dog and begin again.

Don't make the common mistake of telling your dog how good it is when you're still at the other end of the leash. This serves only to signal it to come to you. Wait until the exercise is over and you're back in place with the dog on your left. Then say, "What a good dog!" Exercise over.

■ STEP FOUR: LONG SIT/STAY ■

Now you're going to teach your dog to sit quietly for a longer time. It will learn to stay in place while you make several trips to unload groceries from the car or put the baby in a carriage, for instance. Or you can even tie it to a fence or parking meter while you go into a store for a few minutes.

Long Sit/Stay

Go through the training routine from the beginning. This time, however, when you come back to your dog after the Stay, don't go to the animal's right side to signal that the lesson is over.

Stand in front of the dog and hold the leash in your left hand at your waist level and repeat the Stay signal and command. Stand quietly for several minutes. As you continue to hold the leash in this position in front of the dog's face, begin with your right foot and walk in a counterclockwise circle around the dog and back to the Starting Position. The dog will probably pivot its head to watch you, but if it begins to get up, jerk the leash and repeat the Stay command and your hand motion. Go back to position in front of the dog. Begin again when the dog is quietly sitting in place. Once you've made the circle successfully, go back to Starting Position and praise the dog.

■ STEP FIVE: DOWN/STAY/SIT ■

People sometimes think they've taught a dog to lie down if they wait until the animal is "in the mood" and then give the command. Not so—your dog should learn to lie down when you want it to and stay quietly until you tell it to move.

I give Beau the Down hand signal.

Down/Stay

After you've run through the routine this far and are standing at your dog's right-hand side, hold the leash in your right hand and crouch down to your dog's level. The dog will be sitting looking at you and you will say "Down" while you make an exaggerated downward motion with your left hand, palm facing the ground. At the same time, put downward pressure on the leash and collar with your right hand to show the dog what you want it to do.

Now, some dogs will get the idea right away, but others may not understand. To help this dog know what you want, you may have to grasp both front feet and pull them out in front of the dog while at the same time you push down on its shoulders. This should be accompanied by repeatedly saying "Down" in firm tones.

Sometimes a stubborn, powerful, or aggressive dog simply refuses to go down at all. You cannot allow a dog to get away with this, so tougher measures are called for. Give the hand motion and the verbal com-

BRUCE PLOTKIN

Sometimes you have to use your foot on the leash to emphasize Down *to a stubborn or large dog.*

mand, put pressure on the leash with your hand, and, if the dog still won't lie down, take your left foot and step on the leash and push it down. The dog may struggle and fight, but you're going to win this battle. When the dog finally lies down, say a brief "Good dog," to reassure it that you are pleased. With an extremely stubborn dog, you may have to repeat this procedure again and again until the commands alone do the job.

Stay

Give the dog the Stay command.

Sit

After the dog has remained down for a few minutes, give the Sit command with an upward sweep of your right hand and simultaneously slap your left thigh to make it clear what you want. When the dog sits, praise it.

BRUCE PLOTKIN

I give Hud the hand signal to Sit *from a* Down *position.*

■ STEP SIX: LONG DOWN/STAY/SIT— FROM THE SIDE AND FROM SIX FEET ■

Now that your dog's learned to lie down on command, you want to teach it to stay in that position until you give it a signal to get up. Once your dog has learned this, it will know how to behave anywhere, under any circumstances, no matter what the distractions—a party at your house, children visiting, or strangers working. People will be able to walk around it and even step over it and it won't move. An overly exuberant dog can be calmed down with this command, and a fearful dog is reassured that everything's all right when it's quietly in its place. At the same time, you will be able to signal to your dog when it's all right to get up, no matter how far away you are. Second only to the Come command, the next step, this is the most important command to teach a dog. It is also the precurser of the "Go to your place [or bed]" command that many people teach their dogs.

Long Down/Stay

Once the dog has learned the Down command well and is in the Down position, tell it to Stay, using a flash of your left hand in front of the dog's eyes. Walk backward to the end of the leash and pause for several minutes. Go back to the dog and reinforce the Stay with another verbal command and hand motion. Walk around the dog, holding the leash in front of it just as you did in the Sit/Stay exercise. Praise the dog when it does well.

If the dog breaks at any time during this exercise, reinforce the command with a snap of the leash and go back to the Starting Position and begin this step again. If your dog had difficulty learning the Down command originally, a reminder may be helpful. While you say "No," lift your left foot as if you were going to step on the leash as you did before. The dog will probably go right down again. Have the dog Sit.

Down and Sit from Six Feet

This last step is usually not included in beginners' classes, but I feel it is such a wonderful technique for establishing control that I always teach it to my beginners. If this exercise is learned well, the important Come step will always be successful.

Walk back to the end of the leash and give the Down/Stay command from there. After a few minutes, give the Sit command and signal. If the dog doesn't respond immediately to either command, give an appropriate leash correction. This time, go to the dog and praise it.

■ STEP SEVEN: COME/SIT (RECALL) ■

Many people ask why I don't teach this lesson at the beginning of a dog's training. The reason is—you cannot afford to fail when you teach this lesson, for both your pet's sake and your own. If you've gone through the basic training routine up until this point, you will have built up a structure of trust and obedience with your dog and taught it you are its leader at all times, and this last lesson will be a successful one.

When it's learned this command, your dog will stop whatever it's doing and come straight to sit in front of you when called. Along with learning the word "No," Come is the most important command that a dog can learn. A dog that's thoroughly learned this command is under your control at all times, no matter what. If there's danger the dog can't perceive—for instance, from the dog warden, an oncoming truck, or whatever—your Come command will stop your pet in its tracks and bring it to you. If your dog is following a friend, or another dog, and the situation is such that this is not a good idea—same thing. You'll use this command over and over.

Come

Go through all of the steps of the basic training routine. Once you have completed the Long Down/Stay/Sit from six feet, give an exaggerated beckoning motion. Sweep your right arm and hand toward your body while you hold the leash in your left hand. At the same time call, "Come, Muffin," and give a little tug on the leash (this time you do use your dog's name).

The dog will usually come running to you. As it does, grab the end of the leash with your right hand and pull steadily as the dog approaches you, while you let the leash slide through your left hand. You will be reeling in the dog, so to speak.

Sit

When the dog is in front of you, give the Sit signal and command and, when the dog sits down, praise it.

After your dog has performed the Come successfully a couple of times, walk backward as you continue to reel in the leash and call the dog, so that it keeps on coming to you as you move away. As your dog becomes better at this, you can use a long, twenty-six-foot re-

BRUCE PLOTKIN

LEFT: *The* Come, or Recall *signal.* **BELOW, LEFT:** *Ben sits in front of me in proper position after the* Recall. **BELOW, RIGHT:** *I praise Clancy after he comes on signal.*

BRUCE PLOTKIN

BRUCE PLOTKIN

tractable leash—the slight pull of the leash works well to encourage the dog to come to you. Each time you do this you will increase the threshold of your dog's ability to respond to your command. Always end up with the dog sitting directly in front of you, and praise it.

■ STEP EIGHT: THE FINISH, OR "COME TO HEEL" ■

When your dog learns to return to the Starting Position after the Come/Sit exercise, the animal realizes that after it's come to you it can't run away until you let it go. It puts a tidy end to the training routine. It is also necessary in many kinds of advanced training because it puts the dog back into "ready" position.

Finish One

With the dog sitting in front of you after the Come/Sit, adjust the leash so it's taut, and say "Heel." At the same time, make a swooping counterclockwise motion with your left arm and slap your left thigh. Grab the leash with your left hand, close to the dog's collar, and pull the dog around in a counterclockwise circle next to you while you move your left foot back a bit. Step onto your left foot, tell the dog to Sit, and it will end up sitting at your left side. Praise the dog.

Finish Two

If your dog is large, it won't be able to make the small, tight turn described above. It will have to go around you, clockwise, in order to return to your left side. First, make a swooping clockwise motion with your right arm. Then, with the leash taut, hold it in your right hand, while at the same time you slap your left thigh and say "Heel." Step back with your right foot and bring the leash down to your knee level. Pull it toward your back and guide the dog around your right side while you step

BRUCE PLOTKIN

Beginning of Finish Two. Note how I am guiding Betty around my back so she'll end up in proper finishing position at my left side.

back on your right foot. When the dog is in back of you, take the leash in your left hand and step forward on your left foot. As the dog comes around your left side, put your weight on your left foot and bring your right foot forward into alignment. Change the leash back into your right hand and voilà! The dog will be at your left side in perfect Heel position. Have the dog Sit, and praise it.

PRACTICE MAKES PERFECT

I'm always amused, if a bit annoyed, when clients come to me and complain, "Susie did well last time in class, but this week she seems to have forgotten everything." That's a dead giveaway. The only way Susie could "forget everything" is if she didn't have any practice between classes.

The only way that your dog will be able to really

learn a training routine is through practice and reinforcement. There is no such thing as a dog that cannot learn. If a dog is not learning properly it is because the owner hasn't put enough time into the teaching and learning process. With proper practice, the average dog should be able to master each step of the training routine in about five days and be ready to go on to the next step.

It's not enough simply to go to a group class once a week if you don't practice in between. A group class is a great place to socialize and to learn the routines, but practice should take place in private where there are fewer distractions, so the dog really becomes programmed. Then the newly learned lesson can be tried out in the next group class with all of its distracting activity.

I also tell my clients it's extremely important to practice obedience training in all kinds of settings—outdoors and indoors, alone and with other people and dogs around. You can also provide your own distractions while a dog learns to Stay, for instance, by moving around, calling to other people and so forth (don't ever call the dog, however, or you'll confuse it completely). A dog must learn that proper obedience is something it does wherever it is and no matter what is going on around it.

What constitutes enough practice? Obviously, the more practice the better, but for practical purposes, a ten-minute session three or four times a day is fine for most dogs. It can go like this for most people. When the dog is taken out for its usual walk, practice the routine for five minutes on the way out. Then let the dog have some free time to go to the bathroom and play and, on the way home, practice for five minutes again. If you do this every time your dog goes out for a walk, it will have had thirty or forty minutes of painless practice each day.

If, instead of going to a group class, you decide to train your dog by itself at home with or without a professional trainer's help, make sure you take your dog out into the world to practice where there are other people, dogs, and noises. A dog isn't truly well trained until it learns to listen and react properly in the midst of distractions. It does no good if your dog is an angel in the solitude of your apartment and goes nuts when it goes out in public.

So be sure to combine both kinds of lessons: repeated drilling alone for serious programming, and practice amid distractions as a final reinforcement.

DON'T BE DISCOURAGED

A lot of times dog owners say to me, "OK, I followed the guidelines you gave me and I did practice, but my dog still doesn't get it. What is wrong with this dog? He doesn't listen." I reply, "Every dog learns at a different pace, just as different people learn at different speeds. Certain individual dogs, and certain breeds of dogs, learn quickly. Others need more time and repetition in order to learn the same lesson." I've seen many instances when an owner has, say, a shepherd that learns the entire training routine in three weeks perfectly. Then the same person gets another shepherd and the dog needs three months to learn the same routine. So, you must work comfortably and easily at your own dog's pace and not rush it.

CHECKLIST OF BASH DIBRA'S STEP-BY-STEP BASIC ON-LEASH OBEDIENCE PROGRAM

I suggest that you copy each step on an index card or page of a notepad for easy reference when drilling your dog.

Correct Starting and Finishing Position

- Dog sits at your left side, facing front, its feet in line with yours.
- Leash is held firmly in your right hand.
- There is a slight "bow," or slack, in the leash.

Step One: Heel/Stay/Sit (Heel/Automatic Sit)

- With dog in Starting Position, slap your thigh, say "[Dog's name], Heel," get dog's attention, and begin to walk with your *left* foot.
- Praise dog when it does well.
- Stop walking, put open right hand in front of dog's face, and say "Stay." Tug up on leash for emphasis. Praise dog when it does well.
- Move your right hand in an upward scoop and say "Sit," while you pull up sharply on the leash with your left hand. Push down on dog's rear if necessary.
- Praise dog when it sits.
- If dog sits automatically when you stop, praise it.

Step Two: Heel/Turn (Figure 8)/ Automatic Sit

- Begin to Heel in proper position (dog's front feet in alignment with your feet).
- Right Turn: Take up slack in leash. Slap thigh and say "Heel." Turn to right, your left foot ("follow me" foot) leading. Do an about-face and walk in opposite direction, dog still in proper heel position. Encourage dog.
- Left Turn: Take up slack, slap thigh, say "Heel." Turn left, left foot leading. Bring right knee into dog to push it around. Do an about-face and continue to walk. Encourage dog.
- Figure 8: Put both turns together to walk in a Figure 8. Stop. Dog should Sit. Praise dog.

Step Three: Sit/Stay

- Begin to Heel in proper position. Stop and have dog Sit.
- Flash your left hand in front of dog's eyes and say "Stay."
- Begin to move away on your *right* foot.
- Repeat signal and command ("Stay") and turn counterclockwise to face dog. Repeat signal and command ("Stay") and back up to end of leash.
- Return to position at dog's right side.
- Praise dog.

My timber wolf, Mariah, who taught me so much about dogs and their behavior. (BRUCE PLOTKIN)

ABOVE: Students pet Mariah while I hold her. We were at an endangered species seminar at the Horace Mann School in New York City. (KITTY BROWN)

LEFT: Mariah and me with the late Dr. Marlin Perkins in 1983 when we were on tour for the Wolf Canid Survival and Research Center, Wolf Sanctuary. (COURTESY CAROL PERKINS [MRS. MARLIN])

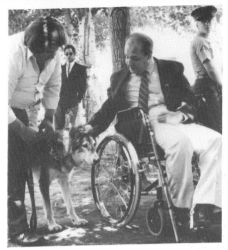

ABOVE: Mariah and I are greeted by President Reagan's White House press secretary James ("The Bear") Brady at the First Annual Celebrity Dog Parade in Washington, D.C., in June 1985. It was Mr. Brady's first public appearance after the Hinckley shooting. (KITTY BROWN) **BELOW:** President and Mrs. Ronald Reagan and Rex, their cavalier King Charles spaniel. (COURTESY PRESIDENT AND MRS. RONALD REAGAN)

ABOVE: Ana-Alicia, star of *Falcon Crest*, on a walk with her beautiful, obedient German shepherds, Helden and Ersehnen, whom I helped her choose and train. (COURTESY ANA-ALICIA) **BELOW, LEFT:** Well-known women's sportswear designer Gloria Sachs and her feisty little Scottish terrier Alexandria. (BASHKIM DIBRA)

RIGHT: Myra Finkelstein, wife of Macy's CEO Ed Finkelstein, practicing obedience training with distractions in Central Park with her golden retriever, Candy. Note the highly distracting squirrel right in front of Candy's nose! (STEVE HILL)

LEFT: Henry Kissinger walking his Labrador retriever puppy, Amelia, in a picture that appeared in the *Daily News* on July 12, 1989. (TED LEYSON)
BELOW: Interior designer J.P. Molyneux with his full-grown, well-trained "boys," Neapolitan mastiffs Tiziano and Palladio. (CARLOS EGUIGUREN)

A group on-lead obedience training class. My sister, Meruet, is on the right with German shepherd, Orph. (BASHKIM DIBRA)

Four of my dogs demonstrate a perfect Down/Stay in the park with a baby for distraction. Clockwise, they are Fluffy, an Old English sheepdog; Pinka, a Doberman pinscher; Orph, a German shepherd, and Brenda, a German shorthaired pointer. (BASHKIM DIBRA)

For dear Barb
"Sally" Ballard's
Trainer.
Love from
KAYE
x
Big Shirl
Punky
Rockets

Actress Kaye Ballard and three of her dogs. (COURTESY KAYE
BALLARD)

Me and four of my shaggy canine stars (left to right), Duncan, Blondie, Muffin and Chelsea. (BRUCE PLOTKIN)

MARIAH
Training & Exercising Machine

ABOVE: My German shorthaired pointer Ellie Mae has her daily workout on a treadmill. (BASHKIM DIBRA) **RIGHT:** Muffin demonstrates the use of a platform for trick work while on the set of the soap opera *The Edge of Night*. (KITTY BROWN) **BELOW:** This picture was taken during the time we were deprogramming Bruno, a German shepherd that was trained as an attack dog. My sister, Meruet, is restraining him. (BASHKIM DIBRA)

ABOVE: Faith Stewart-Gordon, owner of New York's famous Russian Tea Room, relaxing on the pond in Washington, Connecticut, with her Norfolk terriers, Teddy and Gypsy. (COURTESY FAITH STEWART-GORDON) **BELOW:** Edward Asner with my German shepherd, Orph, as they appeared in a public information spot on television. (COURTESY RALSTON PURINA COMPANY & EDWARD ASNER)

Smile! Muffin demonstrates how to hold "an object" in his mouth.
(BRUCE PLOTKIN)

Muffin filming a commercial. (BASHKIM DIBRA)

Here I am working on a Burlington socks commercial with bloodhounds. (MERUET DIBRA)

Practicing advanced stunt work with Orph. (L. EDMONDS, COPYRIGHT BASHKIM DIBRA)

Beauty and the beast. My Doberman, Pinka, bares her teeth for Carol Alt, her costar in *The Chantilly Express*. (STEVE HILL)

ABOVE: My German shorthaired pointer Brandy and I demonstrate an attack by a protection dog. (MERUET DIBRA) **BELOW:** Jim Fowler, host of Mutual of Omaha's *Wild Kingdom*, with his Turkish Akbash, Sashee. (COURTESY JIM FOWLER)

ABOVE: My puppy, Monty, makes friends with a young actor between takes filming the soap opera *All My Children*. (BASHKIM DIBRA) **RIGHT:** Millie, a Bichon Frise, and me at a recent seminar for groomers, Grooming Plus II. The title of my talk was "Jaws. How Not to Be Bitten." (COURTESY FAUNA FOODS CORPORATION)

ABOVE: Pet therapy: My Yorkshire terrier, Kimberly, and Chihuahua, Goldie, bring cheer to residents of a long-term care facility. (COURTESY CENTER FOR PET THERAPY) **BELOW:** Me with actress Paula Trueman, Muffin, and Bronx Borough President Stanley Simon when he proclaimed the first borough-wide Pet Therapy Week in March, 1985. (KITTY BROWN)

Step Four: Long Sit/Stay

- Repeat above steps, but as you stand in front of dog, hold leash in left hand at waist level and repeat Stay signal and command. Stand quietly for several minutes.
- Continue to hold leash in position and begin to walk with your *right* foot, counterclockwise, around the dog.
- Circle the dog completely.
- Go back to Starting Position and praise dog.

Step Five: Down/Stay/Sit

- Begin in Starting Position.
- Crouch down, holding leash in right hand.
- Say "Down." Make exaggerated downward motion with left hand.
- Pull down on leash and collar with right hand.
- If necessary, slide dog's front feet out in front and push down on dog's shoulders.
- Praise dog when it goes down.
- Give the Stay command.
- After a moment or two, slap your left thigh and give Sit command.
- Praise dog when it sits.

Step Six: Long Down/Stay/Sit—From the Side and from Six Feet

- With dog in Down position, give the Stay command.
- Walk backward to end of leash and pause for several minutes.
- Go back to dog and give Stay command.
- Hold leash in front of dog (just as in Sit/Stay) and walk around dog counterclockwise.
- Praise dog.
- Go back to end of leash and give Sit command. Snap leash up if necessary.
- Return to dog and praise it.

Step Seven: Come/Sit (Recall)

- After the Long Down/Sit, do not return to dog but remain at end of leash.
- Make exaggerated Come motion with your right arm and call "[Dog's name], Come."
- Tug leash if necessary.
- Reel dog in until it is directly in front of you.
- Give Sit command and signal.
- Praise dog.
- Later on—continue to move further backward as dog approaches.

Step Eight: Finish (Come to Heel)

- With dog sitting in front of you after Come/Sit, make a swooping, counterclockwise motion with your left arm.
- Tighten leash in your *left* hand, slap your left thigh and say "Heel."
- Grab leash near collar and pull dog around to your left side.
- Give Sit command.
- Praise dog.

Alternate Finish

- Begin as above.
- Make a swooping clockwise motion with your right arm.
- Hold leash in *right* hand, slap thigh and say "Heel."
- Pull dog around your right side to the back.
- Change leash hands and continue to pull dog around you until it is on your left side. Change leash hands.
- Give Sit command.
- Praise dog.

7

BASIC OFF-LEASH OBEDIENCE TRAINING

Even though they may agree with the need to teach a dog to behave while it's on a leash, city and suburban dog owners in particular often feel there's no reason for off-leash training. Their arguments go like this, "Bash, Fred has a fenced-in yard and never goes anywhere except in the car with me." Or "Susie never leaves the apartment without her leash on."

To both of these remarks, I begin by saying, "Never say never." What if someone leaves the gate to Fred's yard open, or Susie jumps out of your arms, leash and all, in the middle of a busy street? Fred, suddenly finding himself free, would probably bolt off down the road like a deer, and Susie would dash down the sidewalk. In both cases you'd have to give chase and, with some help, hopefully catch the dog before it was hurt. It's also not beyond the realm of possibility that you might visit a friend in the country or at the beach and would like to let Fred or Susie take a walk with you without a leash.

Even if you discount such possibilities, wouldn't you like your dog to obey you inside your home so it doesn't have to be closed up whenever company comes or you have a party? Wouldn't it be nice to be able to control your dog with just a simple gesture, so it would go quietly to its bed in the corner, or underneath a table, and lie there until you signaled it to get up?

Off-leash training is necessary if you are going to go on to any kind of advanced work with your dog, but even if you don't plan on hunting with your dog or showing it, it is also very useful for you, the average dog owner, if you want your pet to be well behaved and tuned in to you both inside and outside your home.

HOW TO KNOW WHEN YOUR DOG IS READY FOR OFF-LEASH WORK

If you follow all of the steps for on-leash training outlined in the previous chapter, sooner or later you'll realize your dog performs the steps almost automatically, without a combination of exaggerated signals and commands.

You may also notice that when your dog is in the house without a leash, it responds perfectly when you tell it to Sit or Stay.

If you haven't done so yet, now is the time to practice all of these exercises with a twenty-six-foot lead. I find the best kind of lead to use for this work is a retractable leash. Put the leash in the locked position so that it doesn't exert any pull on the dog at all while you work from a distance (the spring mechanism will be deactivated and the leash will simply be extended to its fullest length). If the dog makes a mistake or becomes tangled up in the leash, you can easily unlock the leash so the spring comes back into action, reel it in and deal with the problem. This kind of leash is also handy when you walk your dog. It allows you to give the animal some freedom to sniff and explore when it's appropriate and then reel it in and continue to walk.

After you have full control over your dog from a distance, you can begin the transition to off-leash work.

As with on-lead work, you must always begin with Step One of the Basic On-Lead Obedience routine and work through all of the steps *before* you introduce new off-lead techniques. This puts your dog in a receptive frame of mind for learning. Not only that, but this way you are building on success. When your dog has just gone through its paces well it will be pleased with itself and eager to learn more.

By the same token, if your dog makes a mistake during any more advanced step in training, always go back to the Starting Position and have the dog Heel for a few minutes before you begin with the new step again. Each time you do this, you reinforce your control and build on it.

USEFUL STIMULANTS FOR OFF-LEASH TRAINING

After a sense of smell, hearing is the second most highly developed sense in both wolves and dogs. A large section of cranial nerves direct sounds to a canine's brain, supplying it with its well-known ultrasonic hearing; that is, they are able to hear much higher-pitched sounds than humans can. What's more, they apparently differentiate between sound frequencies better than humans, and they are obviously expert at detecting the direction from which a sound emanates and focusing on it.

When you work with your dog off-leash, you utilize this keen sense of hearing. Your voice substitutes for the control of the leash. Sometimes, however, your dog may have become so accustomed to your voice that it alone is not enough to make your dog focus on you, especially in the beginning of off-leash training when other stimuli may divert its interest. You may need additional sound stimulants to get your dog's undivided attention when it becomes distracted.

■ A THROW CHAIN ■

A throw chain is simply a length of metal chain that makes a sharp metallic "chunking" sound when it's thrown. If you can't find an item labeled "throw chain" in your pet-supply store, buy a long metal collar (thirty inches or more), and tie two knots in it so that it's weighted.

A throw chain is a tool used to make an off-leash dog respond to you. The principle of a throw chain is to utilize a dog's excellent sense of hearing to startle it and make it pay attention to you. No matter what it's doing—looking at another dog, chasing a squirrel, or running after a child on a bike—the throw chain will immediately make a dog focus on you and then respond to your commands.

It works like this. Say I am working outdoors with Muffin off-leash when he begins to sniff some delicious-smelling garbage on the ground. All of a sudden he's not focusing on me at all and isn't coming along with me as I walk. I say "No, Muffin. Heel." He pays no attention, doesn't even look up, but goes right on root-ing around in the garbage. I aim the throw chain at a spot right beside his rump and throw it. At the same time I again say "No!" The chain makes a loud noise as it lands, and if it accidentally hits him on the rump that's OK, too. Muffin is shocked. He doesn't know where this thing came from. I haven't telegraphed to him that *I* threw it. Immediately he turns to find safety— me—and comes running to me as I call him. I've suc-cessfully recaptured his attention.

A throw chain can also be used when you're training an aggressive dog.

■ A LARGE KEY RING AND A SHAKE CAN ■

These are two other handy devices for capturing your dog's attention and making it focus on you. A key ring, of course, is almost always available to everyone. And one with lots of keys on it is an excellent device to use as a throw object, or simply to rattle to make a dog pay attention to you. Many of my clients find that once a dog has been startled by a thrown key ring a couple of times, all they have to do is rattle the keys in order to stop the dog in its tracks.

I used keys with great success recently when I worked with a New York socialite's golden retriever, Aspen. After we'd successfully trained the dog to do everything right on-lead, Aspen's owner wanted to be able to let him off-leash so she could walk with him in the park to play ball and Frisbee, or even walk on the beach in the Hamptons with her.

We had to teach him to walk off-leash. First, we walked Aspen with leash. Then we dropped the leash and let him drag it while we told him to Heel. Once while we were doing this, Aspen demonstrated typical Chase behavior as he began to bolt after a squirrel in the park. Just as he began to go after the squirrel, I quickly took out my keys, threw them at his rump, and said "No." Startled, he ran back to us, and I praised him.

Then we resumed Heeling while I held the keys in my hand, and no matter what the distraction—children playing all around and so forth—Aspen stayed right with us. His owner was pleased at Aspen's intelligence, but I knew our success was due to his early good training and desire to please us. After that she was able to take Aspen anywhere off-lead. At first she also carried keys and rattled them if his attention seemed about to stray. But soon she didn't even need the keys anymore.

Another simple attention-getting device is a shake can. This is simply an empty soda can filled with pennies or pebbles and taped closed. It works on the same principle as a throw chain or key ring and can be tossed at a dog or rattled loudly to make the animal stop what it's doing and focus on you.

■ **HAND CLAPPING** ■

Hand clapping and thigh slapping are signals that are not accepted in formal training circles, but they are extremely useful tools for off-leash work and even advanced training. When you call your dog to Come, if you squat down and clap your hands at the same time, your dog will almost always stop what it's doing and come to you. The same is true if you bend down and slap your thighs when you call.

The principle is much the same as the throw chain. A loud, sharp clap or slap will capture the dog's attention and make it focus on you. Once it does, and if you're squatting or leaning down in a welcoming position at the same time you call the dog's name, it will invariably come running to you.

USING BODY LANGUAGE AS WELL AS YOUR VOICE

In addition to using your voice and other aural attention-getting devices for off-lead training, you will use a great deal of body language to signal your dog from a distance. Because wolves and dogs have such superior senses of smell and hearing, their vision is often thought of as poor. This is not quite correct. Although their color vision is limited and they don't see as well as we do in bright light, they do see much better in dim light or darkness. This is because their eyes contain more rods—tiny cells that respond to dim light—while human eyes have more cones than rods, which enables them to see better in daylight.

The range of vision of wolves and dogs also differs from that of humans. Because their eyes are set farther apart than peoples' are, wolves see farther to the side than we can. Depending on the breed and the shape of the head, most dogs also have a wide angle of vision. What they gain in visual range, however, they lose in depth perception. Humans' binocular, or 3-D, vision allows us to judge depth and distance better than dogs or wolves can.

Despite her supposedly inferior vision, Mariah constantly surprised me with her ability to see things I couldn't. When we were outdoors, she would suddenly look up, far away, where if I looked very closely, I could finally see a bird sitting in a tree branch miles away, preening itself. This is because of the canine ability to detect even the slightest movement very far away, a talent that has been cultivated in sight hounds such as greyhounds and salukis and hunting dogs as well. Combined with good peripheral vision, this extreme sensitivity to motion serves them well. I used this ability of Mariah's when I was training her outdoors. No matter how far away from her I went, she could always see me raise or lower my arms or give other visual signals.

You can also use body language and your dog's superior vision to stimulate its instinctive Chase behavior and get it to come to you when it's off-lead. It works like this—if you suddenly want your dog to come to you quickly and it's some distance away, begin to run in the opposite direction. As your dog begins to chase you, slow down and allow it to catch you. Then you can leash it immediately while you praise it lavishly for its "good" behavior.

HOW TO BEGIN OFF-LEAD WORK

Again I must emphasize that you always work with your dog in a safe location—in the house or a fenced-in yard. In the beginning, you should work in a place with no distractions until you're sure that your dog understands what's wanted. Later on you'll need to introduce lots of distractions to test your dog.

■ FIRST STEP: DON'T PULL ON THE LEASH ■

The first step in preparing for off-lead work is to let the dog know you're not holding the leash tightly. Use a regular leash (not a retractable one) and attach the clasp to the dog's collar. Put the leash behind your head and drape it over your shoulders so it rests lightly around your neck like a scarf. Let the handle of the leash hang down in front of your right shoulder so it's within easy reach of your hand.

With the leash in this position, practice Heel/Sit/Stay, and walk with the dog in Heel position for a long time (several minutes to start). Don't give any leash correction unless it's absolutely necessary. The dog shouldn't feel any tension in the leash at all. Cut back on elaborate signals. Let your voice be the only means of communication between you and the dog. Do Figure 8's and turns. Work up until your dog walks in perfect Heel position without any correction or reminder for at least five minutes at a time.

■ **STEP TWO: DROP THE LEASH WITHIN REACH** ■

When your dog has the feel of responding without any leash correction at all, go on to the Long Down/Stay/Sit from six feet. With the dog sitting in front of you, say "Stay." Walk to the end of the leash and put the handle down on the ground in front of you, within easy reach of your foot so you can step on it if the dog moves. Tell the dog to go Down and Stay, then Sit and Come to Heel.

After the dog has performed these exercises well at a distance of six feet, switch to the longer retractable leash and gradually increase the distance between you until you're working twenty-six feet from the dog.

If your dog bolts at any time during these exercises, stop it immediately. Grab the leash, give it a snap, and say "No!" Turn quickly away from the dog and have it Heel right away. Walk for a few minutes and begin again. Don't ever go after a dog and then punish it. This will not teach it anything. Remember, any correction must occur at the precise time of a transgression, not later. Instead, catch the dog in the act of running away and go right back into a training mode. You're letting it know, "No hard feelings. I know you didn't understand, but now we have to try again until you get it right."

A throw chain, keys, or shake can are also useful reinforcing tools to use in this situation to stop the dog and make it focus on you.

READINESS TESTS

Once your dog responds well while working without feeling the leash, you can begin to test it to find out if it is really reliable enough to begin to work without any leash at all. I'm a firm believer in making sure. Don't take any shortcuts in this respect.

■ THE THREAD TEST ■

Attach a foot-long piece of lightweight, easily broken string to the clasp of the leash and tie the other end to the dog's collar.

Then go through all of the heeling and turning paces with the dog. If the dog goes through the entire routine without snapping the string, you'll know it's so responsive that it could easily perform the same thing if the leash and collar were attached with only a single thread.

This test is a very good indication of whether or not your dog is ready to go on to the next step in off-leash work. If it is not, go back and repeat the steps in "How to Begin Off-Lead Work" above.

■ A LOOP LEASH ■

The next phase of off-leash training is a loop leash. Don't snap the leash onto the collar, but slide one end of it under the dog's collar and bring it up so both ends are even and you can hold them in one hand. You'll have both the handle and clasp ends of the leash in your hand.

Have your dog sit by your side in Starting Position and say "Heel." As you begin walking, let one end of the looped leash slip through the collar while you hold the other end, and let the rest of the leash dangle by your side in front of the dog's face, not attached to the collar (you'll have to take up any slack in your hand so it doesn't trail on the ground). Keep on walking and let the leash hang next to you while the dog goes through its paces.

As you do this, your dog retains the illusion that it's still attached to the leash. In fact, however, you are testing its responsiveness. If the dog doesn't perform this exercise well, you have to go back to the beginning and drill more.

▪ A HANDLE LEASH ▪

If your dog has done well with the preceding tests you can be pretty sure it's in good control when off-leash.

To be perfectly sure, however, use what I call a handle leash for a while. This is simply a short length of strong, light rope made into a looped handle that you slip through the dog's collar.

The dog can't feel the loop hanging from its collar because it's so light. As you work with the dog in a Heel, however, you will be able to grab the loop and snap it easily if the dog begins to stray. I often use this device when I first take an off-leash dog to the park, for example. Of course, your dog must remain within reach for this to be at all effective.

DRILL AND DISTRACTIONS

The next important steps in off-leash training are to drill repeatedly and introduce distractions. No matter how well your dog does off-leash in the privacy of your home or backyard, you have to drill it repeatedly amid all kinds of distractions in the real world.

This interim stage may pose difficulties, since you still need a secure setting. If you can find a safe fenced-in place to practice where there are other dogs, children, and people walking around, this is ideal. If not, you have to create your own distractions. For instance, have your family engage in all kinds of activities in the area when you're working with your dog. Invite other people and their children over to your yard to play. Ask any friendly neighborhood dogs to come in for a while. I even suggest to clients that they have an off-leash obedience "show" to demonstrate their dog's prowess at the same time they give it practice with people around.

All of this may sound difficult, but remember what you are gaining. Soon your dog will be programmed to obey perfectly off-leash, no matter what happens.

SAFETY FIRST

At this point I must remind you of several very important safety measures. Once you've gone this far and your dog has responded well, it's very easy to become overconfident. Don't ever lose sight of the fact that your dog is just a dog and doesn't have the judgment to know when it might be in danger.

You must continuously be alert for possible distractions and anticipate their potential effect on your pet. If you see something that might frighten or attract your dog and make it run off, immediately get the dog under control. At the same time, stay tuned in to your pet. Even if you don't see or hear something, your dog may. Learn to read its body language so you can react *before* your pet rushes off beyond your reach. A group of boys setting off firecrackers, a horseback rider, a loud truck, or another dog—any of these things and many more might startle or interest your dog enough to make it run off.

At the same time, use common sense about where

you allow your dog to run free. More important, *no matter how well trained your dog is, never, never, allow it to be loose without proper supervision.*

Although my own dogs are perfectly trained off-leash, I never walk them on a city street without a leash, for instance. Too many things might come up that I can't foresee. A car could backfire, a skateboarder whiz by, or another loose dog that is not well trained might suddenly appear—any of these things could make even a very well-trained dog bolt and run off because of instinctive flight behavior.

I have a very sad story to tell that illustrates this danger. A former client of mine who lives in New York City had a beautiful collie. The dog was impeccably trained, both on- and off-leash. The owner always rode her bicycle to and from work in the city and, much against my strong objections, she decided she'd like to take her dog to work with her and let it run alongside the bike in heeling position, off-leash. Several months later, the owner called me to report this routine was working well. Every day she and her dog went about twenty blocks, to and from work, without incident. The dog was in perfect control. What had I been worrying about?

A month afterward I received a quite different call. The dog was dead. It seems that as they went along the street one day, a loose dog suddenly ran out and began to attack and chase the collie. Before the owner could intervene, her startled and frightened dog bolted off in typical mindless flight behavior, right into the path of an oncoming car. Although I managed to avoid saying "I told you so," it was hard for me to disguise my anger and disgust for this thoughtless former dog owner. If only she'd understood canine behavior better, she could have averted this tragedy.

EXTRA CONTROL—STAND/STAY

At this point you may want to think about what methods *you* can use for extra control if it's needed when your dog is off-leash.

■ MAKE YOUR DOG FOCUS ON YOU ■

One of the best ways to cope with either Flight or Chase reactions on the part of your dog is to immediately stop and make it focus on you. I found this out when I worked with Mariah.

The first time we went into the city together, I thought I'd take her for a walk in Central Park to get her used to the city a little at a time. The minute she jumped out of the car onto the sidewalk, she went into complete, unheeding panic. Her eyes rolled back, and she began to thrash around at the end of the leash in an effort to get loose. If I hadn't held her tightly, her instinctive flight behavior would have taken over and she would have bolted and run away.

I had to act quickly to take her attention away from all of the frightening sights, smells, and sounds of the city. Holding her leash tight, I sat down right on the pavement on Fifth Avenue at eye level with Mariah and forced her to focus on me. I talked to her and made her continue to look at me for five minutes until she calmed down. The frightening stimuli receded and she was only aware of me. Each time her attention began to stray, I forced her to look at me again. We stayed there on the sidewalk for a half hour until I thought she was ready to go on with the walk. If she began to tense as we walked, I stooped down again, touched her gently, and made her focus on me once more.

A throw chain or other sound device can be a useful tool to make your dog focus on you in case of a sudden problem. Carry one with you all of the time when your dog is off-leash, even if you think it is completely under control.

■ STAND/STAY, OR STAND FOR EXAMINATION ■

The off-leash exercise called Stand for Examination is actually designed for show use, but you'll find it useful for everyday purposes, too. It works well for visits to the veterinarian or groomer, and is especially good when you groom your dog yourself and need it to stand still. In addition, you'll find it handy when people come up to your dog on the street and want to pet it. A dog that's been taught to stand still and allow itself to be touched all over is safe whenever an unknown adult or child touches it.

I recommend it mostly, though, as a method of control when a dog is off-leash, because it freezes the dog and forces it to focus back on you. For example, if an off-leash dog is some distance away and you suddenly see another dog approaching, signal your dog to Stand/Stay. Then you can either tell it to Sit and go to it and attach the leash, or you can call it to you and leash it. You have thereby avoided a confrontation between the dogs.

Stand/Stay is a variation of the on-leash Sit/Stay command. To teach your dog Stand/Stay, follow these steps.

Heel with the leash on and stop. Give the dog the Stay command with your left hand (palm facing the dog's face) and say "Stand/Stay." If it starts to sit, say "No." Don't jerk up on the leash, because this is the signal to Sit. If the dog does sit, put your arm underneath its stomach and lift it up into a standing position. Once it is standing still, turn and walk to the end of the leash and face the dog. Give the Stay motion and command again. Return to the dog and walk around it holding the leash in front of the dog in your left hand, just as you would do the Sit/Stay exercise.

Then go back to the end of the leash and drop the leash. Return and stand in front of the dog. While the dog stands quietly, stroke it gently all over as you continue to say "Stay." If the dog starts to move, say "No," and repeat the command. Return to Heel position and praise the dog.

Once the dog is able to stand still when you stroke it, have someone else come over and handle it while you stand six feet away and hold the leash. Do this as many times as necessary until the dog stands perfectly still when a stranger approaches it. When you've reached this point you can drop the leash. This completes the necessary steps to teach Stand for Examination for shows. It also has taught your dog to allow friendly strangers to touch it when you are nearby.

Now you can go on to Stand/Stay off-leash for control. After you have taught your dog to Stand for Examination with a dropped leash at six feet, use a retractable leash and continue to move back gradually. Each time you increase the distance, drill until the dog is able to stand perfectly with just a verbal command and drop the leash. When you've reached a distance of twenty-six feet, your dog has learned the command. Continue to practice at every opportunity; you never know when you might need to use this command for extra control and safety.

TWO EXAMPLES OF OFF-LEASH TRAINING

A couple of anecdotes about dogs that I've recently worked with illustrate two very different practical applications of off-leash training.

■ WALKS IN THE PARK ■

One client of mine, Mrs. Louis Marx, lives in New York City near Central Park. Since she likes to take daily walks around the Reservoir, she wanted to take her two golden retrievers, Beau and Melinda, with her for companionship and protection, but she didn't want to have to keep them leashed. She asked me to help her train them so they could walk safely off-lead with her.

The dogs were well trained on-lead, but I knew I had my work cut out for me. This is a most difficult location in which to train a dog to behave well off-leash. Literally hundreds of squirrels scamper about, as though saying, "Chase me, chase me!" Dozens of off-leash dogs frolic nearby, a steady stream of joggers pass on the right and left, bicycles whiz by in all directions, *and* horses and riders are usually trotting past on the nearby trail. To add to the difficulty, Beau is an unaltered male with a natural inclination to protect both his mistress and Melinda from any other male dog that might approach.

I knew I'd have to help Mrs. Marx develop very firm control. She had to agree to work right along with me during the entire training process. We began with a complete review of the dogs' on-leash training until I was sure they had it down perfectly on six-foot leads. Then, using retractable leashes, we went on to drill on-leash with longer and longer distances between the dogs and us.

Next we went through all of the steps outlined above to test the dogs' readiness, but instead of using a handle leash, I attached the dogs together with a coupler so both animals could be controlled at the same time if needed. (A coupler is designed so that two dogs can be walked on one leash. It is in the shape of a triangle with one ring at the top connected to two straps, each of which attaches to one dog's collar so the two animals can walk together as a pair, or brace.) I used a coupler with Beau and Melinda, but I didn't attach a leash to it. Instead I used it like a handle leash—so the owner or I could grab it quickly if necessary. In addition, the coupler served to make the two dogs walk together.

With Beau and Melinda I learned the true usefulness of the Stand/Stay command. As soon as I saw a horse and rider approaching, for instance, I would make the dogs Stand/Stay so they were focused on me and the owner *before* it came into either of their heads to run off after the horse. At first, if it became necessary at this point, we could hook the dogs up to the leash for a few minutes until the horse went by.

It took about three months of intensive training, five

BRUCE PLOTKIN

Golden retrievers Beau and Melinda Marx wearing a Coupler *for off-leash work in Central Park.*

days a week, but now Beau and Melinda are able to walk perfectly with Mrs. Marx in the park, off-leash.

■ DON'T CROSS THE ROAD! ■

Sometimes circumstances dictate that even a dog that's perfectly trained off-leash has to learn one more lesson. I mentioned training Mr. and Mrs. Finkelsteins' golden retriever, Candy. Well, once Candy was well trained both on- and off-leash, there was one more thing her owners wanted to do. They wanted to teach her not to cross the road.

The Finkelstein property in Connecticut spans a country road. Although it is not a busy road by any means, cars do come along it, and Candy's owners were afraid she might be hit if she was allowed to cross the road at will. At the same time, they wanted to allow her the freedom to run loose on the property. So they

asked me to help them train her not to cross the road
unless her collar is grabbed and she's walked across—
just as a small child is taught not to cross a street unless
its hand is held by a grownup.

Again, this was a difficult situation, and I knew the
only way to teach Candy was to make the lesson very
clear. Because I knew she would often be tempted to
cross the road, we had to train Candy through programming and by giving her intentional mixed messages. With her owner along, I had Candy Heel and
then told her to Stay by the side of the road. Her owner
would then cross the road and call her from the other
side while I stayed with Candy. As soon as Candy began
to make the smallest move, I snapped the leash and
said "No!" very harshly. The aim was to teach her *never*
to cross that road, no matter what happened. Even if
a rabbit ran across in front of her nose, or someone
called her from the other side, she was not to set foot
on that road until someone took hold of her collar and
led her across.

With Candy on the leash, we did this again and again.
Then, when she stayed in place well on-leash, I dropped
the leash and moved away from her side and her owner
made a beckoning gesture from across the road. If
Candy made a move toward her owner, I tossed a throw
chain at her to startle her into attention while I shouted
"No!" We did this over and over until she finally understood she was not to set one foot on the road no matter
what. After that, one of us would take hold of her collar,
lead her across the road, and praise her when we got
to the other side. This clearly *showed* her that this was
the only acceptable way for her to cross the road.

If these steps seem harsh to you, remember that Candy's safety depended on her learning the lesson well.
We had to do everything possible to program her and
reinforce the training. Now nothing can lure Candy out
onto the road, and she is allowed to run freely in her
yard in perfect safety.

GO TO YOUR PLACE

Many dog owners with whom I work have no particular need for outdoor off-leash training, but they do want to teach their pets to be responsive to their wishes inside the home. They want to be able to communicate with their dogs with just a single gesture or verbal command from a distance.

One of the most useful indoor applications of off-leash training is the Go to Your Place (or Go to Your Bed) command. Many times you don't want a dog underfoot, especially when the dog is large or active. For instance, when you have a party or meeting, you may not want the dog to mingle. Or you may not want it nearby when you're eating at the dining room table.

One solution, of course, is to close a dog up in another part of the house, but many owners want their pet in the room with them as long as it's not in the way. You can find an out-of-the way spot in almost every room.

To teach this lesson, first you have to train your dog to respond to you when it's off-leash. Then tell it to Heel and as you say "Go to your place," walk it to the spot you've chosen. When the dog is in place, give the Down/Stay signal and praise your pet when it obeys. Walk across the room and sit down. If the dog starts to follow you, immediately say "No!" Go back and put the dog Down again. Go about your normal activities, and if the dog begins to get up at any time, go back and reinforce the Down/Stay command. After a while, give the dog the Sit and Come commands from across the room. Praise it lavishly when it obeys.

Practice this every day when you have dinner, for instance. If you want your dog to learn to go to different spots in different rooms, begin with one location first, and once the dog has learned that place, move on to another room.

I taught Go to Your Place to Mr. and Mrs. Marshall Cogan's standard poodle, Homer. (They're owners of New York's famous 21 Club.) Recently I received a number of telephone calls from people who wanted to become my clients. They had attended a luncheon Mrs. Cogan gave at her apartment and were amazed at Homer's wonderful manners. He had greeted everyone nicely as they arrived, and when it was time for the food to be served, Mrs. Cogan said to him, "Go to your place." Homer immediately ran to the corner, and his owner quickly gave the hand motions Down/Stay from across the room. He lay down quietly and never moved until coffee was served later on and his mistress signaled him to Sit and Come to her. He ran to her happily and sat at her feet.

It's really not hard to teach your own dog to do this. All it takes is the right approach, the appropriate commands, and some time and patience.

CHECKLIST OF BASH DIBRA'S OFF-LEASH OBEDIENCE TRAINING

Most Important Reminder: Safety First

Stimulants: A Throw Chain/Large Key Ring/Shake Can Hand Clapping/Thigh Slapping

Steps in Off-Leash Training

1. Don't pull on leash—wear it like a scarf and go through training routine.
2. Drop leash within reach—work from a distance. Switch to retractable leash.

Readiness Tests

1. The Thread Test: Use a light string to attach collar to leash.
2. A Loop Leash: Don't attach leash to collar. Pass leash through collar. Let it hang while working.

3. A Handle Leash: Attach a short, lightweight loop to collar—
   grasp if needed for correction.

Drill with Distractions

How to Teach a Dog to Stand/Stay (Stand for Examination)

- Heel. Give Stay command and say "Stand/Stay."
- Don't allow dog to sit.
- Work to end of leash. Handle dog. Have others handle dog.
- Drop leash. Move back. Give Stand/Stay command.

How to Teach a Dog to "Go to Your Place"

- Have dog Heel.
- Lead it to chosen place.
- Give Down/Stay command.
- Leave dog.
- When you wish, give Sit and Come commands from a distance.

HOW TO SOLVE
DOG BEHAVIOR
PROBLEMS

8

YOU *CAN* TEACH AN OLDER DOG NEW "TRICKS"!

The well-known saying that "You can't teach an old dog new tricks" has appeared in writings again and again. As early as 1545, John Heywood was of the opinion that "it is harde to make an olde dog stoupe lo" (*Proverbs and Epigrams of John Heywood*), and in 1605, William Camden's *Remains Concerning Britain* contained the statement, "It is harde to teach an old dog tricks." By the early 1700s the sentiment approached its modern form when Thomas D'Urfey wrote in *Quixote I*, "An old dog will learn no new tricks."

This chapter and the four that follow are based on the premise that the old adage simply isn't true. In my observation, dogs continue to learn throughout their lives as long as they are given the opportunity. To hark back to their ancestors the wolves again, those of us who have studied their habits know that they have to learn continuously. If they didn't, they wouldn't survive, because their hunting environment constantly changes. For example, they must learn how to hunt in times of draught, flood, and blizzard. They must also learn how to adjust their hunting habits when their principle prey is decimated by disease. In his book

Never Cry Wolf, Farley Mowat describes how the wolves that he was observing survived on a diet of field mice, for instance, when the caribou they normally hunted were scarce. Necessities of environmental change make learning essential for wolves throughout their lives.

Given the proper encouragement and training any dog, no matter how old, can learn to do new things or to do old routines in a new way, as long as it's in good physical condition (neither deaf, blind, nor genetically impaired). I find that sometimes an older dog learns faster than a youngster because older dogs are, naturally, more mature. They are less easily distracted and better able to focus on you when you are teaching them. They also have better muscle control and are usually calmer than puppies.

However, teaching an older dog "new tricks" is far easier if it has been properly socialized and has already learned the rudiments of obedience. For instance, a bloodhound that I worked with in a Burlington sock commercial had been trained in tracking early in his life, but he had never been a performer before. His early training stood him (and me) in good stead when we worked on the commercial together, and he was able to perform well in front of the camera after only a couple of weeks of advanced training.

In this chapter I'll talk about how to go about changing a mature dog's entire lifestyle to suit a new location, mode of living, or new owner. In subsequent chapters I'll address specific unwanted behavior traits of older dogs and how to alter them.

I find it helpful to think in terms of a computer when I approach the problem of changing the behavior of an older dog. A mature dog has been either taught or allowed to do certain things and act in particular ways. Based on all of its early experience, that dog has created its own behavioral "program" that is fixed in its mind. So before you can begin to teach it a new set of behavior traits, you first have to erase the existing behavior mode in order to create a receptive field for the new "program" that you want to enter.

IF YOU ADOPT AN OLDER DOG

Any dog past the age of three or four months old is, in reality, an "older dog," in the sense that it has already learned a lot. Hopefully the dog has been raised lovingly and socialized well, and will fit into your household with a minimum of adjustment. If, however, the dog has been neglected, spoiled, not trained at all, or a combination of all three, you have your work cut out for you.

When you adopt a pet from a shelter, for instance, it can be very difficult to judge just how well a dog may have been trained or socialized. Some of the temperament tests that I recommend for puppies in Chapter 2 will at least help you to choose a good-natured pet. But shelter dogs often have developed into fairly self-sufficient animals for various reasons, and once you get the dog home it may prove to be very dominant. Other shelter dogs have been made fearful by mishandling. Because you have no way of knowing a shelter dog's past and what bad or quirky habits it may have acquired, you should be prepared to spend time with it training and socializing it, just as you would with a puppy.

I mentioned in Chapter 2 that you can sometimes adopt a well-trained older dog directly from a breeder. In this case you will probably not have to worry about temperament or socialization.

However, even a well-trained and socialized older dog cannot be expected to walk into the door of your home and immediately know where things are and what the "rules of the house" consist of. In order to avoid confusion and accidents, I always recommend that you keep a new animal confined for a short time while it becomes acclimatized. A crate works well in this case and gives the animal a sense of security. Provide your new older dog with a comfortable crate for sleeping and resting when you're not around, and gradually introduce it to each room in the house. With a leash on, give the dog a "guided walking tour" from room to room so that it gets a chance to see everything. If there's a room or area that you never want the dog to enter, don't take it in there. Stand at the door and simply say "Muffin, no" in a firm tone.

If you want to have the dog in the room with you while you work or watch TV, for instance, that's fine. But keep it confined with you until you're sure it's learned where it can and can't go in the house. When the dog needs to let off steam, go out into the yard or play with it in the den or playroom. After about a week or so, most adult dogs will be fully acclimated to their new home and can be allowed the run of the house. Of course, if there's a problem, you will have to continue to confine the dog until it's solved.

HOW I TURNED MUFFIN FROM A SAVAGE INTO A STAR

A perfect example of a dog that had to be completely deprogrammed and reprogrammed is Muffin, my own dog that I turned from an insufferably spoiled, undisciplined brat into a wonderfully responsive, perfectly socialized animal.

Some years ago, I received a call from a woman who asked me to come to her apartment because she was having problems with her five-year-old dog. When I arrived at the apartment, I found this adorable shaggy dog that the lady said was a Tibetan terrier (I think he was actually a cross-breed). It didn't take me long to see that he was a complete nut. He ran around the house continuously barking like mad and had completely destroyed the furniture and rugs, digging and ripping them with his nails and teeth, and soiling all over the place.

Muffin had originally been bought as a pet for the family's only daughter. Both parents worked outside the home, and no one in the household had ever taken the time to give him any training or structure. When he misbehaved or acted wild, they gave him anything that he wanted in order to quiet him down. He was allowed to jump up onto the kitchen counters and eat the family's dinner—I was told that he had filet mignon regularly—on the mistaken assumption that if they let him do this, he would be "grateful" and behave himself. In short, they had made the common mistake of believing that love alone was enough. They reasoned that if they were nice to the dog, he would respond by behaving well. Instead, he was completely undisciplined, confused, and had no idea what was expected of him.

Now that the daughter had grown up and was about to go away to school, the parents wanted to do the apartment over. This was what had prompted them to call me—it was clear something had to be done about Muffin's destructive behavior before they began to fix things up.

I knew right away that Muffin could be trained. He was obviously responsive, energetic, and bright. But at the same time it was obvious that he was very set in his ways and wanted his own way all of the time. He had been allowed to become a willful brat. Retraining him would be a real challenge and take a great deal of time and effort. When I explained this to the owners, they said they really didn't have the time or interest to invest in retraining Muffin. And since they couldn't keep him the way he was, they decided they would have to give him up. So I decided to adopt him.

As a professional dog trainer, I knew that the first thing I had to do was to let him know that his old mode of behavior wasn't acceptable—I had to deprogram him. Then I had to reprogram him in more suitable behavior. He had to learn to respond to my desires, and to help him do that, I had to communicate effectively in return.

I took him home with me and said, "Nice Muffin, here's your new home," and plop! I put him into a crate. He was stunned at first and then he started to bark and scream and go crazy. Here was a five-year-old dog that had been used to having the run of an apartment suddenly closed up in a crate. He didn't know what to make of it, but I knew I had to give him structure. In order to begin he had to learn to pay attention to me—to focus on me—and he wasn't going to do that if I allowed him to run around mindlessly.

So each time he screamed, I took him out of the crate, put him on a leash, and went outdoors for some training. I started at the very beginning and did the drill—Heel, Sit, Stay, and so forth, to tire him out and force him to start to see that he was no longer the leader of his pack. Then I'd take him back, put him in the crate, and he'd start to scream again—this was a very high-energy dog. I'd take him right out and drill again, and again, until he finally calmed down and would go to sleep in his crate. After a few days he began to settle down. Then, when he was quiet, I'd take him out of the crate and socialize him. I'd play with him and pet him. But if he began to go wild again, I'd immediately drill him again, over and over, until he calmed down. Soon he saw the pattern. When he was well behaved and calm, he got to play and run around, but as soon as he began to get out of control, he'd have to drill again.

During this time I trained him four times every day. His walks and training were scheduled, just like a puppy's. At first everything had to be simple. Commands had to be repeated again and again, and he had to learn to focus on me. I was reprogramming him my way at the same time I was teaching him that his former mode of behavior was unacceptable to me. He had to learn that I was the Alpha leader and that there was a new format in this environment which he had to learn to live with. As he became more obedient and responsive I began to let him work and play with my other well-trained dogs, and this, too, served to reinforce his training.

Now we started to have a basis of understanding and communication. For instance, begging had become a terrible habit for Muffin because his former family always gave in to him. As soon as he would start to beg, I'd say "No" and put him on his leash and into the Down/Stay position until I finished eating. When I finished, sometimes I would put a treat or biscuit in his bowl and sometimes I wouldn't. Soon he understood that the decision rested with me, not him. Getting a treat had nothing to do with his begging behavior.

At that time I owned a number of dogs that were performers. Muffin responded so well to training that I soon realized he had the potential to be a wonderful professional animal, too. He was bright, cute, shaggy, cuddly, and eager. So after we completed the leash work we went on to off-leash training and tricks. He was a quick study and soon could speak on command, sit up pretty, hold an object, make gestures with his paws, and respond to situations on camera.

Until his death at fifteen, ten years after I had adopted him, Muffin worked as a performer and became a real star. He was in over four thousand commercials and print advertisements and was so popular with audiences of the soap opera *The Edge of Night* that the producers signed him to a two-year contract!

Muffin's "second life" with me is a perfect example of how, with patient, persistent kindness and structure, an older dog can be changed from an undisciplined brat into a well-mannered mature animal.

HOW I DEPROGRAMMED AN ATTACK DOG

Sometimes it becomes necessary for a highly disciplined and well-trained adult dog to "unlearn" its previous training and learn to act in a completely different way.

This is what happened when clients of mine moved back to the States from overseas. They bought a house in Scarsdale, an affluent suburb north of New York City that abounds in children and dogs. They brought their five-year-old German shepherd, Bruno, with them.

When they had purchased Bruno, they had lived on

a closely guarded company-owned compound in Africa. For the family's protection the dog was sent to Europe to be trained as a guard dog. There he was taught the military approach to obedience. His role was to keep everything and everyone away from the property—not only people but cars and other animals as well. He literally attacked anything that moved.

While this was highly desirable on the compound, it clearly wouldn't do in a friendly suburban town, and the owners knew that if they couldn't modify Bruno's behavior, they would have to give him up. In his present mode he was a lethal weapon. So they called me to help them.

The dog had to be desensitized and socialized to a normal environment and learn that everything and everybody who approached couldn't be perceived as a threat. Because his protective instincts were naturally stronger when he was in his own home, we began to work outside of his "turf." Also, because he had been trained to protect his owners as well as his territory, they both had to work along with me during the entire process.

First, we took him into busy public places such as congested shopping malls, parking lots, and city streets. For everyone's protection, I kept Bruno on a very short, strong lead because his instinct was to lunge at anyone who came within ten feet of his owners. He was an extremely ferocious animal. Each time he tried to leap at anyone, I had to snap him back into place beside me and say "No" in a fierce tone of voice. When he was finally able to walk quietly with me, the owners took turns walking him with me right beside them, ready to step in if necessary. After many weeks of this he was ready to graduate to the next step. He was gradually becoming deprogrammed from his former aggression toward strange people and learning to accept them in a public situation.

The next step in his reeducation was to teach him to accept strange dogs. We accomplished this by having him attend group obedience classes in an outdoor setting along with his owners. Again, each time he showed aggression toward another dog, he had to be corrected immediately. After several weeks he was able to tolerate the nearby presence of other dogs without trying to chase and kill them. He could now be safely walked in the neighborhood.

Now came the hardest part—we had to help him translate his new tolerance for strange people and animals when they were in neutral territory into an ability to accept them on his own property. He had been well taught to defend his family and property against all comers with his own life, if necessary, and now we were going to ask him to sublimate that training.

We didn't want to prevent Bruno from barking at strangers altogether, but we did want him to be able to accept friendly visitors. When the owners were at home, his job now would be to alert them when someone came and then to take his cue from them. If they were friendly toward the visitor, he would be too. But if they commanded him to attack a stranger, he would do so.

In order to teach him to accept friendly strangers in his home, we had to drill. With his collar always on and his leash ready on the hall table, we enlisted the aid of various neighbors and family friends who acted as visitors. As soon as the doorbell rang, Bruno would bark loudly, which we allowed. Then one of his owners or I would snap the leash on and someone would go to the door and open it. As soon as Bruno began to growl and/or go for the visitor, he was severely reprimanded and made to sit quietly in Heel position while the visitor came into the house and sat down. Still under complete control on the leash, the dog was walked into the living room or den where the visitor was, told to Stay, and allowed to observe the social interaction that then took place, still under leash control. This was repeated many, many times, at first only while I was there; finally, when he seemed to get the idea, the owners practiced with him alone. When we were sure he was ready, we continued to practice using voice control alone, without the leash. Because he was an intelligent, well-disciplined dog, he was very responsive to training, and once he had been successfully deprogrammed not to attack everything in sight, he responded well to new commands.

Now Bruno's owners are able to control him successfully. His early guard-dog training made him receptive to instruction, and with a great deal of patience and persistence I was able to modify his aggression and make him into a socially acceptable animal.

FROM COUNTRY TO CITY LIFE

A more common occurrence in many older dogs' lives is a move to a completely different environment. Although a move may not seem as dramatic as a change of ownership or a complete alteration of behavior, it entails a totally new physical setting that can be difficult for an older dog to accept without help.

Michael, a cocker spaniel belonging to William Paley, chairman of the board of CBS, Inc. is a good example of this. For eight years Michael had lived at the Paley home on Long Island. Mr. Paley usually spent the weekend in the country with the dog, but during the week he stayed in New York when he wasn't traveling and Michael remained in the Hamptons, where he was cared for by the household staff.

Recently, Mr. Paley began to spend more time in the city. His daughter knew how fond he was of Michael and thought it would be nice if the little dog could be with her father more. So she called me to see if I thought that Michael was too old to be taught to adjust to this new lifestyle. In order to give her an honest answer, I had to meet Michael first. When Michael came in to New York, I found that he was a bright, friendly, responsive little dog and told her that, yes, he could learn to live in a different environment. But I also told her that it would take some intensive work at first in order to restructure him and teach him how to act in his new home.

Because he had never even been in the city before

but had lived in a house where he could go in and out at will, the first thing we had to do was socialize Michael to city noise and confusion and give him a refresher course in leash-walking. In addition, he had to learn to eliminate on schedule—when he was walked and not whenever he felt like it.

In order to make this easier, we changed Michael's diet and put him on a feeding schedule. In the old days in the country, he had eaten at random, whenever anyone was free to feed him, and he was often given left-over human food. Of course, he was also free to run outside to eliminate whenever he felt like it. So the biggest change in his life was that he had to learn to eliminate on schedule, in direct relationship to meals. We began to feed him regular meals consisting of a highly nutritious, easily digested diet so that the volume of his stools was reduced.

At first we had to cooperate in an intense dog-walking project—to teach him to eliminate outdoors and also to accustom him to city sounds and sights. On the first day I took Michael out with one of the staff eight times. After that the staff did the same number of daily walks for a week. While we walked, I demonstrated how to calm Michael's fears and make him less nervous. Just as I had with Mariah when I was socializing her to the city, whenever he began to get frightened I would stop walking, make him focus on me, and reassure him that everything was all right with soothing words and petting. Soon he began to calm down, look around, and enjoy all of the hustle and bustle on the street. At the same time, Michael was getting the idea that he would earn praise and approval when he eliminated outdoors.

Slowly we eased back on the number of walks, and soon various staff members were able to take him out successfully without me. After several weeks Michael was on a normal schedule of four daily walks.

Mr. Paley and Michael have become firmer friends and good companions and now Michael regularly travels back and forth from the city to the country with his master. He still likes the country house, but he also loves the city and isn't fazed by the cars and other street activity. It took a lot of work at first, but with patience and calm persistence, eight-year-old Michael was able to adjust to a completely new environment. In the process he developed a wonderful new relationship with his owner.

FROM OUTDOORS TO IN

One more story comes to mind about a dog that had to learn a new "trick." In this case, the dog did not have to learn how to change her entire lifestyle, but she did have to be reprogrammed in respect to an important part of her everyday behavior—elimination.

Mia Farrow was living in New York and had a lovely little bichon frisé named Maggie. I had helped her to pick out the dog, and together we had taught her to be perfectly house-trained to the outdoors. She was taken on regular walks four times a day and never made a mistake in the apartment.

But one freezing December day when Maggie was almost a year old, I had a telephone call from Mia. Things in the household had changed and she needed my help with Maggie. Mia had just had a new baby (Woody Allen's son Satchel). On top of that, Christmas was around the corner, and everyone in the house was extremely busy. Unfortunately, Maggie's walks were becoming a problem and Mia was worried about her. She had tried to get Maggie to "go" on paper indoors, but Maggie was so well trained to the outdoors that she didn't understand. She would hold it, sometimes all day, until someone could take her out. Would I please come over and retrain Maggie so that she would understand that it was all right to use paper in the house?

In this case, my job wasn't too difficult. Maggie is not only a smart little dog, but she already knew me well. What I had to do was make her understand that now she was supposed to eliminate in the house, on paper, instead of waiting until she was taken out.

I timed my visit to the apartment to coincide with the time that Maggie was usually walked. I put her leash on, and she was very eager to go out. When we got to the street, I walked her until she was about to eliminate, but I didn't let her do it. Instead I quickly picked her up, took her upstairs in the elevator, and immediately put her onto the papers that were ready in place. She just looked at us and walked away. Nothing happened. Maggie was just too well programmed to go only outdoors!

I waited about a half-hour, knowing that by now the little dog must have to go badly. We went through the same routine and, again, no results. After another wait I tried again. This time Maggie could wait no longer. The walks had excited her too much and she just could not hold it any more. Finally she went on the paper. I praised her lavishly, Mia praised her lavishly, and Maggie understood. She was programmed in a new behavior. From then on, she went on the paper whenever she had to.

Now, when Mia's lifestyle changes again—when the baby is older and ready to go outdoors, and the weather is nicer—there will be no problem. Now it will work both ways. Because Maggie was originally programmed to eliminate outdoors, she'll do so when she has the opportunity to go out. But when she needs to go and is not walked, she'll know enough to use the paper.

I was able to reprogram Maggie's behavior in a humane and logical way to suit both her needs and those of her owner. I was successful because I followed steps that she could understand and timed the training to coincide with her usual (already programmed) elimination schedule.

9

HOW TO BREAK BAD HABITS

Sometimes dogs develop bad habits. Often an owner has allowed the dog to get away with something as a puppy that is no longer acceptable now the dog is grown. A bad habit can also be due to a complete lack of training, or poor early training. Many so-called "bad habits" in dogs are behaviors triggered by separation anxiety, but this is a different subject.

Whatever the reason, people sometimes think they have to grin and bear it. This simply isn't so. It's almost never too late to reprogram a dog and modify its behavior to get rid of its bad habits.

SOME TOOLS TO USE TO BREAK A DOG OF BAD HABITS

In many instances, a successful method is what I call a "set-up." It works this way. You set the stage so the dog does the very action you don't want it to do. Then you arrange for the dog to have an unpleasant experience as it performs this action. In effect, it has brought the unpleasant result upon itself. With several repetitions the dog soon learns that no matter what the encouragement, it does not ever want to perform the action again. Its behavior has been modified.

In addition to a throw chain, large key ring, shake can, or water balloon, all of which startle a dog in the middle of an action, I've found that a pump-style container of bitter-tasting liquid is a handy tool in modifying a dog's behavior. It's also useful in solving a destructive chewing habit. The liquid is not designed to hurt the dog, just to taste horrid. It can be a commercially available product or a combination of lemon juice, vinegar, and/or rubbing alcohol you can mix yourself and put in a plant sprayer or water pistol to squirt into the dog's mouth. I'll explain how I've used this later on.

Another tool that's useful in restructuring a dog's behavior is a crate. The crate is never used as punishment, but it serves as a means of preventing a dog from engaging in a bad habit. Every time a dog performs an action, the action becomes more ingrained in the animal's behavior pattern. When the dog is prevented from performing the action (bad habit), you can more easily redirect its activity and substitute a new, approved action for the bad habit.

HOUSEBREAKING PROBLEMS

Housebreaking problems can arise if a dog was never properly house-trained in the first place. Or they may surface when a male dog feels his territory is being threatened and indulges in urine-marking behavior. Sometimes an owner doesn't notice the problem for a long time and then, when she moves or has the house redecorated, it becomes all too evident. I've known many people who were amazed to find a wood floor underneath a carpet ruined by urine stains, for instance.

■ MARTIN SCORSESE'S CAPTAIN NEMO ■

In this situation, the dog had never been properly socialized or housebroken and had to be completely reprogrammed in order to understand what was wanted of him.

Film director Martin Scorsese, a very kindhearted man, had a female bichon frisé and he really loved her a lot. One day he walked into a pet shop and saw a miserable dog in one of the cages. He recognized it as a bichon frisé and asked the clerk how long it had been in the shop. When the clerk answered, "Eighteen months," Mr. Scorsese was horrified and felt that he had to save the dog. He bought him, took him home, and called him Captain Nemo.

Soon afterward I received a frantic telephone call. Captain Nemo was "going" all over the townhouse, and to make things worse, Mr. Scorsese's other bichon, a perfectly trained female, had decided that it was all right to make mistakes all over the house, too. Mr. Scorsese was understandably *very* upset and, what's more, he had to leave for Morocco the next day to shoot *The Last Temptation of Christ*. He'd be gone for quite a while and was afraid that by the time he got back the house would be ruined. Could I help?

I went over and began to work with the people who were now taking care of Captain Nemo. I soon realized, however, that Captain Nemo's problem was so ingrained that I needed to reprogram him completely. In fact, the situation was so severe I decided to take the dog home with me so I could work closely with him every day. If Mr. Scorsese had been home he would have been able to do this, but under the circumstances it was best for me to take over.

I had to work out a strict schedule for Captain Nemo and re-create the physical conditions that had created the problem in the first place. Captain Nemo had been caged for so long in a little space with nowhere else to eliminate that I had to restructure his behavior to make him realize his cage (den) was for sleeping and outdoors was the place to eliminate.

First, I gave him a crate to sleep in. Then I made up a timetable for him just like the schedule you would create for a puppy you're housebreaking. I fed him, watered him, and walked him at the same time every day. At first he didn't understand he was supposed to eliminate outdoors—he couldn't wait to get back indoors to go in his crate. Because I had to program his elimination behavior so he would become conditioned to going outdoors, I used suppositories.

At first I walked him six times a day, and whenever he eliminated outdoors I praised him lavishly. Praise is very important for a dog that's been in a shop for a long time and hasn't had the opportunity to socialize with people. It needs constant reassurance that it's pleasing you, and this reassurance helps it learn to please you faster. Gradually I was able to cut back on the number of walks until we went out four times each day. I continued to praise Captain Nemo every time he went outdoors, continuing to reinforce the lesson so he wouldn't lapse into his old ways.

Finally I thought that Captain Nemo was ready to go home. He no longer needed to be crated in order to remember his house-training. I took him back and instructed his caretakers to be sure to walk him on schedule and stressed the need to praise him a lot when he did well. By the way, without Captain Nemo's bad example, the little female returned to her normal housebroken behavior.

■ MODESTY PROBLEMS ■

Sometimes a dog develops the bad habit of eliminating in the house because it's overly modest. Recently, Philip Farley, member and former President of the Board of Trustees of New York's prestigious Animal Medical Center, called me because he was having a problem with his mixed-breed terrier named Amos. The dog was perfectly house-trained when the family was in their country house, but in the city he refused to eliminate on the street and went in the apartment instead.

I immediately recognized this as a problem I'd dealt with before—Amos was embarrassed to eliminate in front of anyone. In the country he had privacy, but on a leash in the city it was different.

In this case, we had to gradually desensitize the dog. I advised Mr. Farley to keep Amos in a crate when he was in the apartment so he wouldn't have the opportunity to eliminate indoors during the time we were working to cure him of his shyness. Then I had him buy a long, retractable leash. When Amos was walked in the city, we let him go to the very end of the leash to a private place to eliminate. This satisfied the dog's sense of modesty, and he eliminated on his walks. Then we gradually shortened the leash a foot at a time. Each time we made sure Amos was happy with the arrangement before we shortened the leash any more. At the end of a month Amos was able to eliminate when he was only six feet away from his walker, and later on the leash was shortened even more. Now Amos is a perfectly housebroken dog, in both the city and the country.

■ DOGS THAT URINE-MARK ■

A friend told me a story about a feisty West Highland terrier named Nappy (short for Napoleon) she once owned. He had many bad habits and was extremely territorial, but he *was* well housebroken, or so she thought.

When Nappy was about seven years old, the family redid their house. They put in new carpeting and re-upholstered all of the furniture. Shortly afterward they bought a male Labrador puppy who spent most of his time outside in an enclosed yard. Nappy seemed to accept the new dog with little protest, but about a year later, my friend noticed a pale stain on the blue carpet in the bedroom, right next to a chair. It looked as if the dye had been taken out of the carpet by some kind of bleach. Then she saw something sticky on the pedestal base of a table. It took awhile, but she finally figured out what it was. Nappy had been raising his leg against all of the furniture in the house. He had left such a small dribble of urine it was hardly visible, but it had removed the color from the carpet and left a sticky residue on the table base.

The arrival of the new male dog in the household had prompted Nappy to urine-mark everything in the house to claim it as his territory. This highly territorial dog was responding to an inborn male canine need to mark off the perimeters of "his" house, just as a male wolf urine-marks the bushes and rocks at the edge of its home turf.

By the time my friend told me this story, Nappy had long since gone to dog-heaven, but if he had still been alive I would have told her to have him neutered. This would have helped to offset his urine-marking behavior and many other territorially induced bad habits he had. Even though neutering a male dog later in its life doesn't always undo a bad habit, it certainly can make it easier to reprogram a dog that's highly territorial due to an excessive amount of male hormones.

La Toya Jackson had a similar problem with her dog, a one-year-old male bichon frisé. This time it was the arrival of an eight-month-old female bichon in the household that set the male off. Inspired by the presence of an unspayed female he wanted to impress, he began urine-marking all over La Toya's apartment. In this case I recommended that both dogs be neutered. We also worked out a schedule for the dogs so they were fed and walked at the same time each day. After a short time the dogs were well housebroken and the male didn't feel the need to urine-mark any more.

DESTRUCTIVE CHEWING BEHAVIOR

Destructive chewing also stems from many causes. It can occur if owners allow, or even encourage, a puppy to chew.

Recently a well-known New York bank president came to me for help. He was infuriated with his poodle because it had taken one of his four-hundred-dollar Gucci loafers out of the closet and chewed it up. When I arrived at the apartment, I asked the man if his dog had ever chewed shoes before. "Well, last year when he was a puppy I gave him an *old* shoe to teethe on," he said. "But this is different!" I couldn't help but smile as I politely explained to him that he really couldn't expect a dog to know the difference between an old shoe and a new, expensive one—as a matter of fact, the new leather probably smelled and tasted better to the dog. I told him we could work out a training program to desensitize the dog from shoe-chewing, but he decided he'd rather just keep his closet door closed from then on. I think perhaps he felt annoyed at himself for becoming so angry at his dog for doing something he himself had actually allowed and encouraged.

Dogs will often chew or tear an absent owner's clothing when they are distressed and upset due to separation anxiety.

I dealt with a classic case of destructive behavior due to hearing defects a few years ago. A woman called me after she had worked with a number of other trainers who had not been able to help her. It seems that her year-old Australian sheepdog, Gracie, had destroyed four living room sofas. Every time the owner went out, Gracie went to work, chewing the cushions and gnawing on the legs.

The first thing I discovered was that Gracie was deaf. Her owner didn't know if she had been born with hearing or not because for a long time they hadn't realized she was deaf.

I knew that deaf dogs often have oral problems— they bark constantly or chew a lot. Because of the severity of the problem, I decided we needed to use a crate for Gracie, not as punishment but as a temporary preventive tool to keep her away from the sofa. Each time she successfully chewed the sofa it perpetuated the bad habit, and I wanted to modify her behavior by preventing it from occurring altogether. I told her owner to leave Gracie in the crate whenever she went out and to take her out and give her a good walk as soon as she returned so the dog would know she hadn't been forgotten. Gracie also needed an outlet for her energy, so I told her owner to give Gracie plenty of acceptable things to chew whenever she went out— rawhides, toys, and beef marrow bones (with her veterinarian's approval). After several weeks of this, I told the owner to leave Gracie out of the crate when she was going to be out for only an hour or two. (With most dogs a week or two in a crate will do the trick, but I had to use the crate for longer than usual with Gracie because the severity of her deafness had exacerbated her chewing habit.)

Gradually we allowed her to be out of the crate for longer and longer periods of time. If she regressed, we put her back in the crate for three days and then tried leaving her out again. Each time she was able to go longer and longer without a relapse, and finally we were able to leave her out of the crate altogether. Now the owner felt safe enough to buy yet another new sofa.

Some trainers would have opted simply to crate Gracie every time her owners went out for the rest of her life. This is what I call a Band-Aid approach to dog training—it solves the problem by taking away the opportunity for the dog to misbehave. But it doesn't get to the root of the trouble and cure the problem. Our aim here was to turn Gracie into a well-trained dog with a normal lifestyle, and we achieved our goal.

TOO MUCH ENERGY

Sometimes a dog gets into mischief because it's bored, restless, and doesn't get enough exercise.

Rembrandt, a Manchester terrier belonging to billionaire Saul Steinberg and his wife, Gayfryd, was a classic example of a dog with this kind of problem. He lived in a New York apartment with a busy family. Although he was always walked enough to relieve himself, he still had plenty of energy to burn. He began to develop destructive habits, chewing things and messing up the apartment when his owners were out.

One day when I was at the apartment working with Rembrandt, I noticed there was an exercise room with a treadmill in it. I decided his owners should use the treadmill to exercise Rembrandt every day. With his collar and leash on, I put him on the treadmill and stood next to him so that he was in Heeling position. I started the treadmill up slowly and encouraged him to Heel. As he began to walk along, I gradually increased the speed so he was trotting along next to me. Soon he got into the rhythm and began to enjoy the "walk" we were taking.

Once I'd taught him to walk on the treadmill, I suggested to his owners that they give him a five-mile walk on it every day. It worked wonderfully. Rembrandt became much more relaxed and forgot all about his destructive habits.

A treadmill is also useful if you have a breed of dog that naturally requires a lot of daily exercise. Ellie-Mae, my German shorthaired pointer, suffered when she moved from the country into a city apartment. Designed for running, she needed daily work to be happy and it was impossible for me to give it to her in the city. I decided to teach her to use a treadmill, and it has kept her trim and happy.

If you decide to try this with your dog, always keep a leash on the animal for safety and never leave it on the machine alone, even for a moment. You must stay by the dog's side with the off switch in easy reach, because the animal could be hurt if it fell or decided to get off by itself. Have the dog stop walking as soon as you turn the machine off and don't allow it to move until the treadmill has come to a complete stop.

CAR CHASING

Chasing cars is not only an annoying habit, it is also dangerous. Some dogs seem to have a strong propensity to do this, probably due to a highly developed Chase instinct—the turning wheels seem to incite these dogs.

Of course, if a dog is under your control and has learned not to leave its property, this shouldn't happen. But sometimes even the best-trained dogs find the urge to chase cars irresistible. The best way to break a dog of this habit is to startle it sufficiently so that it associates something unpleasant with the action and stops in its tracks.

Of the various methods to accomplish this, I find the most successful is a water bomb. Enlist the aid of a friend to drive by in a car, and as soon as the dog begins to give chase, have him throw a water-filled balloon right in the dog's face at the same time both of you shout "No!" in your loudest and crossest voices. After a couple of experiences of having water thrown in its face, a dog will usually give up car chasing.

I had a slightly different situation with Mr. and Mrs. Howard Sloan's two-year-old bearded collie, Lizzie, who had been trained both on- and off-leash and was extremely well behaved in all ways but one. When the Sloans were at their home in Connecticut they liked to have Lizzie outdoors with them while they gardened and puttered around. Lizzie had been trained not to leave the property and they felt secure in allowing her to be out on the grounds without a leash.

But one day when Mrs. Sloan left in the car to do some errands, Mr. Sloan suddenly realized that Lizzie was missing. He called her to no avail and finally decided to get in the other car and look for her. There she was, some way down the road! He scolded her and brought her back. The next time Mrs. Sloan went out, she told Lizzie to Stay. The dog sat quietly for a minute, but as Mr. Sloan watched, she began to walk slowly to the end of the driveway and then out onto the road. There she ran down the road after the car. When she lost interest in the car she began to wander along the roadway.

They asked me to come up and help them to deal with this problem and we cooked up the following scheme to cure Lizzie of her wanderlust. We set her up in this manner. Mrs. Sloan got into the car and told Lizzie to Stay and the dog sat quietly. Meanwhile, I hid behind a gatehouse at the end of the driveway with a throw chain in my hand. As soon as Lizzie stood up and started to go out of the driveway onto the road, I threw the chain at her rear and said "No." Lizzie was very startled, and then I called her, and she ran back to me. After two more sessions with the throw chain, Lizzie was completely cured of her car-chasing habit.

JUMPING UP ON PEOPLE

Although it can be endearing when a puppy demonstrates its joy at seeing you by jumping up enthusiastically, no one finds it endearing when an adult dog jumps up. Neither guests nor family members appreciate the torn hose, snagged sweaters, and soiled skirts and trousers that are the inevitable result of an assault by a dog's front paws. What's more, even a small adult dog can bowl over a toddler or throw an elderly person off balance with an overexuberant greeting.

For example, Susie the bulldog used to jump up happily on her owners when she was a puppy, and they thought it was very cute. But when Susie became a powerful adult dog she enjoyed jumping up and hitting people with her chest, as all bulldogs do. One day a neighbor's child came into the house, and Susie greeted her enthusiastically with a chest blow that knocked the child flat on the floor. The dog then grabbed the child and began to play with her roughly. At this point Susie's owners became concerned and called me.

I told them we'd have to go back to the beginning, when Susie was allowed to jump up on people, to resolve the problem. I wanted her to learn by association never to do this, no matter what the provocation. So I showed the owners how to set Susie up. I encouraged her to jump up on me by patting my chest and saying, "Come on, Susie, up, up, up." As soon as she began to jump I simultaneously kneed her sharply in the chest, said "No," and put both open hands, palms down, in front of her face. Susie was shocked. Next time, even with encouragement, she stopped in mid-jump because she thought she might be hit by a knee again. When she didn't jump, I immediately crouched down to her level, praised her, and gave her a lot of petting and hugging.

Susie's owners were amazed at how well this worked. Five days later, however, a family friend came over. Susie had always jumped on this friend to show her delight at his arrival. When Susie failed to jump up in greeting, the friend was surprised and actually took Susie's front paws and placed them on his chest. The owners were horrified because they were afraid the friend had undone all of our work and had restructured Susie's penchant for jumping. I told them not to worry, but to have the friend go through the basic encouragement-knee routine the next time he arrived to let Susie know it wasn't all right to jump up, even on him. It worked fine, and now Susie's feet never leave the ground when she's greeting people.

If a big dog jumps up, you have to do much the same thing on a different scale. Bosley, a male boxer, was adopted by a client after he was found in a basement, badly treated and unsocialized. He was a beautiful dog and his new owner wanted to train him to be a show dog. But Bosley had a temperament problem. He regularly jumped up on his handler and tried to dominate her in an aggressive manner. So, in addition to giving him obedience training, she had to learn to stop him from jumping with a knee in his chest. But this time the knee action had to be especially swift and hard because Bosley was a very strong dog. So I showed her how to turn her body slightly before raising her knee so she could twist as she thrust with her knee and put her entire body into the action as she firmly said "No!" and used the blocking hand action described above. When Bosley learned his lesson and stayed on the floor, his owner went down to his level and praised him.

KNOCKING INTO PEOPLE

Greta, a Bernese mountain dog, performed a different version of the too-exuberant greeting. When someone arrived at *her* house, she would run around madly in circles and then slam into the person's legs from the side with all her might. Her strength was considerable and she often knocked unaware people over.

The solution was similar to the one I used for the jumpers. As Greta finished her circling and began to race toward me, I turned and kneed her firmly in the chest as I said "No!" and held my hands out in front of her face. Countering the momentum of her forward progress, this served to knock her completely off balance and really startled her. After her owners performed this corrective action several more times, Greta was cured of her "tackling" routine.

STEALING FOOD FROM THE KITCHEN COUNTER

One more type of jumping up occurs when a large dog that has become accustomed to being given handouts as you prepare food at the kitchen counter decides to get up and see for himself what's there. He'll stand up and put his front paws on the edge of the counter to look. As he does this, turn toward him, meet him with your knee in his chest and say "No! Don't *ever* do that!" Again, your sudden action will startle the dog and make him get down.

This is fine if you're standing at the counter alongside the dog. But what if you're across the kitchen when the dog jumps up? Again, a set-up works well to cure this bad habit. Put some tempting food on the kitchen counter and wait until the dog starts to get up to investigate. As soon as he does, toss a throw chain, large key ring, or shake can right at his rear end and say "No!" in a loud voice. Startled, he'll immediately get down. Usually only one or two such experiences will cure the dog of his potential food-stealing habit.

ROAMING/RUNNING AWAY

Dogs kept in outdoor runs or fenced yards often decide they want to have a bit more freedom. Active, medium-to-large males, in particular, are apt to become talented "escape artists." This is especially true if they are not altered and a female somewhere nearby comes into heat. Other culprits are animals that do not get enough exercise or social interaction with their owners. They naturally become bored and restless and look for excitement outside their confined yard.

Buck, a male Akita, regularly jumped the fence of his yard and roamed the neighborhood, terrorizing other dogs and frightening children. His owners had to do something, and they called me.

The first thing I did was train Buck in obedience so that his owners could control him. After we had completed the course, though, I still had to teach him not to jump his fence. Again, we set the dog up, but this time more subtly. The owner and I stood right outside the fence talking, then we moved off, around the side of the house out of Buck's sight. As soon as he saw us go, Buck decided to go, too. But we had hidden around the corner, and as soon as Buck began to jump, I rushed out, grabbed his collar, and corrected him severely, shaking him by the side of his neck and shouting "No!" I then told him, "Down/Stay" and left him. Every time he tried to jump the fence I did the same thing. After five tries Buck gave up and stayed in his yard. His owners had to follow-through on a regular basis, however, because the dog's urge to roam was strong.

BOLTING

Sometimes indoor dogs feel the need to escape, too. A dog like this may bolt out of the door as soon as you open it and run off. This can pose a problem when visitors come to the door—the bolting dog flies into them like a guided missile and knocks them over.

One solution is to have your dog Sit/Stay or Down/ Stay before you go to answer the door. But if your dog is not well trained or regularly breaks out of the Stay when the door is opened, you have to take firmer steps. Put on its leash and let it drag it around the house. Then go to the door, open it, and at the same time step on the handle of the leash. When the dog bolts, it will be caught up short when it reaches the end of the leash. Immediately snap the leash in a sharp corrective action and say "No! Stay!" as you do.

Another cure is to open the door slightly and allow the dog to put its head into the crack. Then gradually apply pressure on its head with the door while you say "No!" *Be careful*: The aim is not to hurt the dog but to make the experience unpleasant enough that it realizes it might get stuck there.

On the same principle—the anticipation of possibly being caught in the door—you can set the dog up by opening the door and, as soon as the dog begins to move toward it, slam it hard and fast. Again, *be careful*. Your timing has to be perfect in order for this to work well without injuring the dog.

WHY DOGS BARK

Dogs bark to communicate and to warn other animals off their territory. Their keen sense of hearing often causes them to bark at things we cannot possibly hear.

Walking in the woods with Mariah, I was immediately struck by the way she would prick up her ears and turn each one this way and that. Wolves and dogs are able to move their ears independently of each other to locate the source of a sound. Not only could Mariah smell things that I couldn't, but she was able to hear things that weren't there as far as I could tell. She obviously heard something long before my straining ears could finally pick up the cry of a bird far away or the scuffling of a small animal in the undergrowth.

Dog owners are often startled and annoyed when a

dog that's been sleeping or resting jumps up and begins to bark at "nothing." Usually the dog has heard something outside that human ears can't detect.

On the contrary, the same owner is delighted when his pet always greets him the moment he walks in the door—another example of dogs' ability to differentiate between sounds and recognize his master's step (or the sound of the garage door being raised).

■ EXCESSIVE BARKING, OUTDOORS AND IN ■

Although you want your dog to bark an alert when people come onto your property, some dogs that are closed in a yard or tied up outdoors on a trolley bark at everything that moves in their range of vision—from squirrels to passersby to passing cars. And often such a dog keeps on barking and barking and barking until it drives you and all of the neighborhood crazy. It's developed an excessive barking habit.

To stop this, you must startle the dog every time it begins to bark excessively. A sound stimulant such as beating on a pot with a spoon may work. If not, a throw chain, large key ring, shake can, or water balloon tossed at the dog will make it stop its barking. At the same time, always say "No!" in a particularly firm, harsh tone. If the weather is warm, a sudden spurt of water from a garden hose also does the trick. The secret is to stop the dog every single time it barks too much. This can take some effort on your part, but it will be worth it in the end.

When a dog barks at you incessantly in the house in order to get you to do something—let it out, play with it, give it a treat, for instance—you have probably created the problem yourself. If you jump to "obey" your dog and comply with its wishes immediately each time it barks at you, the dog will soon have you well trained.

In this case, you need to discover when the dog is barking for a legitimate reason. If it's time for it to go out, for instance, let it out when it barks. But if it was let out just a half-hour ago, stop it with a firm "No" and *don't* let it out again. If the dog is well fed, don't give it a treat each time it barks for one. Stop its barking with a "No" and perhaps a sound stimulant (loud noise) and ignore the request for a tidbit.

DO DOGS FEEL GUILTY WHEN THEY MISBEHAVE?

One of the biggest misconceptions dog owners have is the belief that a dog knows when it's done something wrong because it "looks guilty" when they come home. I constantly have to explain to people that a dog cannot possibly feel guilt. Guilt is a human emotion; in order to feel guilty, you have to be able to distinguish between right and wrong. If a dog "looks guilty," it is probably anticipating a reaction on your part to something it has been trained not to do.

There's a story I use to illustrate this to my clients. It goes like this:

A man owns a dog and every day when he comes home after work at six o'clock, the house is destroyed. The rug is soiled, sofa cushions and throw pillows are all over the floor, books have been knocked down, and as he comes in the door, the dog rolls over onto its back and looks guilty. The man has been told many times how to cure this problem, so he yells at the dog, pushes its face in its excrement, opens the door, and throws it outdoors.

One day the man has a half-day at the office and gets home at three o'clock. As he opens the door, he's amazed to find the house in perfect order and the dog asleep in its bed. The dog is startled by the owner's early return and immediately goes into a frenzy. It runs around the room, pulling down cushions and knocking things over, goes into the corner and urinates and defecates on the rug, and then runs to the door and flings itself out.

The moral of this is—the man had not cured his dog

of its bad habits. Instead he'd programmed it to act guilty when he came home. The dog had no idea why, but it anticipated the man's displeasure at the same time it relished the attention it received, even though the attention was negative. Therefore, it acted in a destructive way and "looked guilty" when the man surprised it, in order to get attention.

10

HOW TO SOLVE AGGRESSION PROBLEMS

Few sights fill a person with fear faster than a snarling, aggressive dog. If you're the owner of a dog that becomes aggressive toward you, you'll usually experience a feeling of helplessness, and you may also become furious at your pet.

Dogs, wolves, and other wild animals display aggression as a natural and often necessary level of communication. Aggression is sometimes the only recourse to protect family, home, and food, or to establish dominance over another animal. However natural, though, this tendency must be under control for a dog to be accepted in our human society.

Entire books, including Conrad Lorenz's *On Aggression,* have been written on this topic. Here I can only skim the surface of the subject and tell you how I've dealt with individual cases of aggressive dogs. Hopefully, these will give you some insight into the problem and help you ascertain what the cause of your dog's aggression may be. Remember, every case of canine aggression is different and should be approached individually. There are no "rules" to follow when dealing with aggression.

There are conflicting theories among behaviorists as to whether aggression in dogs is a learned or an inherent trait. In my opinion it can be either or a combination of the two. The bottom line is this—if you see a hint of aggressive behavior in your dog, no matter how young it is, get help to cure it right away. If you allow a dog to get away with aggressive behavior it will only become worse. This applies especially if there are children in the household or even if youngsters visit regularly—never allow a child to go anywhere near a dog that has exhibited any signs of aggression.

KINDS OF CANINE AGGRESSION

Aggressive behavior is labeled agonistic (combative, competitive, argumentative) by behaviorists. In this scientific mode, aggression falls into three categories: fighting (intermale, territorial, etc.) behavior; dominant/subordinant behavior; and defense/escape, or fear, behavior.

To make the subject clearer, however, I'll break it down further to suggest the underlying causes of some kinds of aggression in dogs.

Dominance-related aggression is, of course, competitive and is related to pack mentality. Aggressive behavior is seen in both male and female animals. It arises from a need to establish, or protect, an individual's role in the hierarchy of the pack. When a dog is a pet, its pack includes humans. Some dogs are more inherently dominant than others, males usually more so than females.

Fear-induced aggression occurs when an animal is so frightened it becomes panicky and irrational and strikes out when a feared creature, man or dog, approaches. Even a very submissive wolf, for instance, will strike out at other pack members if they gang up on it and corner it. Stories of wolves attacking humans can usually be explained by this instinct. If a group of hunters surrounds a wolf, the wolf will fight to save itself. With dogs the reaction has usually been brought about by a previous frightening experience or experiences, and is probably the single most common reason that owners and other people who handle dogs regularly are bitten.

Lowered ears and tail, or a tail between the legs indicates fear and apprehension: the animal is trying to make itself as small as possible, hoping perhaps to escape notice. Experienced dog handlers learn to recognize these signs right away because a frightened dog can easily become a *fear-biter*.

Food-guarding aggression often goes along with territorial aggression. A dog will guard anything at all it perceives as its possession. It can be either a learned or inborn response. In a wolf pack, for instance, each individual must guard its portion of food against even family members. In times of scarcity, only the strongest pack members survive and eventually are able to establish a new pack.

Idiopathic aggression may occur in a dog that is born brain-damaged or otherwise genetically unsound; this abnormal form of aggression always surfaces early in the animal's life. A puppy that won't allow itself to be turned over onto its back, snaps at you if you pick it up a certain way, looks in your eyes and snarls, or is overly protective of its food bowl, is probably a genetically aggressive animal whose rage can be triggered by anything.

Inter-male aggression is closely related to dominance aggression, but it is usually confined to dog-to-dog problems and is often hormone-induced.

Learned aggression occurs when a dog is mishandled or badly trained. Incorrectly taught protection and/or guard dogs become aggressive. So do dogs that are treated harshly, punished severely, or harassed and teased continuously. If an older adopted dog displays aggression, prior experiences may be the cause.

Maternal aggression often occurs in mother dogs (dams) with puppies. This kind of aggression cures itself when the pups are weaned.

Physically-induced aggression, including *pain-induced aggression*, is self-explanatory. A dog in pain may lash out mindlessly at anyone who comes near. That's why you should never approach an injured dog without protecting yourself. Dogs with systemic illnesses, such as epilepsy or hormonal disorders, may develop aggressive tendencies. There can also be *chemically induced aggression,* triggered by medication, chemical sprays, and even food additives. Scientists are studying this area, about which little is known.

Predatory aggression is actually instinctive hunting behavior and causes a dog to chase and seize another animal (usually smaller) that it perceives as prey. It can cause a problem in society if a dog decides the neighbor's cat, for instance, is literally "fair game."

Territorial aggression occurs most often in dogs that are, by nature, highly territorial, but it is often exacerbated by poor early handling and training. As in intermale aggression, neutering of males can often alleviate severe territorial behavior.

■ RAGE ■

While we're on the topic of different kinds of aggression, I have to mention rage. "Rage syndrome" is a term that's recently come widely into use.

True rage in a dog is not related to most of the kinds of aggression mentioned above. It is a tantrum that suddenly occurs for no apparent reason. Quite rare, it is usually thought to be brought about by some idiopathic, genetic malfunction.

Unfortunately, people who don't know, or can't figure out, what's causing a dog to be aggressive have of late tended to label its aggression under the convenient umbrella term of "rage syndrome."

Because true rage syndrome is difficult, if not impossible, to treat, most dogs that are diagnosed as suffering from it are put to sleep.

If your dog is diagnosed as having rage syndrome, I urge you to get a second opinion before you give up on the animal. Your dog's aggression may have a perfectly logical, curable cause.

HOW TO AVOID CREATING AGGRESSION IN A DOG

You can't help prevent aggression in every dog, but you can take steps to help your dog grow up in control of its emotions. This doesn't mean that a situation might not arise that could trigger an aggressive reaction in your dog, but it does mean you can avoid raising a dog with an aggressive personality.

First of all, follow the recommendations of a qualified breeder about when to take your puppy home. For the long-term social development of a puppy, it should remain with its mother and litter mates for the proper length of time unless you're willing, able, and knowledgeable enough to act as a surrogate mother, as I did with Mariah. Don't be tempted to go against a breeder's advice because Susie's birthday is tomorrow or some such reason. The breeder isn't being arbitrary. He only wants the best for his puppies and their new owners.

On the other hand, be careful about adopting a puppy that's been in a kennel for too long, unless it's been socialized to people. A puppy that grows up solely with other dogs will become very territorial in time.

If a dog has been well trained in obedience it rarely, if ever, develops a severe aggression problem. Once you've established that you are the Alpha in the pack, your secure pet does not need to prove itself.

Build up trust and confidence in your dog. Socialize it early in life to other dogs, other people, and especially to children.

If your dog is naturally possessive and territorial, work with it in the ways I described in earlier chapters to make it less so. Do not ever allow a dog to decide that one area in the house, or an item such as a food bowl or toy, belongs to it.

Don't ever punish a dog harshly or subject it to ha-

rassment or lengthy confinement. Be sure to obtain professional help if you are going to train a dog in serious protection. If you don't, you will probably create a seriously aggressive dog and a potential tragedy.

Last, but certainly not least, if you have a male dog that is a naturally dominant breed, have it neutered at an appropriate age. Dominance-related aggression, inter-male aggression, and even territorial aggression are all exacerbated by testosterone, the male hormone.

SIGNS OF AGGRESSION

Aggression is clearly signaled by body posture. A stiff-legged stance or walk accompanied by a straight back, erect head, ears, and tail are immediate indications that a wolf or dog is feeling aggressive. An animal that feels threatened usually wants to make itself seem larger and more imposing, so it will also raise the hairs on the back of its neck and along its spine. This is known as *pilo-erection*. If an animal is frightened and aggressive at the same time, the ears will be back.

A dominant wolf also sometimes mounts a submissive animal, not to indulge in sexual activity but in an apparent effort to press it down to the ground. Dog owners are sometimes puzzled at this seemingly sexual behavior when a dog mounts another of the same sex, or even a household cat. The dog is not confused, however, but just showing its dominance over the other animal.

Aggressive growling usually communicates a well-understood warning to both wolves and dogs. When Mariah was a tiny cub she would growl to warn off one of my dogs if it became too rough, and she even growled at me when I approached her food bowl. If an aggressive growl is ignored, it will soon escalate from warning to outright threat.

Along with tail, ear, body position, and vocal warnings, wolves and dogs use their mouths and eyes to communicate their feelings. A friendly, relaxed animal has its eyes fully open and mouth closed or slightly ajar, giving it an alert, receptive expression. If it meets a nonaggressive, nonthreatening stranger, both animals lower their ears and tails slightly to indicate mutual submission and possibly some anxiety while they explore each other by sniffing. If all goes well they usually then either go on to playful behavior or simply ignore each other and walk away. Rarely one or the other animal breaks the truce and acts in an aggressive manner, lowering its ears and tail, opening its mouth to show its teeth and emit a low warning growl, wrinkling its brow, and narrowing its eyes to stare the other animal challengingly in the eye. If the other animal wants to avoid a fight, it looks away.

This brings me to an important point. Elsewhere in this book I have mentioned that I made Mariah *focus* on me by looking her straight in the eye. I was able to do that because I had already established a dominant relationship with her. This should never be tried with an unfamiliar dog, though, because it will be perceived as a challenge by a dominant animal and may lead to an attack. Wolves often display their dominance over another animal by staring fixedly at it. If you meet a dog that acts aggressive, immediately avert your eyes to avoid a direct confrontation.

IF YOUR DOG SHOWS SIGNS OF AGGRESSION

Act at the very first sign of aggression in a dog. You may think it's "cute" when your puppy growls at you, but it won't be later. Unless you nip aggressive behavior in the bud, a dog will decide it's the boss and can get away with anything. This is a dangerous lesson for a naturally aggressive dog to learn. Don't delude yourself into thinking that if you give an aggressive puppy enough love, it will magically change into a nonaggressive animal—love alone won't work.

Although it may be difficult to do, don't react to an aggressive act on the part of your dog by becoming aggressive yourself. This only makes things worse. It acts as a challenge to an aggressive dog and excites it further. Curb your anger and act in a calm, controlled manner to make your dog focus on you and stop its aggressive action.

You should consult with two people if your dog seems aggressive—a veterinarian and a professional dog trainer. First, have your veterinarian check the dog over thoroughly for a possible physical cause of the problem. If the dog is taking any kind of medication, double-check to be sure that it isn't *possible* the drug could cause behavioral side effects.

■ "JUST THE FACTS, MA'AM" ■

There are no easy answers to most aggression problems. A professional trainer or animal behaviorist can only help you solve your dog's aggression problem if he or she has all of the facts. Prepare a complete "case history" of your dog's life. Don't omit anything—something that may seem trivial to you may help a professional figure out what the problem is.

You'll notice I use the term *desensitize* in this chapter when I describe my work with aggressive dogs, whereas in previous chapters I talked of *deprogramming*. Let me explain the difference. I deprogram a dog when I want it to "unlearn" a response or behavior that it's been taught so it can learn a new or different response or behavior. Desensitizing a dog, on the other hand, is a gradual process through which it becomes less sensitive to and more tolerant of certain stimulants that trigger an aggressive reaction.

A High Collar

I always needed complete control over Mariah when we were out in public, so I used what in dog-show language is called a "high collar." Instead of placing her collar low around her neck, I put it in the sensitive area right behind her ears. This allowed me to correct her with very slight pressure. This method is often used by professionals when they work with highly aggressive dogs.

HOW TO ACT WITH STRANGE DOGS

A knowledge of canine body language can protect you and your children around strange or threatening dogs. If you understand how the animal will interpret your body movements and facial expressions, you will know how to act in a nonthreatening way and avoid a possible aggressive attack. Here are a few rules to follow:

1. *Never* approach an unknown dog without first asking its owner if it's all right. If the owner is not around, don't approach the dog.
2. *Never* run up to a dog, or make quick, jerky gestures toward it that might be interpreted as a threat. Act like the famous mime Marcel Marceau, and move slowly and deliberately.
3. Many people immediately squat down to be at a dog's eye level. *Don't do this.* As I have already told you, staring into a strange dog's eyes may be considered a challenge by the dog—an invitation to fight. If you get down low, you're telling the dog, "Look, I'm submissive to you." It's the equivalent of another dog going onto its back to signify submission. Naturally the dog thinks, "OK, I'm going to challenge you." You always want to avoid a challenge with a strange dog. I like to use the example of St. Francis of Assisi, the friend of animals. He obviously knew all about body language: when he approached the wolf, he stood erect and held his hand out calmly to it.
4. When you meet a dog for the first time, make your hand into a loosely closed fist, fingers down, and extend it slowly to allow the dog to sniff your knuckles. *Never* put your open hand over the dog's head as if to pat it, because this is interpreted as a threat

by many dogs. If the dog is calm and friendly, you can then turn your hand over, palm up, but continue to keep your fingers curled in lightly; then you can gradually uncurl your fingers and let the animal nuzzle your hand if it wants to.

5. If a strange dog approaches you, *stay still*. If you're standing, put your arms at your sides. Don't raise your arms—the dog may think that you are threatening it. If you're on the ground, lie facedown. Let the animal sniff at you—soon it will lose interest and go away.

6. Adults should *never* snatch a small child away or up from a dog, because the animal may then perceive the child as a toy—a stuffed animal to run and grab. If an adult calmly places herself between the child and the dog, the dog will understand that she's being protective—that's pack-related behavior.

7. Running away is interpreted by a dog as Flight behavior and almost always triggers an instinctive Chase reaction in a dog, in which it sees you, the runner, as potential prey.

To sum up, *stay calm* and *use common sense around any dog*. It will understand by your reactions and body language that you are not a threat and will leave you alone.

DOGS THAT PICK ON PEOPLE

Sometimes a dog that hasn't been socialized to live with people but has been encouraged to be aggressive with other dogs will try to dominate his owner or another person. The picked-on individual is often a child or frequent visitor to the household—someone the dog perceives as not being a strong pack member. But sometimes it's the owner.

For example, Pamela Murdock, socialite and public relations woman, called me for help. Her fox terrier, Bentley, whom she had bought when he was about a year old, was waking her up several times every night. He was sweet and loving all during the day and she wanted him to sleep on the bed with her. But every time she moved in bed, Bentley would jump up, stand over her, and growl and snarl at her. She wasn't able to get much sleep and was becoming really upset. She loved the little dog, but she couldn't go on like this.

I learned that Bentley had been raised by a breeder as a show dog. He was kept solely for showing purposes and had not been handled much or socialized to people. What's more, for show reasons he had been encouraged to be feisty and growl and snarl at other dogs in the ring. (This is considered a good quality in show terriers, because terriers are judged on their courage and bravery.)

As soon as I heard his history, I knew Bentley was simply trying to tell Miss Murdock he was boss. When she lay down, she assumed a submissive posture in his eyes, and he was demonstrating his dominance over her.

Because male terriers are dominant and territorial by nature, the first thing I suggested was to have Bentley neutered. Then we went through a complete obedience training program. Miss Murdock learned to be firm with him, and they developed a wonderful, companionable relationship.

To deal specifically with the nighttime problem, I had her leave Bentley's collar and leash on when she went to bed. The minute he began to growl at her, she grabbed the leash and corrected him with a quick snap of the leash and "No!" After she did this for two or three nights, Bentley became calm, relaxed, and never tried to dominate her again. Now they can both sleep through the night.

In another situation in which a dog tried to dominate a person, I worked with a male husky. The dog was as nice as could be with his family, but every time one of their good friends came into the house, the dog rose on his hind legs, put his paws on her chest, looked her in the eyes, and growled threateningly. The dog's owner was concerned and asked me to see if I could figure out what the problem was.

I found out that the friend had a male dog of her own, and reasoned that the smell of her dog made the husky feel the need to dominate her. I told the owner the friend had to learn how to assert her dominance over the dog the moment she came into the house. I suggested that as soon as the dog began to jump up on her, she should knee the dog in the chest and forcefully say "No!" If the dog came back again, I told her to squirt a bitter-tasting spray in the dog's mouth as he opened it to growl at her at the same time that she said "No!" and kneed the dog again.

This has two effects. The knee reminded the dog that no jumping was allowed (he had already been taught this) while the spray had a negative taste that stopped him in his tracks. The result was to stop the dog's aggression immediately. He now saw the woman as a dominant force, not to be bullied. The dual actions desensitized the dog's feeling of dominance over the person and at the same time reprogrammed him and reshaped his behavior so he acted in a different manner toward her.

THE DOG WHO WAS AFRAID OF POLICEMEN

A fearful dog can become aggressive out of sheer self-protective terror. Dogs often develop seemingly irrational fears of certain types of people—tall men with boots on, women in red coats, people in uniform, and so on. But their fear isn't irrational. It always has a cause. If a dog has been teased or harassed in the past it can develop a deep-seated fear of anyone who resembles the person who frightened it in the first place. This can be an embarrassment as well as a worry to the owner.

One day I got a call from a man who asked me to solve a problem concerning his male cockapoo (cocker spaniel/poodle mix). Put simply, the dog was terrified of policemen. Whenever he saw an officer in uniform, he would cringe behind his owner, and if the policeman came near, he would growl and snap at him. Now, most people's contact with uniformed policemen is rare, so this would not be a serious problem for them. The irony of the situation was that the dog's owner was himself a police officer! The dog had never seen him in uniform, however, because he always changed into civilian clothes before he came home. But his buddies often came to the house in uniform and he was afraid someone would be bitten. What's more, he was upset to have his dog snarling and snapping at his friends.

At first I was sorely puzzled. I asked the owner a number of questions, and finally he remembered an incident I thought was the key. When the dog had been a puppy, some of his friends had come over in uniform. They were playing with the puppy in the backyard, and, when he looked out the window, he noticed they were being rough with it, teasing it and tossing it around. He reminded them it was still young and asked them to stop. As soon as they did, the puppy scuttled into the house and hid under the sofa until they left. They had unwittingly frightened the puppy very badly.

Now that I knew the cause of the dog's fearfulness, I could desensitize it. First, I had the owner work on obedience with the dog until it developed trust and confidence in him. Then I told the owner to bring his uniform home for the next training session. When the dog saw his owner dressed as a policeman, he was amazed! But soon he became used to it and played and socialized with the owner with no fear.

Then I asked the owner to ask the same buddies who had teased the dog to come over in civilian clothes. When they arrived, I gave them food treats for the dog and told them to socialize, play gently, and pat the animal. Soon the dog responded to them and showed it liked them and trusted them. It had a positive experience with them. The final step was to have these same buddies don their uniforms and again socialize, feed, and play with the dog.

Now the owner tells me that the dog not only is no longer fearful of policemen—he runs up to every officer he sees and tries to make friends!

FOOD GUARDING

As a young cub, Mariah provided me with insight into the dynamics of possessiveness. Some dogs develop a very possessive attitude toward their belongings and, most particularly, toward their food. This is usually not evident in young puppies. In Mariah's case, though, right from the beginning she would not let me come anywhere near her when she was eating from her bowl. She would growl, bare her teeth, and even snap at me if I persisted. I realized then just how strong her food-guarding instincts were. Nevertheless, I couldn't tolerate this kind of behavior in Mariah. I had to have her complete trust in order to work with her successfully.

So, I devised a simple but effective ploy. Instead of giving her her food in a bowl and then walking away, I began to feed her entirely by hand. I put some food in the palm of my hand and held it out to her. At first she didn't know what to do and backed away, expecting me to put the food down. When I patiently sat still, calmly holding out my food-filled hand, she gradually approached, grabbed a bite, and backed off again. Soon hunger got the best of her and after a while Mariah was actually eating out of my hand, although she still approached warily. Several tries later, she accepted the hand-feeding as natural. She no longer perceived my hand as a threat.

I performed this routine at every mealtime for several weeks until I felt Mariah was able to eat out of a bowl again without feeling she had to guard her meal against me. At first I sat down next to the bowl, picked up a little food out of it, and let her lick it off my hand. Then I let her alone to eat from her bowl. After that she never minded at all if I came near her while she ate, and she would even allow me to stroke her gently during her meals. She had learned to trust me not to take her food away from her.

While we're on the topic of food, I should mention that I never used food treats as a training tool with Mariah. Because food was so important to her, I didn't think that it was right to give or withhold it on what might seem to her an arbitrary basis. Looking ahead to her appearances in public, I didn't want ever to create a situation in which her food-guarding instincts might surface—when she might feel that she had to protect some food from a stranger and overreact. In addition, I always made it a rule that no food be allowed in the room when we went into schools and other gatherings, just to be on the safe side.

■ THE DOG WHO WOULDN'T LET HER OWNERS IN THE KITCHEN ■

When you raise a puppy you can offset food-guarding behavior, but sometimes when you adopt an older dog this form of aggression already has a firm foothold.

A couple with whom I worked are both lawyers. They wanted a dog, but didn't have the time to devote to raising a puppy. On the advice of friends, they called a breeder and found a ten-month-old springer spaniel available for sale. She had been bought by a family with children, turned out not to be good with the youngsters, and was returned to the breeder. She was totally house-broken and well behaved, and once the couple saw her, they decided to take her.

All went well until the first evening when they gave the dog her dinner. As soon as her food bowl was put down, she became fiercely aggressive and growled and snapped at her new owners if they came anywhere near her. They reasoned she was nervous in her new home and would get better once she knew them, but the problem became worse and worse. She was sweet and responsive all of the rest of the time, but as soon as they fed her they had to literally run out of the kitchen. She was a regular Dr. Jekyll and Miss Hyde! They called the breeder who admitted that, yes, this was why she had been returned in the first place. She thought the children in the previous family had teased the dog and made her nervous and had hoped the behavior wouldn't surface if the puppy lived alone with adults.

Well, it had, and what's more, the couple planned to start a family soon. But by then they had become fond of the dog and weren't willing to give up on her. They called me and we worked out a desensitizing routine to rid the dog of her intense food guarding and modify her behavior so she would trust her owners and allow them to touch her food, pet her, and remove her food bowl without fear they'd take it away.

We had to take strong steps because the dog's behavior was so ingrained by then. We put the dog on a long leash and let her go to her food bowl. One of the owners approached her, and as soon as the dog began to growl, we snapped the leash and shouted "No!" We had to do this time and again until she allowed an owner to come near her. Then the owner sat down on the floor near the dog as she ate. Again, as soon as the dog reacted in a negative manner, she was reprimanded severely. The owners had to work together when I wasn't there.

After several months of daily correction, the dog finally learned to allow her owners to touch her food bowl, stroke her, and move around freely in the room while she ate. On my advice, they continued to reinforce her acceptance of their presence at mealtimes every day. I also suggested that they enlist the aid of friends and family to further reinforce her tolerance of people around her while she ate. This was very important because they were now expecting a child soon.

THE BRAIN-DAMAGED BRIARD

Idiopathic, or genetic, aggression in a dog is usually incurable. All a professional can hope to do is channel it so the dog will be able to live in society under certain conditions. A dog like this must always be kept in firm control and can't be trusted with children and strangers.

I had an interesting case of a genetically impaired dog in New York's Westchester County a few years ago. The owner of a six-month-old briard named Rego hired me to train the dog. He had been told by the breeder that Rego must have early training. On my first visit, Rego tried to bite me when I made him sit. I knew now why the breeder had insisted he be trained right away—he had inborn aggressive tendencies.

I worked closely with Rego and his owner through the obedience routine, showed the owner how to maintain complete control over the dog at all times, and Rego responded well. At the same time, however, the owner's companion was having difficulty with Rego. The dog played with him and seemed to like him, but all of a sudden he would turn and bite the man on the hand hard enough to draw blood.

So I began to work with the second owner. We took Rego to group classes to socialize him and worked with a lot of distractions to help him to focus on his handler. As Rego became older he seemed a lot more manageable and stable, although he still had moments of extreme aggression. But both owners felt they could deal with him now.

Then, when Rego was about a year old, the breeder called the owners from Montana to warn them about Rego. She told them the entire litter had had to be destroyed. The last to go was one of Rego's brothers whom she had kept herself. He had just bitten her badly on the face, and she had put him to sleep. She felt the whole line was brain-damaged and suggested they have Rego put to sleep before he hurt someone.

She was amazed to hear how well the dog had been socialized and agreed that if the owners felt comfortable with him and could control him, it would be safe for them to keep him.

After a while, however, the strain of owning a dog that was literally a time bomb began to get to them. They felt he was really only half a dog because his natural animosity got in the way of their enjoyment of him—he had to be kept under such strict control all of the time. Finally, they decided they didn't want to keep him any longer. They knew the dog couldn't be given to someone else, but at the same time they were fond of him and didn't want to destroy him. So they called me for advice.

We talked it over and agreed that an outdoor life on a sheep farm in Montana would be ideal for Rego. Briards were originally bred as herding dogs, and this kind of environment would be perfect for him. Because of his good training, we were able to convince the breeder not to destroy Rego. She agreed to take the dog back and found him a home on a sheep farm near her.

INTER-DOG AGGRESSION

Let me tell you how I solved an incipient aggression problem with Mariah. In any group of dogs, one individual always becomes dominant. Among my dogs, a Doberman pinscher named Sweet Pea was the dominant female. Sweet Pea was a good-natured dog who had appeared in the movie *The Exterminator* as a stand-in for another Doberman named Strider, who was a trained attack dog. In close-up scenes in which Strider was supposed to fight the actor Robert Gindy and attack him, Sweet Pea did the actual fighting. Then the camera focused in on Strider, baring his teeth and tearing a dummy actor apart. Anyway, as Mariah matured she took over the Alpha role. Not only had she become larger and stronger than any of the other dogs, but her special relationship with me made her particularly possessive of me. She really considered me a member of her own "pack." Also, by virtue of my position in the household, I was the dominant male. In a wolf pack the Alpha female has preference over all of the other females when it comes to the Alpha male. So she wouldn't let any of the other females come too close to me and warned them off with a growl.

Then an incident occurred that really shocked me and clearly illustrated the depth of a wolf's aggressive instincts. Sweet Pea came into heat and, in Mariah's view, instantly became a serious threat to her position as Alpha female. She had to defend her standing. She grabbed Sweet Pea and seriously set upon her. She would have hurt Sweet Pea badly if I hadn't intervened. In the wild, the subordinate female (the Doberman) would have then had to leave the pack, but in this situation that couldn't happen and one, or both, animals might have been seriously hurt.

I realized that I had underestimated Mariah's aggressive instincts and had to act quickly to harness them. What would work with a domesticated dog would not be strong enough, so I had to take extra measures to modify Mariah's aggression. After some thought I worked out a plan that seemed simple on the surface, but would jibe with Mariah's sense of the proper order of things and achieve my goal of showing her I was *not* pleased with her actions.

First, I put Sweet Pea, securely leashed, nearby. Then, with Mariah on a leash, we walked past the Doberman. As soon as Mariah began to growl at Sweet Pea, I stopped abruptly, got down at her level, and made her look at me—*focus* on me—and I actually growled—a long, low, very threatening *Grrrrrrr*. Mariah was shocked, but in her world I was dominant over her, and she knew that I did not like what she was doing. However, *I* knew that the roots of her instinctive behavior were so deep I had to reinforce the lesson repeatedly so that she would realize that she was *never* to engage in this behavior—that she would always incur my strong displeasure if she did. After many, many patient lessons, in which I forced her to concentrate on me and demonstrated that I would never tolerate her aggressive behavior toward another animal, she was able to walk by Sweet Pea with no reaction.

With my exaggerated, repetitive behavior, I had

been able to completely modify and control her strong innate instincts, and from this experience I developed a system that can be used with any dog that is aggressive with other animals.

INTER-MALE AGGRESSION

Here's a story that illustrates classic inter-male aggression.

An engineer in White Plains, New York, had two intact (unneutered) six-year-old male German shepherds. The dogs had grown up together and were great companions. Then the man's mother died, and he decided to adopt her two-year-old male Doberman-shepherd mix.

At first the dogs seemed to be getting along, playing and roughhousing together. But all of a sudden they began to have serious fights. They bit each other so badly they regularly needed numerous stitches, and the owner was also badly bitten several times when he tried to separate them. The veterinarian realized the situation was getting out of hand. The owner could no longer control his dogs, and clearly needed professional help.

The first thing I did when I assessed the situation was to tell the owner to have the younger dog altered (for medical reasons the veterinarian recommended not altering the older two) to at least reduce his hormone-induced aggression toward all other male dogs. Then I explained to the owner that he had to learn to become his dogs' pack leader and develop an authority role if the dogs were ever to listen to him. Without a leader, each dog would continue to vie for the Alpha role.

We went through strict obedience training with each dog, until all three were responsive and under the owner's control at all times. Then we introduced the younger dog to one of the older animals, both on leashes, and corrected them until they could remain in the same room off-leash without bothering each other, each in a Down/Stay position. We then repeated the entire routine with the younger dog and the other older one. Finally we reached the point when all three dogs could be in the same room without incident. But they had to be in Down/Stay with the owner present. That's as far as we could go with these dogs—their innate intermale aggressions still made it too risky to trust them alone together.

AGGRESSION CAUSED BY PHYSICAL PROBLEMS

Sometimes an undetected physical condition can cause a dog to act aggressively. A good example is a lovely little poodle who bit a neighbor's child, apparently without provocation, while she was out in the backyard. I was called in for a consultation because the owners wanted to know if the dog was "vicious," as they put it. I went to the house and met the dog. I could tell right away she lacked any aggressive tendencies. I could also tell right away that she was almost totally blind. The owners were stunned—they had never noticed.

Once I knew this, I easily reconstructed what had happened in the backyard. The child had obviously come upon the dog suddenly and touched or grabbed the animal. The dog, badly frightened because she couldn't see who or what had suddenly "attacked" her, snapped in perfectly natural self-defense. The bottom line here was that if the owners had been more observant and aware of the dog's blindness, they could have prevented the incident. In this case the dog wasn't aggressive at all. Her blindness had caused the seemingly aggressive act.

Pain can also trigger an apparently aggressive action. The owners of a cocker spaniel named Camper called me in to evaluate the dog after he had bitten a dog-walker badly on the hand. The dog seemed perfectly calm and nonaggressive to me when I met him. When I tried to pet him on the neck, however, he immediately screamed and quickly backed off. Questioning the owners, I learned that he had a history of serious ear infections. They told me they had to be very careful when they put on his collar or took it off because he was still very sensitive around his ears.

Then it evolved that the dog-walker who had been bitten was a substitute for the person who regularly took Camper out. I reasoned that, not knowing about his ear infection, she had probably been rough when she put his collar on and he had lashed out at this strange person who was causing him extreme pain. The fault was not Camper's—his regular dog-walker should have told her stand-in about his problem.

The owners were greatly relieved to find out Camper didn't have an aggressive bone in his body. He had simply reacted in a perfectly natural way to pain.

THE CAT-KILLER

A classic case of aggression stemming from ingrained predatory behavior occurred when New York socialite Andréa Portago adopted a cat to become the third member of her animal family.

She already had two wonderful female dogs, Poppi, a five-year-old Siberian husky, and Lulu, a mixed husky-shepherd who was found wandering loose in Arizona and adopted by her as a second dog. I first came into the picture when Lulu was adopted, to help Poppi accept her. I worked with Poppi to make her become less competitive with Lulu, and soon the two dogs became fast friends.

The trouble arose when Andréa fell in love with a beautiful black cat and took it home with her. Lulu accepted the cat immediately, but Poppi began to exhibit tremendous predatory aggression toward the cat. It got so bad that Andréa had to literally pry the poor cat out of Poppi's jaws several times! If she hadn't intervened, the cat would have been killed. So she called me for help.

My job was to try to establish a workable relationship between the husky and the cat. I had to desensitize the dog so her instinctive predatory behavior was modified to the extent that she could see the cat without wanting to chase and kill it. I told Andréa to keep Poppi leashed all the time and showed her how to set the dog up. She was to call the cat into the room and then use an immediate snap correction the minute the dog began to go for the cat, to emphasize that this was not acceptable behavior. After a while, when we thought that Poppi had learned the lesson and was in complete control, we let her off-leash with the cat in the room. She was still under voice control at this time, and seemed to be able to tolerate the cat's presence well. For safety's sake, however, I told Andréa to be sure not to leave the two loose in the apartment when no one was around until she was 100 percent sure that Poppi wouldn't revert to her normal predatory behavior. Now she reports that everything's fine and the three animals are all great friends.

THE RAMBUNCTIOUS TERRIERS AND THE DOG WHO WOULDN'T LET ANYONE LEAVE

Territorial behavior in dogs can assume many aspects, and individual animals will protect what they perceive as their property in different ways.

Faith Stewart-Gordon, proprietor of New York's famous Russian Tea Room, has two Norfolk terriers, Gypsy and Teddy, mother and son. As terriers are, they're high-strung and feisty, but also loving little dogs and good companions. As Teddy matured, however, he became very aggressive. He was extremely protective of "his" pack (his mother and his owner), and it became impossible to walk him without a riot ensuing. Every time he saw another dog on the street, he began to bark and charge at the other animal. And, like all terriers, Gypsy would then feel the need to join in and add to the confusion. It became very embarrassing for their owner to take them out! What's more, when they were in Connecticut they'd run off heedlessly and not come back when called—their owner had no control over them at all.

One day Miss Stewart-Gordon was at journalist Barbara Howar's house and remarked that Barbara's little pug, Max, was a delightful, calm, enjoyable pet. When she found out I'd trained Max, she called me for help to make Gypsy and Teddy more civilized.

She didn't plan to breed Teddy, so my first suggestion was to have Teddy altered to make him calm down and be less protective of his turf. The dogs had never been trained, and we worked together in a regular obedience training program to establish the owner's control over the dogs. Gypsy and Teddy responded wonderfully. They now behave so well that Faith Stewart-Gordon can take them anywhere with her with no fear of a scene. In addition, they always come when she calls them.

Another fiercely territorial dog I worked with was a two-year-old wheaton terrier belonging to a well-known acting coach. Her office was in her apartment and she kept the dog with her for companionship and protection. The problem was, the dog wouldn't allow her clients to leave the office at the end of an appointment. As soon as a hapless actor got up to leave and walked to the door, the dog would jump up growling and attack and bite him.

The dog was a perfect pet in every other respect, but the coach couldn't tolerate this—it was ruining her business. She had worked with six different dog trainers to no avail and was still completely baffled by the dog's behavior. She was reluctantly about to give up on the dog when her dog-walker suggested she call me.

I explained that the dog's actions were a not uncommon outgrowth of highly territorial, guarding behavior. A dog like this will allow a person to enter its territory but will keep him there until the dog (or the owner) gives permission to leave. In this case, the coach remained sitting behind her desk when her clients left and the dog felt it was his duty to detain them.

One way to solve this problem would be to have the

coach get up and escort each client to the door—then
the dog would feel it was all right to let the person go.
But this would have been what I call a Band-Aid approach—solving a problem on the surface but not getting to its roots and curing it. We both felt this could
be dangerous in case the situation changed in the future,
since the dog would retain its aggressive behavior.

So I worked out what seemed to be a simple solution.
I had the owner keep a throw chain on her desk. As
soon as the dog began to tense in readiness to get up
and attack a departing client, she threw the chain right
at his rear. This shocked him so much he stopped in
his tracks and turned around to see where this thing
had come from. At that moment the owner could capture his attention and tell him "No, Down/Stay." The
dog was taken out of his aggressive mode and forced
to focus on his owner and respond to her command. It
worked beautifully for about a week, but then the dog
began to regress and his owner called me again. I wasn't
surprised, because the dog had been allowed to get away
with this behavior for a long time (through six other
trainers!), and it was thoroughly ingrained by now.

This time I made the owner go through the basic
Heel, Sit/Stay routine with the dog on leash. He did it
perfectly three times and then lost interest and began
to goof off—his attention span had been reached. So
then I told her to go through the routine again, fifteen
times. "Fifteen times?" Yes, I told her, "I want you to
be assertive. After going through the same routine fifteen times, you'll get angry and your style will change.
You'll be the boss." I knew, too, that the dog's threshold of response had to be increased. I wanted the owner
to really convey the message to him that "No" is "No"
even if it's the third time she's said it in an hour. We
had to reinforce the training over and over so the dog
would become really trained to control his aggression.

Now the owner reports the dog is doing well. She
doesn't even have to throw the chain most of the time,
but can sit at her desk and rattle it and the dog gets the
message. Needless to say, her clients are pleased, too.

CHANNELING A NATURALLY AGGRESSIVE DOG TO SERVE PEOPLE

Jim Fowler, naturalist and noted wildlife spokesman who worked with Marlin Perkins for twenty years and is now host of Mutual of Omaha's *Wild Kingdom*, came to me for help on a current project of his about which I'm very enthusiastic.

He is very interested in developing some way to help wolves to repopulate areas of the country where they used to abound. The major problem previous wolf repopulation efforts have run into is opposition from ranchers who are afraid their stock will be preyed on by wolves and will shoot any wolf they see on sight.

Even though the chances of wolves ever increasing in such numbers to be anything but a minor threat to livestock are slim, Jim feels that if somehow we could go back to using dogs to guard livestock against wolves, the ranchers would be happy and the wolves could live and breed in peace. Because dogs "speak" a language wolves can understand, they would keep the wolves away from the livestock and the wolves wouldn't have to be killed.

The problem was to find the right kind of dog. The dog must be strong, have the natural territorially aggressive instincts of a guard dog, but at the same time, it must be safe around people.

Jim has a wonderful female livestock guard dog, a Turkish Akbash named Sashee, who he thinks will fit the role and can become the foundation for breeding a strain of dogs to be used for this purpose. She is one of only about four hundred Akbash in this country. In Turkey, Akbash are raised with sheep so they think they *are* sheep when they grow up. Naturally, they then protect their "family" from wolves. The same thing would work in this country and the dogs could be raised with any type of livestock a rancher wanted to protect.

Sashee was naturally highly aggressive and territorial and we began to work to socialize her to a variety of people and desensitize her attack mode toward people she didn't know. At the same time we had to be very careful not to deprogram or diminish her natural territorial aggression, because then she would no longer be a good livestock protector.

So we took her out among crowds of people to socialize her. Just as I did with Bruno the attack dog (see Chapter 7), we worked and worked with her, correcting her severely every time she began to act aggressive toward anyone. Soon she got the idea that humans were not on her attack list. At the same time, we allowed her to act aggressively toward other dogs—we wanted her to retain her instinctive distrust of all other animals. We also encouraged her to use her guarding instincts when she was in her yard at home—to bark at intruders and visitors.

When Jim finds a proper mate for Sashee, he is going to breed her. Her puppies will have an inborn tendency to be territorially aggressive, but they will learn to trust people from her. Hopefully, this will be the beginning of a whole new strain of dogs that will use their natural guarding abilities to protect livestock from wolves and any other animal predators while at the same time they will be able to live peacefully among people.

If this old/new form of protection is accepted by enough ranchers, perhaps the wolf will have a chance to live unmolested in the wild again.

■ **OTHER APPROACHES** ■

There are other programs designed to utilize dogs' natural instincts to guard their pack and train them to protect livestock. In one such program in Italy, dogs have been selectively bred to look like sheep and the puppies are raised in pens along with lambs in order to make their bonding and pack instinct very strong. When they grow up, these puppies literally become sheepdogs.

The important difference between this and other programs and the one devised by Jim Fowler is the relationship of these guarding dogs to people. The dogs described above are not bonded to human beings but to sheep, and might create a problem in all but an isolated setting.

11

PROBLEMS CAUSED BY SEPARATION ANXIETY

Separation anxiety in dogs is a topic about which much has been written. True separation anxiety is a very real condition in dogs and often leads to antisocial, or "bad," behavior.

Contrary to the belief of some dog owners, a dog that acts its anxiety out by barking incessantly, indulging in destructive behavior, or even urinating and defecating in the house is not "trying to get back at me for going out." Dogs don't think that way. And in most cases, severe punishment "to show the dog it can't get away with this behavior" only makes the dog more anxious and exacerbates the "bad" behavior. This doesn't mean, however, that you have to put up with it.

WHAT IS SEPARATION ANXIETY?

As I've pointed out throughout this book, dogs are social, pack animals. By nature they need other members of their pack around them. In the wild, an individual wolf may wander off by itself, but it will always keep in touch with other pack members. From time to time it will communicate with a howl to say, "Here I am, where are you?" Answering howls will ensue.

Except for the first few nights home when a puppy is settling in, full-blown separation anxiety problems never surface when a puppy is young. When you take a puppy into your home, you and your family become that puppy's pack. At first someone is always there to care for it, feed it, walk it, play with it, and nurture it throughout the day. The puppy becomes strongly bonded to you. Then, when the puppy grows up to be an adult dog, it's left alone for a longer time. Or perhaps it's left without you in a strange place. It becomes anxious and fearful. Will you come back? Have you abandoned it?

It's just like a small child who's been nurtured and cared for since infancy, never far from her parents' loving presence. All of a sudden a strange baby-sitter comes into the house and the parents go out. Or, later on, one day her mother takes her to a new place and leaves her alone with a lot of other children and unfamiliar adults in nursery school. A child who has not been prepared for these experiences becomes frightened and anxious. She tries to run out after her parent, cries inconsolably, sometimes becoming hysterical, feverishly clutches a favorite toy or other security object, may throw a tantrum and even wet her pants in her distress.

A dog in the throes of separation anxiety acts in much the same way. It cries, whines, howls, yodels and barks incessantly and sometimes hysterically to call you back. In an effort to get out and find you, it may scratch the door. Or it may find a piece of your clothing and chew or tear it for security and to feel closer to you. In its frustration and distress it may also chew furniture or other objects, pull the cushions off chairs and sofas, and knock things over. Finally, a dog can actually become physically sick from anxiety and may soil in the house, have diarrhea, or throw up.

HOW TO PREVENT SEPARATION ANXIETY IN A DOG

The key is preparation, or socialization. If a puppy has gradually become used to your absences a bit at a time, it won't be so anxious the first time you're out all day. Similarly, if you've followed my advice and socialized your puppy so it's comfortable staying in the groomer's shop or a boarding kennel for short periods of time, it won't be traumatized when you board it for a week when you go away.

This is common sense, but I'm constantly surprised at the number of dog owners who fail to prepare a pet for their absence. For some reason people sometimes think they will never have to be separated from a dog. This is foolish because things can and do change in people's lives during the course of an average dog's lifespan. It's far better to prepare your dog ahead of time for all sorts of eventualities—a dog that's been well socialized as a puppy will get along better as an adult dog, no matter what comes up.

CREATING ANXIETIES

An owner can unwittingly create severe anxieties in a dog. A few years ago, I was called by a lovely older woman because her little terrier-mix, Schnapsie, was destroying her apartment every time she went out. I went to the apartment, met the dog, and made friends with him for about a half-hour. Then I said to the owner, "All right. Let's go out and see what happens. Come on." She looked horrified, became almost tearful, and told me she couldn't just go out like that, she wasn't ready.

First she said to the dog, "Schnapsie, I'm going to go out in a few minutes, but I'll be back soon. Don't worry." She then proceeded to go all around the apartment and gather up dozens of dog toys and put them in a pile in the middle of the living room, all the while reassuring the dog while he sat and watched her. After that she went to the kitchen and came out with a box of dog biscuits and put a bunch of them on the floor in the hallway. She took the dog's face in her hands, kissed him on the nose, looked at him intently, and said, "All right, now. Everything will be fine. I won't be long." Smiling, she said to me, "Now I'm ready to go."

But I looked at her and said, "I don't want you to go. I'm afraid." She stared at me, shocked, and I said, "You've just made a forty-five-minute production of leaving. You've said good-bye to me five times. I don't think you'll ever be back. Please don't leave." Now she understood what I was getting at. She began to look at her actions from the dog's perspective. Rather than reassuring him by her elaborate leave-taking, she had made him more and more anxious. By the time she actually did leave, poor Schnapsie's stomach was churning and he was on the verge of hysteria because he felt something terrible was going to happen.

Although this was an extreme case, owners often alarm their dogs needlessly by making their leave-taking too elaborate. You don't want your dog to think it's at all out of the ordinary when you go out the door. The animal should be able to accept it as a normal everyday event when you leave and understand you will be back.

WAYS TO SOLVE SEPARATION ANXIETY PROBLEMS

If a dog has been allowed to develop separation anxiety problems because it hasn't been properly trained and socialized, or if you adopt an older dog that already has this problem, you have to desensitize the dog so it can accept your absence at the same time you reprogram its undesirable behavior.

A dog that's a "foundling," either abused or abandoned before adoption, often forms a particularly strong bond with its new owner and may require special help in order to get over severe anxiety whenever the owner leaves.

The classic way to treat an extremely anxious dog is to desensitize it to your absence gradually by regularly leaving it for increasingly long periods of time until it becomes accustomed to being alone.

Sometimes a crate is also useful. The security of a crate can help a dog to calm down and become used to staying quietly by itself. Also, if a dog becomes destructive because of anxiety, a crate helps deprogram the destructive behavior, just as it did with Gracie the Australian sheepdog.

If excessive barking or howling is a symptom of anxiety, devices on the market can help while you work on the underlying problem. One is a sound-activated box that makes a high-pitched noise whenever a dog barks. It works on a negative-sound principle and shocks a dog enough that it stops barking. This works especially well when a dog still barks when it's in a crate. Another device is hand-held and emits a loud screaming noise. This works well if you're home in another part of the house and can run in and use it the minute the dog begins to bark. If you're not able to be home, perhaps you can enlist the aid of a neighbor, the elevator operator, or the doorman to rush into your home and use the device when the dog barks in your absence.

A pump spray-bottle of bitter-tasting liquid can also help stop anxiety-related barking and destructive behavior.

Separation anxiety problems are rarely simple, and often require a combination of approaches before they can be completely solved.

FRANTIC NOISE

If you need to cure a dog of making excessive noise when you go out, remember that you probably don't want to stop it from barking altogether. If you want your dog to continue to give an alarm when it hears a strange noise or someone comes to the door, for instance, you have to differentiate between normal barking and distressed, frantic noisemaking. Otherwise, you'll confuse the dog and it may stop barking altogether.

A young woman called me a while ago about a serious barking problem she was having with a six-year-old standard poodle. The dog, Mimi, had been her mother's constant companion and had always been perfectly behaved. When the mother died, my client had adopted the dog. As soon as she left for work each day, though, Mimi would set up a horrible crying, screaming, barking noise.

The owner had tried everything she could think of. She reassured Mimi that everything was all right each time the dog barked, but this only seemed to make her bark more. She had been told by someone else to close Mimi up in her bedroom when she went out, but this solved nothing. Mimi simply barked and screamed in the bedroom.

Obviously, we had to modify Mimi's behavior and let the dog know this was not acceptable behavior. So the client and I stepped out of the apartment into the hall and closed the door. The moment Mimi began to bark, I rushed in, grabbed her by the loose skin at the sides of her neck, shook her, and screamed "No!" Mimi was shocked. She had wanted to bring us back with her noise, but she hadn't expected this kind of reaction—she'd expected reassurance. The next time it took a little longer before she began to wail. This time I told the owner to perform the scolding routine. Soon Mimi realized her screaming and barking brought nothing but negative results. The owner continued to repeat the lesson every day when she went out, and encouraged and reinforced Mimi's good, nonbarking, behavior with lavish praise.

Smokey, a sweet female beagle-shepherd cross, was a found dog that was babied and nurtured by her owners. She became intensely bonded to them, and whenever they went out, Smokey barked and barked continuously. A mixture of two vocal breeds, she barked so loud and so much she would be hoarse, almost voiceless, when her owners came home.

We tried the routine I'd used with Mimi—setting her up by leaving, waiting outdoors, and returning to scold her severely, but this wasn't enough for Smokey. Because she was a found dog, she was just too bonded to her owners and too upset when they left. She continued to bark frantically each time.

Stronger measures were called for. The next time we set Smokey up and rushed in, I grabbed her again and immediately pumped a bitter-tasting liquid right into her mouth. That one time it worked—she was quiet when we went out again. But because her behavior was so entrenched and her anxiety level so high, I advised her owner to continue to reinforce the deprogramming every day for a while. She had to get up fifteen minutes earlier than usual so she could set the stage. She would leave, wait outside the door, and rush back inside with the pump-can if Smokey began to bark. After several weeks Smokey learned her lesson well.

PANICKY DESTRUCTION

I worked with a Siberian husky named Jack who exhibited a combination of anxiety-induced behaviors. When his owners went out he would set up a horrible howl. At the same time he scratched and scratched the inside of the front door until it was in splinters.

His behavior was so hysterical I knew he had to be calmed down in order to break him of his anxiety. I got him a crate and had his owners put him in it whenever they were going out. This accomplished two things: First, it prevented him from indulging in the door scratching and deprogrammed the action; second, it quieted him and provided him with a sense of security—it desensitized him. He no longer howled. (If he had continued to howl, a noisemaking gadget such as I described previously might have helped.) After a while, because the crate was so calming for him, I told the owners to put Jack in the crate as usual and to leave the door closed but unlatched. A week later they reported that he had figured the unlatched door out. When they came home they found him peacefully sleeping in the hall by the front door. The security of his crate had successfully taken the trauma out of their actual leave-taking and kept Jack calm. Once they'd been gone for a while, he was no longer anxious and could safely wander the house at will.

Jim, a golden retriever, had a different reaction to his anxiety. When his owners weren't home, he chewed paper. Any paper he could find, from toilet tissue and grocery bags to newspapers, magazines, and books. He even began to strip the wallpaper off the kitchen wall. In Jim's case the behavior was more deliberate than hysterical and required reprogramming. I used the bitter-tasting-liquid approach and set Jim up. As the owners and I prepared to leave the house, we put all of the paper in the house out of reach except for one piece. We saturated the one piece of paper with the liquid and left it within easy reach. Then we went out the door and immediately came back. Jim was sniffing the paper, but he didn't like its smell. I went over to him and put the paper in his mouth and gently but firmly held his muzzle closed. He struggled to spit out the bitter-tasting paper but had to swallow it. I left the liquid with Jim's owners and they reported that after several more enforced tastes of bitter-tasting paper, Jim was completely cured.

DESTROYING CLOTHES

A dog sometimes chews shoes or clothing because it's been allowed to develop this habit when it was a puppy.

But often a dog tears or chews its owner's clothes in an effort to immerse itself in its owner's familiar body smells.

Alex, a toy poodle, was devoted to his owner and followed her everywhere. When he was about a year old, his owner went out and left her closet door ajar. She was horrified when she walked in the front door with a friend to find her silk nightgown and a pair of underpants lying in the hall, ripped to shreds, with Alex sound asleep on top of the ruins. From then on she always made sure that her closet door was tightly closed when she went out. But several weeks later, she changed her clothes quickly and left them on the bed when she rushed out to play tennis. Again, Alex took her things, but this time a favorite cashmere sweater was among the items he destroyed.

Annoyed, she called me for help. I used a set-up once more. I told her to leave a T-shirt that she'd worn on top of her bed, but this time to douse it with bitter-tasting liquid. We went out and came right back and ran up the stairs. As Alex jumped up on the bed, I took the T-shirt, jammed it in his mouth, and held his muzzle closed gently but firmly. As it did with Jim, this did the trick with Alex too. We had deprogrammed his action by making it unpleasant.

An interesting note: Sometimes the instinct to find comfort by dragging around or chewing an owner's clothes is helpful to a dog. If it runs off and becomes lost in the country or the woods, I always suggest that the owner take a piece of clothing he's worn and leave it in a clearing overnight. Nine times out of ten, the lost dog will be asleep on the clothes the next day. The dog's keen sense of smell leads it to the clothing.

COMPLETE FRENZY

Sometimes a dog exhibits complete frenzy when it's left alone. Usually a dog like this has become exceptionally strongly bonded to its owner(s) for one reason or another.

Mary Ann Crenshaw, author and fashion editor, was having a problem with her bichon frisé, Millie. Millie had been found, abused, in the East Bronx, and friends gave her to Miss Crenshaw, who nurtured and cared for the dog until she became physically well. In the process, Millie became immensely bonded to her mistress and didn't want to let her out of her sight. It was so bad, Millie wouldn't even allow anyone else to hold her.

One day, for instance, Miss Crenshaw went to do a few errands and left Millie at a friend's apartment. The minute she left, the friend reported that Millie flew into hysteria. For the entire half hour her mistress was gone, Millie literally threw herself at the apartment door, crying and screaming all the time, and nothing the friend did could reach her—she was inconsolable.

Miss Crenshaw realized she really needed some help with Millie's behavior, however, when she took the dog in the car with her to visit some friends in the country one day. When they arrived at the house, her mistress decided Millie should stay in the car because her friends had a dog. It was a cool December day and she parked in a shaded spot and went indoors. A short time later the doorbell rang. It was a concerned neighbor. There was a dog screaming in a car parked in the driveway and it sounded hurt. When Miss Crenshaw went outside, Millie was literally throwing herself against the window glass, shrieking at the top of her lungs. She looked like one of those stuffed Garfield cats with the suction feet. With assurances to the concerned neighbor that the dog was really all right, Miss Crenshaw said good-bye to her friends and made a hasty retreat. (She told me later she was sure the neighbor thought Millie was abused and would have called the police if she'd left Millie in the car any longer.)

When she was back in the city, she called me. Millie's anxiety was so severe I knew we'd have to work hard to desensitize her. At the same time we had to be careful not to be too harsh with her. Because of her history of abuse we didn't want to frighten or alarm her. I was therefore very firm with both Millie and her mistress. I told Miss Crenshaw that this was a situation in which she'd have to practice tough love. She had to be firm and understanding at the same time.

We worked out a routine. I would stay in the apartment with Millie while Miss Crenshaw left. Before Millie had a chance even to begin to become frantic, I would sit on the floor near her, pet her, and hold her still by her collar. If she began to bark, I stopped her with a snap of the collar and "No!" Soon Millie was able to stay quietly with me for longer and longer periods of time without having a problem. She realized that it wasn't a crisis when her mistress went out. She would return. But before she became too dependent on me, I had to leave, too. I started by going to another room in the apartment and telling Millie to Stay. After a while I was able to stay out of the room for a half hour. Then I told her to Stay and went out the apartment door into the hall. She started to bark and I went right back in and said "No." I went out again and stayed for only about five minutes and came right back. This time Millie was still quiet and in Stay position. I praised her lavishly. And so, little by little, Millie learned to overcome her extreme anxiety when her mistress went out.

I had to treat Caesar, a five-year-old Neapolitan mastiff, in somewhat the same way. His severe separation anxiety had been created by his family. Hard as it was for me to believe, from the time they had gotten him as a puppy, Caesar had *never* been left alone without at least one family member at home. Now the family situation had changed. The children were older, beginning to go away to school, and Caesar had to be left alone in the house occasionally. When he was left he would go into a complete frenzy. He screamed, barked, and actually foamed at the mouth.

Because Caesar's anxiety had been created by the family over the years, it had to be diminished gradually.

In this case I used the classic desensitizing approach. Each day, everyone had to leave the house for half an hour and then return. Caesar would go into his usual frenzy, but as soon as they came home he would calm down. After a few weeks he was able to remain calm for half an hour. Then we gradually increased the time away, a half hour at a time, until Caesar was finally able to accept an eight-hour absence without anxiety.

12

HOW TO HELP A DOG ADJUST TO NEW PEOPLE AND SITUATIONS

Dog owners often expect a great deal of their pets. For example, an owner assumes a dog will be able to accept a new family member or person living in the household with no problem. Or perhaps he'll take it for granted his dog will feel no qualms about travel or a move as long as he's with it.

This is an example of anthropomorphism at its simplest. It's based on the belief a dog is able to think like a person, understand the reasons for a change in family makeup or lifestyle, and at the same time figure out that its position in your regard hasn't changed. No matter how intelligent a dog is, or how tuned-in to you, none of these thought processes are in its power.

When you have a relationship with a dog and changes are about to occur in your life, you have to stop and try to look at what's going on from the dog's viewpoint. You need to prepare it for whatever is going to happen in terms it can understand. Only then can you make it clear to your dog that everything is all right. You have to let it know it hasn't been forgotten and that your relationship will continue, no matter what else happens. If you can do this, your dog will be able to accept any new situations that arise. If not, you're courting behavior problems and other difficulties with your dog.

TRAVEL WITH A DOG

Before Mariah and I began our travels all over the country as ambassadors for wolves, she had to learn how to travel by air. She had adapted easily to riding in the back of my van in her crate. Because she had always slept in her crate from the very beginning, she considered it a friendly, safe haven and would jump right into it the minute I opened the door and invited her in. So, motor travel with me was no problem. Mariah would settle down in her crate and usually sleep for the entire trip. Or sometimes she would stand and look out of the back window. She was always calm and completely at ease in her crate in the van, no matter what noisy or frightening things went on outside. But I wasn't at all sure how she would react to having her crate picked up and handled by strangers, or what she would do when the crate with her in it was carried away from me on a conveyer belt. So, well before our first air trip, I took her out to the nearest airport.

With the proper permits and the cooperation and approval of the airport authorities, I put Mariah through a "test run." I unloaded the crate with Mariah in it at curbside, and walked beside her as the baggage handler wheeled the crate to a baggage conveyer belt. When we got there, I told Mariah quietly and calmly to be a good girl and that I would see her later. Then I walked away as the handler put the crate on the moving belt and it slowly disappeared between black rubber flaps. I expected to hear howls or barks of protest from my wolf, but nothing happened. After about five minutes, the crate reappeared through the flaps. Mariah looked up at me from the floor where she was curled up about to go to sleep as if to say, "There you are." The baggage handler was amazed. He said that he had never known a "dog" to be so calm the first time that it traveled by air. And so it went—Mariah became a totally relaxed air traveler and continuously surprised all of the airline and airport personnel by her complete calm every time she and I flew. She was never frightened or unhappy. Travel was a very positive and enjoyable experience for Mariah. Her early acceptance of her crate as a safe haven, or den, stood her (and me) in very good stead.

If you anticipate taking your dog with you on trips, either short jaunts to a weekend house in the country, or longer cross-country or overseas journeys, you'll undoubtedly prepare your pet to travel comfortably when it's young. If a puppy takes short uneventful trips on a regular basis, it will be perfectly calm and at ease when it has to travel for a longer time as an adult dog.

In the normal course of events, however, things don't always work out logically. A dog owner may have had no intention of traveling with her pet when she got it. Extensive travel or a move may arise suddenly. In cases such as these, the owner can't just pick up the dog as if it were a suitcase and go. Conditioning and training ahead of time are necessary in order to be sure the dog knows what's expected of it and is able to accept the experience with equanimity.

■ THE JET-SETTING YORKIE ■

International fashion consultant Cindy Rose, had a Yorkshire terrier named Coco. She was very fond of the little dog but, because she had to travel most of the year, she had to leave Coco at home with a caretaker much of the time.

Cindy went to Paris frequently; there she noticed not only that practically everybody had a dog, but that the dogs went everywhere with their owners—to the best restaurants, hotels, shops, fashion shows, and so forth—and they were very well behaved. She began to think maybe she could bring Coco with her on her travels. It would be very nice to have the little dog along for companionship.

When Miss Rose returned to New York, she contacted me for a consultation. Could I help her teach Coco to be a good traveler and to behave in a civilized way so she could take her anywhere? At the time Coco was not well behaved. She barked and yapped a lot, for instance, and attacked anyone who approached her mistress. She had the tendency of many small dogs to be protective of her owner, but this was exacerbated because she had had an injury when she was young and became especially closely bonded to Miss Rose while she recuperated. Clearly, Coco would require a lot of restructuring in order to become a good traveling companion.

I began to work in several areas at the same time. We started with basic obedience because Coco had to be taught to be responsive to her owner and to walk perfectly on a leash if she was to travel and go to the best places with her owner. She needed to feel secure and calm wherever she was and know what was expected of her at all times. At the same time Miss Rose always had to have complete control over her.

Simultaneously I began to work on Coco's protective aggression. She couldn't be yapping constantly and attacking anyone who came within a yard of her owner. With a small dog the best method for modifying aggression is often the same one used for puppies. When I took Coco out for a walk, she would constantly bark and yap at other dogs and at people. Every time she began to be vocal or aggressive, I immediately picked her up and turned her over onto her back so she was lying belly-up on my crooked arm, and said "No!" Then I'd stroke her gently on her neck and belly until she calmed down and put her back on the ground. As soon as she'd begin to bark and yap again, up she went into my arm with a "No!" Soon she began to understand that as soon as she became aggressive, she'd be flipped over and scolded. Then Miss Rose had to learn to do this with Coco every single time the little dog became aggressive, indoors or out. After a while the word "No!" alone was sufficient to stop her yapping, and within a short time Coco gave it up altogether.

Another area in which Coco's education had been less than perfect was housebreaking. She had been allowed to get away with mistakes from time to time, as many small dogs are, and was not entirely reliable. This, of course, wouldn't do if she was going to be welcomed in the best hotels and restaurants. We decided to teach Coco to use a housebreaking pad—a small, portable version of a bathroom station that can be easily folded up for carrying. It would be convenient for both the dog and her owner, and enable Coco to relieve herself neatly and quickly wherever she was. She took to it immediately and soon learned to signal her owner with a soft yap when she needed to eliminate.

Now Coco was almost ready to travel. The one remaining step was to decide how to transport her. Because she was so tiny, Miss Rose decided not to use a bulky, traditional carrying case, but to get Coco used to riding in a shoulder bag designed specifically for small dogs. Coco loved it right away. She was warm and comfortable and close to her mistress, safely out of the way of people's feet. Whenever she saw the bag she ran into it—she knew it meant she was going to go along with her mistress.

A short while ago, Miss Rose called me to tell me Coco had been the hit of the Continent. The dog enjoyed her travels thoroughly and was so well behaved that she was a welcome guest in all of Miss Rose's friends' villas and elegant townhouses and has been invited back "any time." Miss Rose is delighted with her new traveling companion.

SURVIVING A QUARANTINE

I had trained investment advisor Carolyn Bransford's corgi, Topper, from the time he was a small puppy.

Miss Bransford traveled frequently in her work, and Topper had become used to boarding right from the beginning. He often stayed with me when she was away. He was well trained and very adaptable, so when she called to tell me she was moving to England and wanted me to help her prepare Topper for the move, I wasn't too concerned.

The main thing we had to do was accustom Topper to confinement. To prevent the introduction of rabies to England, all pets entering the British Isles have to be quarantined for six months in an approved kennel before they can live with their owners. Although owners are allowed to visit their pets, the animals must remain in a kennel enclosure for the duration.

Luckily, Topper had been boarded throughout his life and wouldn't be unhappy traveling in a crate. He had never had to stay in a small space for a long period of time, though, and Miss Bransford was afraid he wouldn't like that. So we decided to program him to get used to living in a confined area. There was a section of the pantry/kitchen in her apartment that approximated the size of the enclosure in the kennel outside London that Miss Bransford had chosen for Topper. It was easy to close off with a pressure gate, and we made this into Topper's new home. There he stayed for a few weeks until he became used to it and it was time to fly off to England.

This Christmas I received a card from Miss Bransford with a picture of Topper looking perky and cheerful, sitting on a lawn. She reported he had survived his quarantine very well, thanks to his preparation, and was now happily ensconced in his new home with her.

MACARONI MOVES TO NEW YORK

Sometimes moving to a new place requires a major adjustment for a dog. An example is Mac (short for Macaroni), a Siberian husky. He lived in New York with his owner, filmwriter Gianni (Johnny) Bozzacchi. (Mr. Bozzacchi used to be Elizabeth Taylor and Richard Burton's personal photographer and is now associated with the Fellini group.)

Mr. Bozzacchi was going to Cin Citie, Rome, to make a movie, *I Love NY,* and he wanted Mac to perform in the film. Despite the fact that Siberian huskies are stubborn and can be difficult to train to do stunts and tricks, I worked with Mac and trained him to become a reliable performer and he traveled to Rome with his master. There he lived in a beautiful, spacious villa where he could roam around at will and take daily swims in the pool.

When it was time for Mac to do his scenes, I went over to Italy to help. He acted very well in the film and endeared himself to his costars Scott Baio, Kelly Van Der Velden, Christopher Plummer, Verna Lisi, Jennifer O'Neill, and Jerry Orbach.

Then the shooting was over and it was time for Mac and his master to move back to their New York apartment. Although the apartment was big and had a nice terrace, Mac had a terrible time readjusting to city life—he had been spoiled by the villa. He seemed to have forgotten all of his training, even his house-training. Soon I got a desperate call from Mr. Bozzacchi.

I realized that in Mac's case, the experience of learning to do stunts, travel, living in the villa with its large garden, and the performance itself had caused him to completely lose track of all his early basic training. His behavior had to be restructured.

Because he had traveled, he was accustomed to a crate. So I immediately put him into a crate, not as punishment but to prevent him from reinforcing bad habits by misbehaving when he was in the apartment. Then I began to reprogram him with structured meals, walks, and playtime in nearby Central Park, just as if he were a puppy again. He didn't seem to like the flagstone terrace much, so I suggested that Mr. Bozzacchi put some wood chips on part of it to make it seem more to Mac like the outdoors underfoot.

After a few weeks in which his owner carefully adhered to a strict schedule for the dog, the structure started to put things back into perspective for Mac. He began to adjust to life in New York again and to enjoy the terrace. Soon Mr. Bozzacchi was able to leave him out of the crate for longer and longer periods of time. Now Mac has remembered all of his manners. He still sleeps in his crate, but the door is left open all the time.

JEALOUSY IN DOGS?

I often hear dog owners attribute their pets' bad or unpleasant behavior to "jealousy." "Oh, poor Rex. He wet all over the living room rug because his 'nose is out of joint.' He's so jealous of the new puppy." Again, this is anthropomorphic reasoning. A dog does not know the meaning of the word *jealousy*.

How, then, do we explain the behavior we often see in a dog when it's reacting to the arrival of a new animal or person in the household? Once more we have to make the analogy to pack behavior. A dog that's lived in your household for any time has established its place in the family "pack." If it has been the only dog in the house, it is the number-one dog. When a new animal comes into the house, the dog feels it must work to maintain its position in the pecking order. If a new person comes into the house, the dog feels it must work to maintain its relationship with you, its pack leader.

In the process, a dog may become very stressed and display what is known as displaced behavior. That is, it exhibits all kinds of behavior that doesn't seem to be related to the matter at hand. Instead of fighting with the new dog, or biting the baby, a dog may bark excessively, break house-training, indulge in destructive behavior, or any combination of these. In effect, it feels it has to recapture its owner's attention. This can be confusing for an owner who doesn't realize what's going on. When a formerly well-behaved dog suddenly begins to act up, an owner may be tempted to punish it severely. This only adds to the dog's stress and misery. Although you certainly don't have to put up with this kind of behavior, you can often avoid it or alleviate it if you prepare the dog for the new arrival ahead of time.

Some dogs feel more threatened in these situations than others. It stands to reason that an animal that's been an adored "only child" for years will resent a new arrival more than a dog that's grown up in a house full of other pets and small children. I mentioned in the last chapter that dogs that have been rescued from abuse or abandonment usually form particularly strong bonds with their owners. These dogs have a very difficult time accepting a newcomer into their house.

If you understand this and are willing and able to work with your dog to help it adjust to the newcomer, both before and after its arrival, you'll be able to offset many of the behavior problems that are often attributed to "jealousy."

■ A NEW DOG ■

One of the most frequent problems is this: When a new puppy or dog is introduced into a household, a formerly well-trained older dog forgets all about house-training. This occurs especially with male dogs that feel the need to urine mark to redefine their territory.

About a year ago, I worked with Carly Simon's poodle puppy, Johnny. Miss Simon is often out late because of her busy schedule, so for her own peace of mind and Johnny's comfort and well-being, she wanted to train him to use a bathroom station in her apartment. We worked together with Johnny and soon the poodle was perfectly trained to use a bathroom station, located in a powder room in the hall. Some time later, Miss Simon decided to get a second dog, a female bichon frisé puppy named Patois. Afraid that Johnny might forget his training when the puppy arrived, she asked me to help her make the transition easier for him.

Miss Simon was aware of Johnny's need for extra affection and attention at this time and gave him a lot of reassurance. I also knew it was important for Johnny to continue to be allowed the run of the apartment, including the kitchen where Patois was—I told Miss Simon to let him in whenever she was home. He needed to retain his rights and privileges as the Alpha dog. At the same time we reviewed and reinforced his training to prevent regression.

For convenience, Miss Simon wanted both dogs to share one bathroom station eventually. But at the moment Patois had to be confined to the kitchen with her own bathroom station until she was trained. The time when problems might arise would be when Patois was allowed the run of the apartment. If she then attempted to use the bathroom station in the powder room Johnny regarded as his, he would feel threatened and perhaps resort to urine marking the apartment (displaced behavior). To prevent this, we allowed Johnny to share Patois's bathroom station in the kitchen, while we continued to retain his in the powder room. He learned to share the space with her in the kitchen. Then, when Patois was old enough to be allowed some freedom, we still kept two bathroom stations in the apartment until we were sure both dogs were comfortable with the sharing arrangement. All went well and after a while we were able to remove the bathroom station from the kitchen.

Johnny was able to make the transition smoothly and learned to tolerate Patois in "his" house without serious problems because in his view we had allowed him to retain his number-one position in the household.

■ DON'T TOUCH MY OWNER! ■

Sometimes a dog owner loses track of the fact that her pet feels threatened and displaced by another person.

Josie, a friend of my sister's, lives alone with a tiny Maltese named Arthur. Great companions, they go everywhere together. As many small dogs are, Arthur is fiercely protective of his mistress.

The dog always accepted Josie's friends when they came to the apartment as long as Josie welcomed them. Then Josie started to see a man named David. David was not particularly fond of dogs, and when he was at the apartment he paid little attention to Arthur. This was OK with Arthur, who ignored him, too.

Trouble arose one day when David hugged and kissed Josie while they sat on the sofa. Immediately, Arthur began to growl, pounced at the man, grabbed his pant cuff, and ripped it. Startled and enraged, David lashed out with a kick and sent the dog flying. Josie screamed at him not to hurt the dog, and chaos reigned.

Later, while David plucked at his torn pants and nursed his wounded ego, he told Josie she'd have to get rid of Arthur if she expected to see him again. Horrified by the idea, she asked me what to do. She certainly wasn't going to get rid of Arthur.

I told her if she really liked David enough to bother, she'd have to get him to make friends with Arthur. If he wasn't willing to do this, I suggested she "get rid of" him, not her dog. Clearly, Arthur saw the man as a competitor for his mistress's affections and would fight him every step of the way unless something was done to change their relationship. In this case it was too late to prevent destructive behavior, but fences could be mended with a lot of patience. David agreed to try.

The trick was to make Arthur take the newcomer into his pack so the dog would accept him and become protective of him as well as Josie. I explained to David that he'd have to go slowly, a step at a time, to accomplish this and to undo Arthur's perception of him as competition. He would have to "court" the dog: pet him, play with him, take him for walks alone, and in general reassure Arthur that they were friends. This didn't come easily to David, since he had never known a dog before. But he was patient and tried hard, and soon Arthur began to greet him with enthusiasm when he came to the apartment, and go out on walks with pleasure.

Once David and Arthur had become better friends,

it was time for Josie to join them when they played and walked together. At first Arthur still tried to get between Josie and David when all three were together, but with continued time spent alone with David, the dog gradually began to treat the two people as equals and tolerate their displays of affection with each other.

With all of the work David put in to win Arthur over to his side, I'm pleased to report that Josie and David recently became engaged. Soon all three will be living together as a real family.

Sometimes, despite all the efforts a new adult in a household makes, a dog still refuses to accept him. It may be necessary to restructure the dog—to show it clearly that its aggressive behavior is not acceptable. A crate can be useful in this circumstance. It allows the dog to be present when its owner and her friend are in the room, to observe them acting in a friendly manner, and to learn the newcomer is not a threat. Once the dog has calmed down, the newcomer still has to go through the same steps David did with Arthur in order to become fully accepted by the dog.

DOGS AND CHILDREN

People often assume that in some mysterious way any dog will automatically be gentle and loving with any infant or a child.

This is a dangerous myth, because it's often far from the truth. Unless a dog has grown up with small children and become accustomed to their actions, it can have great difficulty feeling comfortable with youngsters. Children often unwittingly frighten dogs, especially if they're loud and exuberant, and make sudden motions that could easily be perceived as a threat.

Parents are responsible for teaching their children to respect all animals and to treat them with care. Adults set the tone for children, and I'm continuously amazed at the number of people who allow a young child to approach a dog I'm walking without asking if it's all right. Children need to know two basic rules: Never approach or touch a dog without the owner's permission, and even with permission, always treat a dog gently and kindly.

As a dog owner, you can help your pet learn to be comfortable with children. Make a point of taking it for walks near playgrounds and parks where children are playing so it becomes used to the sounds of their voices. If your dog is a bit nervous around children, you can protect it at the same time you allow children to pet it. Pick up a small dog and hold it in your arms while you carefully guide the children's hands to an appropriate petting spot. If your dog is too big to pick up, do the same thing while you squat beside it. The dog gains a sense of security from your nearness and learns to accept children's attentions without fear.

■ CHILDREN IN THE HOME ■

If you have a dog that has lived all its life with adults, visiting children can present a problem. No matter how good-natured your dog, or how well you've socialized it to children outdoors, it can be a different matter when youngsters invade the dog's home. The dog can become confused, upset, and frightened. I have discussed the causes of aggression in dogs, and even if you know your pet hasn't an aggressive bone in its body, an otherwise completely reliable dog can still become so harassed that it strikes out self-protectively.

In this case you have to be alert to the possibility of a problem. If the children set upon the dog, chase it all over, take its toys, and play with its food bowl without any intervention from their parents, you have to remove the dog. Politely take it away and put it in its crate or a room and close the door. This is for both the dog's and the children's protection.

■ YOUNG CHILDREN AND DOGS ■

A young child can present a particular problem for a dog. Toddlers and preschool youngsters move fast, are manually dexterous, and yet often have little understanding of their own strength and ability to hurt or pester a dog. In their concern for a child's safety with a dog, people often fail to consider that a dog can also be hurt by a child.

One way parents can help foster a good relationship between a young child and a dog is to enlist the youngster as an "assistant trainer." This method worked extremely well when Mickey, a golden retriever, came to live with two-year-old Robin's family. Mickey had lived with another family until his adoption and had to be retrained to adapt to his new household. What we did was teach the child and the dog simultaneously. While Mickey learned to be obedient and well behaved, the little girl learned to be loving and gentle to the dog while helping her mother with his training. If her mother was busy and Mickey began to chew something he shouldn't, for instance, Robin would run to her mother and say, "Mickey bad dog."

We decided to use a crate for Mickey. Not only did it help restructure him initially, but it also provided him with a ready-made retreat. Robin learned to leave Mickey alone when he was in his crate, and whenever the dog was tired of playing and wanted to rest, he would go into it and lie down.

Because Robin's parents handled Mickey's introduction into their household and into their young child's life so well, the dog and the child are strongly bonded and have a close, loving relationship.

Not all parents are as perceptive of a dog's needs as Robin's were. Parents often fail to teach children how to treat their own pets. It may not occur to them that most children are insatiably curious, are often thoughtless, and must be taught not to poke things into a dog's body openings, for instance. When I adopted Chelsea, an adorable shaggy mixed-breed, from a shelter, I was told she hated children. Her former owners had brought her to the shelter because she had bitten a young child. I was concerned because I wanted to train her to become a performer and didn't want to have any problems if there were children on the set, so I decided to find out what had happened. I discovered that when the very young children in Chelsea's former family had been playing with her one day, they had decided to poke a pencil down her ear to find out how far it would go. They pushed and pushed until they finally punctured the poor dog's eardrum. Finally, Chelsea could stand the pain no longer, and bit one of the children. Once I knew her hatred of children was based on fear of pain, I was able to reassure her, and as long as I was with her she was perfectly fine when she had to work with a child on a TV set.

■ PREPARING A DOG FOR A NEW BABY ■

It can be just as hard for a dog that's been an "only child" in a household to accept a new baby as to accept a new dog. Most dog owners are conscious of this, but sometimes they don't know how to prepare a dog for a baby's arrival.

Of course, you need to be sure the dog is in good health and free from parasites. Well before the baby arrives, have your dog checked out by the veterinarian and treated for any problems if necessary.

A dog must also be obedient and in your complete control around a baby. So no matter how old your dog is, it must be obedience trained if it hasn't been already. Many expectant mothers find this an enjoyable experience—it's good exercise and can be fun.

Physical changes in a household can be upsetting for a dog. Allow your pet to sniff and explore the nursery and furnishings so they don't alarm it.

Be sure to arrange ahead of time for the dog's care during the time the baby is born and the mother's still away in the hospital. If your dog feels as if it's been deserted or neglected because of the baby, it surely won't feel good about the whole thing.

Murray was ten months old and an "only child" when the baby in his house was born. The young shepherd had been very responsive to obedience training, and now his owners had to introduce him to the new family member. They knew Murray had to receive a lot of love and attention himself, and so they made a point of greeting him enthusiastically as soon as they walked into the door with the baby.

After the baby was settled in her crib, they took Murray into the room to introduce him. They put Murray in a Stay next to the crib so he would remain quiet and wouldn't accidentally paw or scratch the infant in his enthusiasm. (Sometimes a dog thinks a baby is a small animal or a plaything and may jump on it or injure it by mistake.) They let him sniff the baby and then took him out of the room. In order to avoid any problems when they weren't right there, they put a pressure gate across the door—Murray could look, but he couldn't go close without supervision.

Adult wolves and dogs always recognize a mother's nurturing behavior and know instinctively to be gentle with an infant. When wolf cubs and puppies meet an adult animal, they usually roll over onto their backs in a submissive posture and urinate to show they're still babies. Human parents can use this innate behavior to their advantage, as Murray's owners did. Whenever they changed the baby's diaper, they let Murray sniff it. This served as a reminder to him that this was a baby and it also let him feel he was sharing in its care.

When the baby was nursed, Murray sat in a Sit/Stay or Down/Stay and watched. Again, his owners wanted him to feel like a participant in the baby's care so he would learn it was part of his family, to be protected and cared for. They didn't ever want him to feel upstaged or left out.

That's a mistake new parents often make. In their concern for the baby's safety, they close a dog up, away from the child, so the dog begins to feel left out in favor of this new being. This fosters competition between the dog and the child—something you want to avoid. If you follow sensible, commonsense rules of safety and have your dog under your control at all times, it soon learns to treat a baby with restraint and care, just as it treats all people. That's the way it's worked with Murray.

Of course, as their baby grows and learns to crawl and then walk, she has to be taught in turn to treat Murray with care and respect. But when a dog has been properly introduced to and socialized with a baby, it becomes so bonded to the child that it tolerates a lot of unintentional hair tugs or ear pullings with good nature.

HOW TO TRAIN DOGS FOR SPECIAL ROLES

13

DOGS THAT HELP PEOPLE

The list of roles a dog can learn to perform is endless. Over the years people have been able to cultivate dogs' superior senses and innate loyalty in order to teach them to be protectors, guides, assistants, and even four-footed therapists.

DOGS AS PROTECTORS

Historically, dogs have been perceived as our protectors. The theory of how dogs first came to live with early cave dwellers revolves around the assumption that in addition to their help with hunting and obtaining food, they served as guardians of the family and their possessions. In 400 B.C., Socrates said, "Well-bred dogs, as you know, are by instinct perfectly gentle to people whom they know and are accustomed to, and fierce to strangers. . . . It is really remarkable how the creature gets angry at the mere sight of a stranger and welcomes anyone he knows."

In the beginning of their relationship with man, dogs alerted and guarded their human friends against predatory animals. Later, dogs learned to alert their masters when other humans approached. Nowadays, dogs are often trained to keep people and property from harm in a variety of ways.

Entire books have been written on the subject of protection dogs and how to train them. In this chapter I can give only a brief rundown of the different kinds of protection dogs and tell you how to teach your own pet to be a good home watchdog. As in all other kinds of advanced training, protection training on every level builds on the foundation of obedience training.

KINDS OF GUARD/PROTECTION DOGS

You may want your dog to act as a watchdog—to alert your family when someone comes to the house. Or perhaps you want your pet to be a companion and baby-sitter for your children when they're alone in the house or yard (à la Nana in *Peter Pan*).

Other people may need more serious protection. Dogs can be trained as personal protectors/bodyguards for individuals who are highly visible, such as politicians, or as escorts for people who regularly carry valuables and/or cash with them. These dogs are precision-trained animals, alert to their surroundings at all times. They're taught to focus on anyone who comes within their visual range, and stand at the ready to obey any voice command given by their owners/handlers.

Dogs are often trained as guards for businesses—stores, garages, boat yards, etc. Sometimes they're brought in to patrol each evening at closing time and taken away the next morning, or they may live on the premises and be released to "walk the beat" at night. These are also highly trained dogs and are very dangerous. Their job is to keep anyone at all from entering the establishment, and they're taught to chase and attack anything that moves. Business guard dogs are trained/handled/cared for and fed by only one person so that they can't ever be bribed with food.

■ SERVICE DOGS ■

Dogs have been used as soldiers ever since Roman times. Today, military dogs are specifically chosen and trained very carefully and precisely to work with and respond to only one person who is their handler. They never socialize with other people, and are kept in special isolated kennels at the military base. A dog trained as a military animal is very dangerous. It can't be retired to civilian life because it will go into a rage and attack if anyone other than its handler comes near.

Dogs that are trained for police work, on the other hand, are socialized to the civilian world. They are taught to work in a team with their handlers/owners, and when they're not working they go home with their human partners and become loving family pets.

THE SCENTING ABILITY OF DOGS

One of the reasons dogs make excellent protectors is because of their excellent natural scenting abilities.

I learned about this superior sense early in my relationship with Mariah. One night I decided to "sleep out" with her to observe her in an outdoor setting. No sooner did I settle down than she began pacing around the enclosure with her face turned upward, ears pricked, nostrils twitching, sniffing the air and turning her head this way and that to capture the scent better. In a short while she began to make a kind of low whining, murmuring sound in her throat.

She obviously smelled something in the air, but try as I could, I detected nothing. Almost five minutes passed and then the faint odor of a skunk finally reached my nostrils. The skunk must have been at least a mile away when Mariah first smelled it.

On another day, Mariah and I were walking in the woods when she began to sniff the air. She walked to a point slightly off to the right and sniffed, then to the left and sniffed again. She began to walk forward, zigzagging from side to side, each time for a slightly shorter distance, until she finally stopped and flushed a pheasant. If you watch hunting dogs—pointers and retrievers—you'll see them do the same thing. That's because an airborne smell travels downwind from side to side in a conelike, triangular shape, from the vertex (smell) to the open end.

The instinctive ability of dogs to recognize strangers that Socrates mentions is based to a large extent on their superior olfactory sense. Dogs will often attack a frightened person, for example. That's because when a person is scared (he doesn't belong where he is, for instance) his glands secrete adrenalin into the blood stream. This causes his heart to pump harder and accelerates his respiration/circulation, which increases body heat and makes him perspire. When the scent created by the perspiration is picked up by a dog, it triggers a psychological response in the animal. The dog is immediately put on guard—it becomes alert and snarls, growls, and barks at the frightened person.

If the dog's reaction causes the person to attempt to flee, the dog immediately gives chase. The Chase reaction is also an instinctive canine behavior.

Trained guard dogs seem to develop a heightened ability to smell fear and react to it.

WHAT KIND OF DOG MAKES
A GOOD HOME WATCHDOG?

Although some dogs are more vocal than others, almost every kind of dog that barks is capable of becoming a good home watchdog. A barking dog is a great psychological deterrent to anyone attempting a break-in. Not only does he fear the dog might be dangerous, but the bark alone alerts people that something's up. Statistics show that households with dogs are much less apt to be broken into than those without. There is even a popular device on the market that turns on a tape of a barking dog if anyone approaches the house!

■ THE RIGHT TEMPERAMENT FOR THE WORK ■

A dog used for any level of protection work must have the right temperament. If you have raised your dog from a puppy, you probably know what kind of temperament it has. But if you obtain an older dog, it's extremely important to find out before you begin to train it. Certain canine personality/temperament traits are exacerbated by protection training and may cause a dog to go too far.

A very territorial and possessive dog, for example, that growls or snaps at you when you approach its food bowl or favorite toy must have this behavior modified before it can be trained for protection. On the other hand, a skittish dog that jumps and runs at any loud noise is too unpredictable for protection work. It could easily become a fear-biter and lash out in terror at an imagined threat.

If your dog is at all shaky in the temperament department, don't attempt to train it to be a protection animal. If a problem does arise with a dog that has not been properly temperament-tested, it is *your* fault, not the dog's.

A well-chosen, well-trained protection dog never attacks anyone without being told to by its owner, and is therefore completely safe in society. The terrible reports in the news of dogs that attack people "for no reason" are always the result of dogs that were either unintentionally badly trained by uninformed, misguided individuals, or animals intentionally trained to attack by stupid, antisocial people.

■ NATURALLY PROTECTIVE DOGS ■

Some dogs are naturally very protective of their owners and property. Extremely territorial dogs such as most terriers and many working dogs, for instance, may need no instruction at all in order to bark at strangers and act possessive of their property and human families.

Other dogs become highly sensitive to their owners' moods and are able to read their body language. If an owner is upset or frightened by another person on the street, for instance, this kind of dog senses it immediately and reacts in a protective way.

This can be a wonderful asset for a dog owner, who can always feel safe as long as his dog is at his side. But don't encourage a naturally protective dog to go too far. A problem arises if you allow a dog like this to become overly protective without simultaneously being always and completely under your control.

When a dog is instinctively protective, the trick is to harness that natural instinct so you can use it and then stop it. You have to work to make the dog focus on you and learn to stop when you tell it to. Work on-lead and correct the dog as soon as it begins to carry the protection mode too far. Set up situations in which an assistant approaches, for instance, and correct the dog immediately if it crosses the line into aggression or doesn't stop barking the moment you tell it to.

If you fail to teach a naturally protective dog to remain under your control at all times, the dog will become a dangerous animal.

BE CAREFUL!

If you want your pet to be a good watchdog and at the same time be completely trustworthy around children and friends, the dog must always be in your complete control. Before you even consider training your dog to be a watchdog, you absolutely must obedience-train it. A dog that's mastered on- and off-leash obedience training will always respond to your commands.

Take no shortcuts in this respect. A badly trained dog that is taught to be protective can become a lethal weapon. And if you are even *considering* going beyond simple watchdog training, get professional help. Do not attempt to train a dog to be a serious guard dog yourself.

I recently heard about a man who knew nothing about

dogs or dog training, but decided he wanted a dog to guard his house. He bought a book about how to train a guard dog, then got an adult Doberman pinscher. He proceeded to tie the dog up (this fosters and encourages territorial aggression), teased and goaded it to make it bark, show its teeth, and snap at him. One day the man came home and the dog had soiled the rug. He beat the dog, and the dog bit him. Then the man went around telling everyone, "My dog turned on me." Nothing makes me crosser than this. It wasn't the dog's fault, it was the man's own stupidity. He himself taught the dog to go against him. He is very fortunate it wasn't a neighbor's child who was bitten.

If you decide to hire a professional trainer for this kind of work, be sure he or she is well qualified. Talk to a veterinarian who has had some experience with protection dogs and ask for a recommendation of a proven professional. Get references of dog owners you can talk to. Find out if they have children, for instance, so you can be sure that a dog trained by this person won't become a menace to society (or yourself).

HOW TO TEACH YOUR DOG TO BARK ON SIGNAL

Most people, of course, don't require such protection. If you simply want your dog to bark whenever anyone comes to the door, follow these steps. Enlist someone's aid and, with your dog sitting at your side on the leash, have the other person knock on the door. As soon as you hear the knock, call out in an excited voice, "Who's there? Who's there?" If the dog barks, praise it. If not, have the person knock again, and this time wave your arms and move around in an agitated manner while you make a panting "Huf, Huf, Woof, Woof" dog-wolf sound. You want to excite your dog and make it bark, just as an adult wolf does with a cub to teach it to bark— she jumps up and makes excited, agitated sounds. When the dog barks, praise it and go to the door. Tell the dog to Stay and open the door. With the dog still in Stay, have the other person praise the dog, too. The dog will then recognize the person as a friend. Remember, you want your dog to be alert; you don't want it to be a menace.

▪ A STRANGER IN THE HOUSE ▪

Perhaps you don't know the person who just came into your house, and you're not sure how friendly you want to be with him. He may have posed as a salesman or appliance repair person, and once he's in the door, you think he might not be legitimate.

In this situation you want your dog to bark, but don't want to alert the visitor by using a verbal command. Therefore your dog must learn to respond to a hand signal alone. Once your dog has learned to bark when an aural stimulus is given, such as the sound of someone knocking on the door or your spoken words, make eye contact with it and have it focus on you. As you say "Speak," move the tips of the thumb and fingers of your right hand up and down in a "talking" or "quacking" motion (think of making shadow pictures on the wall). Do this every time you give your dog the verbal command to speak. Soon the dog will learn to speak with only the hand gesture.

If you don't want your dog to bark but would like it to remain on guard, you can keep the animal in a Stay position (either Sit/Stay or Down/Stay). Grab its collar and snap it while you say "No. Stay." In this context, "No" means "Stop barking." The dog will continue to be alert and focus on the visitor until you release it— I'll tell you how to do this later in this chapter. This alert mode is also used in police and military work, to keep a prisoner under surveillance while the officer searches him, for example.

■ A SECRET BARKING SIGNAL ■

Another technique used to make a dog bark is twisting its collar. This method can be very useful outdoors. For instance, you're walking your dog in the park late at night and a stranger approaches. You may not be sure if the person is a threat or not, so you not only want to alert your dog to focus on the person, but also give it an unobtrusive signal to bark if necessary.

The dog must already be trained to bark when someone comes to the door. To program your dog to respond to the collar signal, begin as before, with it sitting by your side in your home, on leash. Again, enlist the aid of another person—ideally someone whom the dog doesn't know well. This time, however, you have to synchronize your actions ahead of time. Hold onto the dog's collar and, just as the person begins to knock at the door, give the dog's collar a short, counterclockwise twist to coincide with the dog's bark response and say, "Who's there?" Each time you say that, the person knocks and you twist the collar as the dog barks. Soon the dog has been programmed to bark when its collar is twisted—just like turning on a light switch. It's learned a new bark signal.

To make the collar signal more urgent, add a vocal command. The word or phrase that you choose should be explosive-sounding in order to incite the dog into action. To avoid mistakes, pick a word or words you normally don't use in everyday conversation. Some people like "Watch it!" but this seems a poor choice because you might say "Watch it!" to someone who's about to trip over something or be hit in the head by a ball or Frisbee. I often choose the word "Focus!" when I work with people—it's not used regularly in conversation and it's explosive-sounding, expecially when you pronounce it "fo-cus!" Another good word that many trainers use is "Pasahf"—German for "Look out." My favorite word, however, is one that no one else knows—"Kapea," pronounced "ka-pay!" In my native language, Albanian, it means "Get it!" It's short and explosive, and you're most welcome to use it if you wish.

These same signals are used in more advanced protection work. Recently I worked with a client who had had a terrible experience. She lived alone in the suburbs and had been raped in a parking lot one night as she went to her car. Needless to say, she was very fearful and nervous after this. The therapist with whom she was working suggested her life might be more bearable if she got a dog for companionship and protection. I helped her choose a lovely female shepherd (I didn't want her to get a male because he might be too hard for her to control). We went through all of the steps of obedience training, and then I taught her the collar switch with verbal command procedure. Later we went further and taught the dog to attack on signal, but I won't describe this part of the training. As I said, this should *never* be attempted without a professional trainer.

This collar-switch signal also works well at home if someone unexpectedly comes to the door late at night, for instance. You can answer the door with the dog at your side and signal it to bark if you beome alarmed.

THE RELEASE

When the person who knocked comes in, you can be friendly and put the dog in the Stay mode, or you can release it so that it, too, can make friends. You also need to be able to release the dog from its alert mode if the person who approaches you in the park turns out to be no threat. Once the dog is alert, you have to give it a signal to let it know it can stop focusing on the person.

To release the dog, you need to say another command. As the friendly person comes into the house, or the seemingly threatening person in the park retreats, praise your dog and say "Out," or "Oust" in German.

The dog will then relax, go to your friend when it's called, or continue to walk at your side.

Again, practice this in the house. Act friendly and relaxed at the same time you praise the dog lavishly and tell it everything's OK. Say "Out" and let go of the dog's collar. Have your assistant call the dog to him and pet it. After a few times the dog will be programmed to let down its guard when you say "Out" after an alert mode.

The release ensures you your dog is really safe and will never make any trouble for a friendly person or a guest in your home.

I must repeat once more, be very careful when you work with a dog to make it a protector. You want to end up with a safe animal, not a problem dog that has to be locked up all the time.

OTHER WAYS DOGS USE THEIR SENSES TO HELP PEOPLE

In addition to their keen sense of smell, dogs are taught to use their other senses to help people. They learn how to serve as the eyes, ears, and even hands of disabled owners and to communicate with elaborate body language.

Each type of helping dog goes through lengthy training in which it hones the senses it will require to fulfill its particular role. It must become sensitive to certain signals and stimuli and learn the appropriate response to each. It must then communicate with its owner via body language in the form of touch or posture. As time goes by, owner and dog invariably develop personal signals and gestures to meet their individual needs.

Seeing Eye dogs, for example, are carefully taught to recognize obstacles and other potential dangers in order to help their visually impaired owners negotiate safely around them and be able to function in the world independently.

Hearing dogs learn to identify a number of important

sounds—the doorbell, telephone, teakettle, a baby crying, smoke detectors, and alarm clocks—and communicate each one in a different way to their hearing-impaired owners. Their help makes a world of difference to their owners, who are cut off from the aural world without them and often become fearful in their isolation.

Still other dogs are taught to find and retrieve lost or dropped objects, open doors and cabinets, and turn on switches for wheelchair-bound individuals.

Dogs that perform these specialized tasks are tested for temperament and ability to learn and are chosen and taught by the organizations that place them. If you want to know more about these dogs, their training and availability, contact your veterinarian, local SPCA, or humane society.

■ EMERGENCY ALERT DOGS ■

In the early 1980s I was instrumental in developing a system in which dogs were trained to respond to a crisis by activating a special pull-cord alarm. Some (Medi-Alert dogs) were taught to react to a medical crisis. Other dogs were trained to pull the alarm if an intruder broke in. An advantage of this system is that it does away with the need for an attack guard dog, thereby eliminating the possibility of a tragic mistake. We have not been training Emergency Alert dogs in recent years, but are in the process of reactivating the system.

■ SEARCH AND RESCUE DOGS ■

Search and Rescue dogs are animals that have been highly trained to use their keen senses of smell and hearing to locate people who are missing in the wilderness, help the police to find homicide and drowning victims, and find disaster victims who may be buried under rubble after an earthquake or a building collapse.

They also use what I call an extra, special sense-

thermal sensitivity. Wolves and dogs share this ability to sense a mammal's body heat inside their noses and pinpoint a hidden source of odor. I once watched Mariah as she sniffed along the surface of freshly fallen, untracked snow. Suddenly she stopped and began to dig. Soon she unearthed a mole that had been hiding under a rock. In the wild, wolves use this extra sense to survive in snowy, icy winters. Over the years, Saint Bernards have used this kinetic sense to find people trapped below many feet of snow.

Owner/handlers and their pets go through an intensive training program so they are able to work together as a Search and Rescue team. Shepherds are the breed best suited for this type of rescue work because of their size, thick double coats, physical strength, and receptiveness to training. Because Search and Rescue dogs always work off-lead and are often in wooded areas, the fact that shepherds aren't hunting dogs means they won't be distracted by game in the woods.

Training usually begins when a dog is young. After its initial socialization, a puppy slated for Search and Rescue work is taught to further develop its strong sense of smell. Through an elaborate hide-and-seek game in which the owner hides, the puppy is trained to use its nose to locate people by means of airborne scent. Later, as the dog matures, it goes through advanced obedience training to learn to work off-leash under only voice command. Its tracking abilities are honed, agility developed (rescue dogs often have to go into areas where the footing is treacherous), and its stamina is built up. After all of this intensive training, a Search and Rescue dog and its owner/handler are ready to join a team. For names of Search and Rescue associations, see Appendix C.

■ **DOGS AS THERAPISTS** ■

In 1985, I was instrumental in influencing Bronx Borough President Stanley Simon to proclaim Pet Therapy Week in the Bronx—the first such proclamation in the

United States. The next year New York City Mayor Ed Koch proclaimed a city-wide Pet Therapy Week, and subsequently a statewide pet therapy program was developed under the direction of the Center for Pet Therapy in New York City, of which I am a director.

It's now a well-accepted fact that animals, and dogs in particular because of their loving and responsive natures, have a positive effect on most people, especially those who are cut off from family and friends because of hospitalization, institutionalization, or mental illness. Dogs provide many benefits to people. They act as social catalysts and provide a common ground for conversation and communication. They give touch contact, so missed by individuals who are removed from loved ones. They are nonjudgmental in their acceptance of people—a dog couldn't care less if your hair is messy or your clothes aren't stylish. What's more, they often bring a person who has lost his sense of reality back to the present. These are just some of the reasons why health professionals are in accord about the positive benefits of pet therapy (or pet-facilitated therapy, as it's often called) for institutionalized people.

Dogs that are going to be used for pet therapy must be specially trained and socialized for their jobs. People sometimes think they can go into a shelter, for instance, take out a couple of cute puppies, and bring them to a nursing home to visit the residents. This can be a bad mistake, because no matter how cute they are, untrained puppies can be wild, nippy, "wetty," and so forth. The same type of advanced training required for theatrical work is necessary for a pet-therapy dog. It must learn to be calm while handled and held by strangers. Proper training and handling of an animal makes pet therapy work.

Take Goldie, my chihuahua, as an example. As a rule, these little dogs are very nippy and aggressive. But Goldie was trained in advanced obedience and theatrical work and has appeared in numerous commercials. She is used to a lot of distractions, to being handled by people she doesn't know, and is therefore an ideal pet therapist who responds to everyone with calm love and affection.

Every other week last summer I went to a long-term care facility in Westchester County with Goldie and my Yorkshire terrier, Kimberly, also a trained performer. Let me tell you about a typical visit:

As I step off the elevator with my two pet-carrying cases, about two dozen residents of the facility are sitting in a circle in the lobby. There's little movement or conversation—most of the people are staring into space, their hands folded in their laps or resting lightly on the walkers in front of them. Some are dozing.

As soon as they see me, the residents are suddenly alert. Exclamations of "Oh, good" and "Let me have her" follow when I take the two little dogs out of their boxes. Eager hands reach out to touch the dogs as I walk around the circle carrying them. One lady, however, sits quietly and shrinks back as I approach her with Goldie. "Would you like to hold her?" I ask. "Oh no, I'm afraid of dogs," she says. I show the lady that Goldie is trembling (chihuahuas are sensitive to temperature changes and often tremble unless they're being held close). "Look, she's afraid too. She's trembling. Why don't you hold her so she'll know everything's all right?" She reaches out for Goldie tentatively, and in a few minutes the little dog is in her tight embrace while she smilingly pets her and coos to her.

In the meanwhile, Kimberly is bouncing around in another lady's arms. When I go over to take Kimberly and give her to someone else, the lady's eyes fill with tears. "I used to have a little dog," she says. "I had him for fifteen years. It was so sad to have to give him up." She goes on to tell a nearby therapist all about her family and their dog.

Now hands are reaching out eagerly to pet and hold the little dogs. Many residents are talking to each other and to the therapists and staff. A man in the back of the room who had been quiet up until now suddenly begins to sing "How Much Is That Doggy in the Window?'' Everyone laughs and a couple of people join in the song.

All too soon it's time to leave. Amid a babble of "Good-bye" and "Come back soon," I put Goldie and Kimberly back into their carrying cases. As we get into the elevator I can't help but reflect about the change in atmosphere the dogs had brought about.

Currently I am working on a program to enable ordinary dog owners to train their pets so they can work as animal therapists, but for now pet therapy is best left to dogs that have been specially trained for the work.

A Miracle?

I'd like to end this chapter with a story that illustrates the essence of pet therapy to me.

I went to a nursing home in New York City with my dogs last winter. I had been visiting there on a regular basis for six months and most of the residents knew me well. When I arrived, the recreation director told me of a new resident in the group who was not communicating at all. The staff thought perhaps she might enjoy the dogs.

When I went into the room where all the residents were waiting for me, the new patient's husband was there visiting. He told me how pleased he was I was there, and said his wife had always loved animals. He went on to say she had been an eye surgeon, a concert pianist, and spoke six languages, but now she was suffering from a severe case of Alzheimer's disease. She couldn't remember anything and hadn't spoken for months.

She had a wonderful smile and I immediately felt warmly toward her. I brought Goldie over and, as I stood in front of her, I asked her husband what languages she knew. He told me she had been born in Greece. Having grown up in Europe myself, I speak a little bit of a lot of languages, so I spoke to her in the language of her childhood. I said, *"Te canis,"* which means "Hello" in Greek. While she stroked Goldie she

looked up at me, smiled, and whispered, "*Te canis.*"
Her husband was shocked. All of the health professionals rushed over.

Then I tried another language. In French I asked her, "*Desirez-vous le chien?*" (Do you want the dog?), and she said, "*Oui, je desire le chien*" (Yes, I want the dog). She smiled and smiled with a wonderful expression. Her husband shouted out loud, "Look, she's talking! It's a miracle," and everyone laughed and clapped.

A door had been opened. When I left, the professionals took over and, with therapeutic reconstruction, working from her childhood on by using the languages she had learned when she was young, they were able to get her to communicate again.

This is what pet therapy is all about. Sometimes the touch of an animal can create an area of communication that has been forgotten. It can cause a person to relax, forget the stress of present circumstances, and open up an avenue of memory or feeling so the person is eventually able to come back to the present. I was so happy Goldie and I had been able to accomplish a "miracle" with that wonderful, smiling lady.

14

HOW TO MAKE YOUR DOG A STAR

After you have trained your dog well, you may decide that it would be nice to teach it a few tricks. Its ability to do tricks will add a dimension to your relationship and will provide mutual enjoyment for both of you. You'll gain satisfaction in being able to show off to friends just how bright and well trained your dog is, while your dog will gain satisfaction when it pleases you and earns extra attention. Youngsters especially enjoy working with a pet to teach it to do tricks.

A trick can be simple, based on an action that the dog has already learned, such as "Go to Your Place" with just a hand gesture. Or it may be something more complex, such as fetching the newspaper from the end of the driveway every day or learning how to take food from one hand but not the other.

Many of the actions a dog will learn to do in trick work are the same as the ones that dogs are trained to do in other kinds of advanced work. For example, a field-trained retriever goes through the same routine as a dog that's taught to fetch on command, and a personal-protection animal learns to speak on signal just as a movie dog does. The major differences are that we use more exaggerated and elaborate commands in teaching trick work than we do in dog shows (conformation), obedience, field, and protection training; and we often use food rewards as inducements in trick work—never in other kinds of advanced training. Otherwise they all tie together, and a dog with ability in one field often becomes adept in another. For instance, we often use dogs in theatrical work that have qualified in the Utility class in obedience because the "moves" they have to go through are the same.

If your dog is really good at learning tricks and does them well, you may even decide you want to go further in your training and turn your pet into a performer that can do stunt work.

Well-trained show dogs and animal performers often amaze the public by their "mind-reading" abilities—seeming to know just what a handler or trainer wants them to do with no visible signals. But what the public can't see is highly noticeable to a dog—a raised eyebrow, slight inclination of the head, or minimum hand gesture on the part of the trainer conveys all of the message necessary for the animal to respond.

A classic example was a dog that could apparently solve arithmetic problems: adding, subtracting, multiplying, and dividing while his owner simply sat there. Now, obviously dogs can't possibly grasp the concept of numbers and their relationships, so how could this be? When asked, even the owner seemed genuinely baffled—he apparently believed that his dog actually was a genius. After watching this performance a couple of times, I had the answer. As the dog began to bark his "answer" to each problem, the owner watched intently and nodded his head slightly with each bark. When the dog completed the correct number of barks, the man inadvertently nodded his head a bit harder and the beginnings of a smile showed on his face. The dog interpreted, correctly, that his master was now pleased with him and stopped barking—always just at the right time.

HOW TO JUDGE YOUR DOG'S ABILITY TO DO TRICKS

You cannot teach a dog to do tricks until it's mastered off-leash training well. It must always be in control, ready to focus on you and "read" your signals and commands. Tricks are not tricks if the dog has to be leashed and corrected every time it performs.

You must be realistic about your dog. All dogs are not created equal when it comes to physical ability. Some dogs are better suited for trick work than others, and you can't force a pet to perform physical tasks that it isn't cut out for. If your pet is overweight or has a skeletal problem such as a bad back or hip dysplasia, it simply cannot do a lot of things. If your dog has poor vision, it can't see your hand signals. If it's hard of hearing, verbal commands are a problem—and so forth.

Some breeds of dog have more agility and balance than others. For instance, no matter how hard it tries, a Saint Bernard, Great Pyrenees, or other large, heavy-set breed will never be able to sit up. Nor can a dachshund jump through a shoulder-high hoop. But big dogs can be great at shaking hands or fetching, and a dachsie can learn to roll over and speak with ease.

Recognize your own pet's strengths and limitations and work within them. If you try to force a dog to do something that's beyond its abilities, you'll both end up miserable.

Remember, even if your dog can't become a wonderful performer, it will still be a Star in your own household!

PREPARATION FOR TEACHING A DOG TO DO TRICKS AT HOME

There are a number of fairly easy tricks almost every dog can learn to do at home, for fun. Always begin with the dog on a leash so that you have control and the dog realizes that this is a serious training session, not a play time. Once a trick is thoroughly learned, take off the leash and gradually move farther and farther away from the dog. The aim is to have the dog perform the trick with just a command or signal.

Start work in a quiet place without distractions so that the dog can focus on you and understand fully what it is you want. As the dog becomes more proficient, you can begin to demonstrate the trick in front of family and friends.

As in any other type of training, patience, persistence, and praise are the three most important elements. Let your dog know what you want in a clear, calm way; repeat the commands and signals as often as necessary until the dog understands; and always praise the dog lavishly when it does well. Remember, every dog learns at its own pace. So be patient and understanding with your pet. Not every dog was cut out to be a Lassie or a Benji.

All the beginning tricks presented here are the basis for more complex routines that a dog needs to learn if it goes into professional work, no matter what the media. One essential difference, however, is that in "show biz" a dog must learn to respond to a visual signal alone. What's more, that signal is usually given by its handler from some distance away—from behind the camera, for instance. Commands can't be shouted out loud on a soundstage, nor can a handler get in the camera's way to adjust a dog's pose. I'll talk more about professional work later in this chapter.

SHAKE HANDS

A very popular trick to teach a dog is to shake hands on command. This trick requires no physical strength or agility and almost any dog can learn to do it.

Have your dog sit, on-leash, in front of you, and say "Give me your paw" or "Shake hands." At first the dog won't understand, so tap the center of its chest lightly with your left hand, tug up on the leash so that it becomes taut, and at the same time grab the dog's right paw in your right hand and give the command. (Always begin with the right paw. Later on, if you want to refine this trick, you can add the left and the commands "Give me your right paw" and "Give me your left paw.") The tap is a signal to the dog to pay attention, and the taut leash will cause its head to go up while its foot lifts in a reflex action.

Practice with the leash on and gradually cut back on the jerking action and chest tap until the dog has learned to respond to the verbal command alone. Then take off the leash and practice some more. If the dog regresses, go back to step one and drill again.

WAVE

Once a dog has learned to shake hands perfectly without the leash, you can teach it to wave. Again, almost every dog, no matter what its athletic ability, can learn to do this trick.

With the dog sitting facing you, say "Give me your paw," with your right hand outstretched, palm up. As the dog begins to give you its paw, draw your hand back quickly to encourage and excite the dog. Move back a little and continue to say "Give me your paw." The dog will keep waving its paw in the air in an effort to make contact with your hand. Once it begins to do this, say "Wave." Continue to practice until it has it down.

HOLDING/CARRYING AN OBJECT

This is the first step in teaching your dog to fetch an object, but many owners merely want a dog to be able to carry something—a small package, for instance, when the owner's hands are full. In order to do this, the dog has to learn to have a "soft" mouth so that the package isn't damaged. This, of course, is something that bird dogs and retrievers must also learn to do, but almost any dog can do this with practice.

First, you must have an object to work with. You can purchase a retrieving dummy made for this purpose at most pet stores. If you can't find one, a stick or even an oblong toy will do. If you use a toy, reserve it specifically for this exercise. Don't use a favorite toy, because then the dog will think that this is play time and won't concentrate on learning.

With the dog on leash and sitting at your left in Heel position, crouch down to the dog's level. Hold the object and say "Take it" at the same time that you open the dog's mouth by applying gentle but firm pressure on either side of its jaw. Place the object in the dog's mouth just behind the long canine teeth, where it fits nicely. Gently close the dog's mouth and hold it closed while you say "Hold it." Continue to say "Hold it" and if the dog starts to drop the object close its jaws again and say "No, hold it." Once the dog holds onto the object, say "Stay." Continue to say "Hold, Stay," and stand up. Reinforce the command if necessary.

After the dog has held the object for a few seconds, go back to the dog's level and say "Let go" or "Drop it," and take the object out of the dog's mouth. If the dog refuses to let go, you'll have to force its mouth open by applying pressure to either side of the jaw while you say "Drop it." Praise the dog when it releases the object.

Once your dog is able to hold an object in its mouth for several minutes, stand up and tell it to Heel. Walk in Heel position as the dog carries the object in its mouth. Practice this until your dog can carry the object for some distance with no difficulty. Always praise your dog at the end of the exercise when it gives you the object.

FETCH AN OBJECT

The next step is to teach your dog to go and pick up an object and bring it back to you. This trick is an extension of the kind of training you'd do to prepare a dog for obedience-training competition or field work.

Hunting dogs, especially retrievers, are particularly good at this. The most difficult part of this trick for most dogs to learn is to return to you and relinquish the object. Many dogs have a tendency to run around with an object in their mouths once they've picked it up. That's why you must work with your dog on a leash at first, to prevent this behavior from becoming a bad habit before you can stop it.

With the dog on a retractable leash at your side, show it the object. Be sure the dog is focusing on the object, and toss it as far as you can (but not out of reach of the extended leash). Tell the dog "Fetch it," and allow it to run to the end of the leash and pick up the object. Now say "Bring it to me," and reel in the leash until the dog is in front of you. Then tell the dog to Sit and Drop it. Take the object from the dog's mouth and praise the dog.

When the dog has mastered this so well that it can perform the action off-leash, you can teach it to go and get an object you haven't thrown. For instance, if the morning paper is lying rolled up at the end of your driveway, have the dog focus on you and make a throwing motion with your arm in the direction of the paper. Say "Fetch," and when the dog runs to the paper, say "Bring it to me," then "Drop it" when it comes back, and praise the dog lavishly when you have the paper in your hand. With some practice your dog will learn to go and get the paper each day with just a verbal command.

Many people like to carry this exercise one step further and have their pets catch Frisbees. The principle is the same, but the timing is much more difficult and takes some practice for a dog to master. It must learn to watch the Frisbee and wait until it's on a downward arc before trying to grab it. Some dogs become expert at this, and Frisbee-catching contests for dogs are held all over the country every year.

SPEAK

One of the easiest tricks for any dog to learn (except, of course, a barkless basenji) is to speak on command.

To teach this trick you need a tasty food reward—a favorite dog biscuit, for instance. Have the dog sit in front of you, and hold the food treat in your left hand between your thumb and two first fingers. Make sure that the dog is watching you, and wiggle the treat up and down while you say "Speak, (dog's name)" in an excited, happy tone of voice. As soon as the dog barks, give it the treat and praise it. This works for almost all dogs.

Now, some very low-key dogs won't bark when you hold up a treat, no matter how much you wiggle it or how enthusiastically you say "Speak." A dog like this needs a bit more excitement before it will open its mouth and say something. You may have to jump around, wave your arms in the air, or engage in some other dramatic physical motions in order to get one of these laid-back dogs to bark. Whatever excites your dog and makes it bark, do it. But be sure to say the command and give the dog both praise and a food reward when it finally does speak so it learns what you want. Repeat the exercise until the dog learns to speak on command.

DISTINGUISHING "GOOD" FOOD FROM "BAD"

This is an easy trick almost any dog can learn. It creates the illusion that your dog has the ability to make a judgment about the suitability of one kind of food over another and to choose the correct item. It will astound everyone. When I perform this trick I call it "Poison Proofing" (the dog has learned not to take food from strangers), but other people have different names.

It goes like this. A dog is offered a large, tasty piece of food by a stranger and rejects it. The owner then offers the dog a much less desirable piece of food and the dog eats it. How did that dog know enough not to take food that might be poisoned from a stranger??

Here's how it's done. With your dog sitting in front of you, put a dog biscuit of equal size in each hand. Offer the dog a biscuit with your left hand, but as soon as the dog begins to take it, close your hand and push the side of the dog's head away with your closed fist while you say "No!" Then offer the dog a biscuit with your right hand. Let it take the biscuit, and say "Good dog." Do this over and over until the dog puts two and two together and won't make a move when you offer it food from your left hand. After a while, make the food in your left hand more attractive than the food in your right. When the dog rejects this, you'll know that the trick is well learned.

Now, when a friend comes to the house, put a food treat in his left hand and ask him to offer it to your dog. The dog won't even look at the food. Then feed your dog a biscuit with your right hand. It will take it right away. Amazing! Your dog won't accept food from strangers.

SIT UP PRETTY

A trick many people want to teach their dog is to sit up on its back haunches with its front paws folded down nicely in front of it—to Sit Up Pretty. But this is not a trick every dog is able to do. In order to do this trick a dog must learn to use the muscles in its back. Some terriers, especially Bostons, Westies, and Cairns, are especially good at this, as are small poodles.

Before you begin, test your dog to see if it's capable of sitting up. With your dog on-leash, sitting in front of you, say "Sit up." Hold a food treat in your left hand and wiggle it upward, above the dog's head. Give a tug up on the leash as you speak. If the dog sits up, even for a second, give it the treat and praise it.

Now that you know that your dog is capable of sitting up and understands the command, you have to build up a threshold so that it can stay in this position for more than a second without losing its balance. Have the dog sit up, drop the leash, and step back a few steps. If the dog doesn't stay in position, go back and reinforce the command with an upward tug on the leash and another "Sit up." Hold its front paws up and say "Stay." Sometimes it's helpful to place the dog in a corner when you practice, so that the walls on either side give the illusion of support and help the dog keep its balance. The more the dog practices, the better its muscle control will become and the longer it will be able to sit up.

DANCE

Again, this trick cannot be performed by large dogs, heavy-bodied dogs, or by those with short legs. What's more, it entails the use of leg and back muscles, and some dogs may need to develop these muscles before they can dance unaided. Small terriers, poodles, and toy dogs are usually best at dancing and learn it with ease. If a pet is very good at this and stands up on its hind legs all the time, the main thing that you want to teach it is to learn to dance on command.

With the dog sitting in front of you on-lead, tease it with a food treat held up in the air above its head. This time you want it not to sit up but to stand up on its back legs and turn around. As you dangle the food above its head, pull up steadily on the leash and say "Up, dance."

Once the dog is able to stand up easily without falling over, move the hand holding the leash around in a clockwise circle so the dog turns around in a dancing motion to follow it while you say "Dance." Praise the dog and give it a treat. Continue to practice, giving the command each time so soon the dog can get up and dance without the support of the leash.

ROLL OVER

The last at-home trick I'll describe is roll over. This is a bit harder than some others. It shouldn't be attempted at all if your dog has any kind of spine or joint problems, but otherwise almost any dog can learn to perform this trick.

With a leash on the dog, tell it to go into the Down position in front of you (see chapters 5 and 6); hold a food treat in your left hand in front of the dog's nose. If you want the dog to roll to the right, say "Roll over" and take one sideways step to your right. At first you will probably have to show the dog what you want and physically shift it over onto its right side. Then take one more step while you continue to give the command. Again, you'll probably need to help the dog over. Continue to do this until the dog gets the idea. Then try with only the command and a circling hand motion.

Once your dog has learned to roll over in one direction, you can teach it to roll the other way so it will roll over a couple of times one way and then roll back in the opposite direction, back to its starting position.

STAGESTRUCK

If your dog becomes really adept at doing tricks and you both enjoy the process of learning and performing, you may decide that you want to go further, just as producer Sharen Klein did with her Maltese, Max, who recently appeared on the *Today* show. Your pet could learn to be able to pose for print advertisements or go on to theatrical work on stage and movies, or on television in soap operas, commercials, and dramas. If show business isn't your thing, you can teach your dog to entertain children and adults in schools, libraries, hospitals, and nursing homes.

Whatever the type of performing work, your dog must be taught in a precise, specific manner so it is always in complete control and ready to focus on you and follow your commands no matter what the distractions. Remember, performing at home is entirely different from performing in front of dozens (or hundreds) of strangers and possibly a lot of pieces of camera equipment and other machinery. Don't ask your dog to become a performer unless you are willing to take the time to prepare it thoroughly for the job.

Each action you will teach your dog is an extension and refinement of a lesson it learned in basic on- and off-lead obedience. But this time your pet will have to learn to perform these actions with just a hand signal from you. And it will have to learn to focus on you all the time, no matter what else is going on, so it can interpret your signals from a distance and act on them immediately. I'll tell you how to do some of these things.

The techniques I'll outline below are based on my own years of experience training over one thousand different dogs that have appeared in the media on at least ten thousand occasions.

PERFECT CONTROL—PLATFORM WORK

The first thing your dog has to learn is to stay quietly in place when you walk away from it. This is an advanced level of the Stay command that you taught your dog in obedience. It also needs to learn to work comfortably on a table or platform. This is necessary for a lot of photographic work, but a dog will also often work on a table so that everyone can see it when it is on stage or giving a performance in a large room, for instance. Many stunts can be performed easily on a table or platform.

First you need a sturdy, nonwobbling platform of some kind. A low coffee table, large chair, or a grooming table all are fine. You also need a a nonskid mat of some type such as a large rubber bathtub mat with suction cups or a rubber-backed door mat. Whatever kind of mat you choose, it needs to be large enough for the dog to stand on comfortably, but it should also be portable—you have to take it along with you when you go out to perform in public.

With a retractable leash on, place the dog on the mat on the platform. Tell the dog to Sit/Stay, and walk six feet away. If the dog begins to move, go back and reinforce the command. When the dog stays, give the Down command from the end of the leash. Then give the Sit/Stay command and return to the dog. Praise it.

Repeat this as often as necessary until the dog does it perfectly. Then begin to move farther away. Gradually increase the distance between you and the dog until you are at the end of the leash—twenty-six feet away. Once the dog has gone through the routine perfectly at this distance, drop the leash and begin again— first at six feet, and so on. Finally you can undo the leash entirely.

Before you go on to the next step, provide some distractions while you practice with the dog in place on the platform. You want to be sure it remains quiet, no matter what.

WATCH THE BIRDIE!

Once the dog is able to do Down/Stay and Sit/Stay from a distance while it's on a platform, it has to learn to "pose." You want to make it look alert and happy, at the camera, just as I taught the dog models for Ilene Hochberg's takeoffs on the fashion magazines, "Dogue" and "Vanity Fur."

From a distance of at least twenty feet, clap your hands so that the dog focuses on you. If the dog misinterprets this action and begins to move, you have to go back and reinforce the Stay command. Once you have the dog's attention, squeeze a squeaky toy, or make mouth sounds. A couple of the latter that always work well are a chirping sound or the noise you make when you kiss loudly into your closed fist. The dog will look right at you, cock its head, and perk up its ears so it appears enthusiastic and charismatic.

TAKE/HOLD/CARRY/DROP AN OBJECT

This next stunt utilizes a number of commands your dog has already learned, but it puts them all together into a complete routine that the dog can perform while you give hand commands from a distance.

In order to do this, you must first teach your dog to be able to hold any kind of an object at all without damaging it. In the tricks section, you used a retrieving dummy or toy to teach your dog to hold and bring an object to you. Now you must practice this trick using all sorts of objects of different shapes and materials—metal keys, a tube of toothpaste, a bunch of flowers, and so forth. You want your dog to be able to hold anything the advertising agency might want. I remember once when I was working on a sneaker ad with a little dog. The producer wanted the dog to hold a big athletic sneaker in his mouth, but it was too big for him to get a grip on. Finally we worked it out—the dog held one lace and let the sneaker dangle. The picture was a real winner!

I sometimes demonstrate the ability of my German shorthaired pointer, Eli, to carry anything in his mouth without breaking it. I tell him to Stay, put a raw egg on the floor, and tell him to "Fetch it." He goes and gets the egg, brings it to me, sits, and I say "Drop it." I take the egg from his mouth, and then I crack it open to prove to the audience that it was a real raw egg.

Once you've taught your dog to hold anything at all in its mouth, you have to review the Fetch sequence that I ran through previously. But this time you must have the dog fetch all kinds of objects, and it has to learn to come back to you, sit, and drop the object with just hand signals from you. The Come signal is the same beckoning arm and hand gesture you learned in Chapter

6. Sit is also the same upward-scoop gesture from basic on-leash obedience.

In this sequence, the dog will also learn to drop the object as soon as it sits, without any command. To program this you begin by simply taking the object out of the dog's mouth each time it comes back and sits in front of you. Soon the drop becomes automatic.

You've seen this sequence in films and television many times—when Lassie runs off and fetches a baby kitten and brings it to Tommy, for instance. In one episode of the soap opera *As the World Turns,* Blondie, a cute shaggy dog of mine that's a cross between a golden retriever and a briard, had to perform a complex version of this routine with hundreds of people on the set and numerous distractions. There was an elaborate wedding scene and Blondie ran across the room, between peoples' legs, picked up a shoe, ran back toward the camera with a boy chasing her, and dropped the shoe at one of the actor's feet. She had to do all of this with only hand signals from me while I stood twenty feet away in back of the cameras.

FACIAL EXPRESSIONS/THEATRICAL BARKING

Sometimes a dog seems to be able to make different facial expressions at will. Many dogs smile when they are greeting favorite people—there's a theory that a dog that does this is emulating the expression it often sees on its owner's face. Others grin and grimace in various ways. If your dog naturally does any of these expressions, it's easy to teach it to turn on these "emotions" on command. Simply do whatever you normally would do in order to bring about the expression, say "Smile," or whatever when the dog responds, and give it a treat. Soon your dog will understand and be programmed to put on the desired expression on command. When you want to transfer the command to a silent signal, you can do this by smiling yourself in an exaggerated grimace, for example.

I've already discussed how to make your dog speak on command. But theatrical barking sometimes takes on another dimension. Some dramatic situations call for a dog to bare its teeth. You can do this training yourself, but it's very difficult and best left to professionals. Some dogs naturally pull back their lips and show their teeth in a grimace when they bark however. If your dog tends to do this, you can encourage it to do it on command by saying "Show teeth" at the same time you curl your hand up like a claw. Reward the dog each time it shows its teeth and soon you'll be able to work with only the hand signal. As a reminder during the learning process, you can tuck your dog's lip up with your fingers when it barks.

Pinka, my Doberman pinscher, was taught to do this and has happily bared her teeth on the soap operas *Guiding Light* and *One Life to Live*. She was also in the movie *The Chantilly Express* with Carol Alt and was featured in an article in the magazine *Manhattan, Inc.*

Pinka was originally taught to show her teeth when I trained her to be a personal-protection dog for a diplomat. When her owner died, I decided to turn Pinka from a guard dog into a performer. Because I had trained her originally, I knew she was very bright and basically good-natured. So I deprogrammed her by socializing her. I gave her leash corrections every time she acted aggressively to emphasize that this was no longer the way I wanted her to act. And when she behaved on cue, I gave her a lot of praise and food rewards. Food rewards are never given to a dog that is being trained for serious protection work, so she soon realized she was only play-acting now. Today Pinka performs all of the things she was trained to do in deadly earnest, from showing her teeth to grabbing onto an actor's sleeve and hanging on, but now she knows that it's all in fun. She's completely trustworthy with everyone.

CRAWLING

You've seen the scene—Lassie or Benji is crawling through the underbrush toward the place where the kidnappers are holding Timmy or whoever.

How do you teach a dog to crawl? It certainly doesn't come naturally to dogs, so it takes some work to accomplish.

Have your dog on-leash in Down position next to your side. Take one step forward and say "Heel." The dog will get up and begin to take a step. Immediately stop and say "Down." The dog will go down again. Keep on switching from Heel to Down and back again to condition the dog to this action.

Once the dog begins to get the idea when it's at your side, go out in front of the dog with the leash still on and do the same thing. This time, as you give the verbal commands, make a walking motion with two fingers of your left hand, and then say "Crawl." Keep doing this as you walk backward and make the dog follow you. If the dog stops crawling, correct it with a snap of the leash, say "Crawl," and make the finger motions. Continue to do this until the dog can crawl for six feet, then gradually go farther and farther back until you can remove the leash. Eventually the dog should be able to crawl with just a hand signal.

JUMPING

The final stunt I'll describe here is jumping. This, too, is an extension of an exercise that's part of obedience trials.

Begin with your dog on leash in Heel position. Set up a knee-high hurdle made of sticks (two uprights, one across the top). Have the dog Heel and step over the hurdle as you say "Hup" or "Over" to the dog enthusiastically. After the dog goes over the hurdle, have it sit, and praise it.

Next, stand in alignment with the hurdle and the dog

on one side of it. Encourage the dog to jump over the hurdle and sit on the other side with the commands "Hup" or "Over" and "Sit." Again, praise the dog when it does this.

Then, with a retractable leash, have the dog Sit/Stay on one side of the hurdle while you stand on the other side and call it to Come. Guide it over the hurdle with the leash, if necessary, and have it come and sit in front of you. Praise it. Move back until the dog will do this from a distance and then without the leash.

After the dog has mastered this form of jumping, squat down with the dog sitting on your left, facing its platform. Extend your arms away from your body and make a circle with them, right arm on the bottom. Turn your face to look away from the dog, pat the platform, and tell the dog to Come. It will leap through your arms to the platform. Give it a reward and praise it. Gradually you can move your arm-circle higher and higher off the ground until you're standing upright. Then have the dog perform the jump without the platform.

Once you've mastered this on one side, turn and make a circle with your left arm on the bottom.

LIGHTS, CAMERA, ACTION

The number of other stunts you can teach your dog are far too many to describe here. After you put together a routine, practice as much as possible in front of an audience in order to accustom your dog to distractions. You can volunteer to give shows at school fairs, for the benefit of local charities, and so forth. The more practice the better.

Take pictures of your dog in action and put a portfolio together to show to potential clients. Certain agents specialize in working with professional animals and getting them auditions. If you're serious about doing professional work with your dog, contact an agent and talk to her about the possibilities.

If you and your dog do get a chance to audition for

a job, be sure to pack a bag to take with you. You'll need the practice mat, your dog's favorite noisemakers to get its attention, and treats for rewards and to help your pet focus on you. Also pack a comb, brush, and any other grooming aids you might need to give your dog a quick touch-up on the set.

APPENDIX A

THE WOLF SANCTUARY

Mariah taught me to know and love wolves. Others who also wish to support these wonderful animals may do so through this organization.

In 1971, the late Dr. Marlin Perkins, his wife, Carol, and a group of friends founded the Wild Canid Survival and Research Center (WCSRC), known informally as the Wolf Sanctuary. It is located in Eureka, Missouri, on fifty acres leased from Washington University's Tyson Research Center.

The Wolf Sanctuary is a private, nonprofit organization dedicated to the preservation of the wolf and its habitat through education and captive breeding. In recent years, WCSRC has focused its efforts on the severely endangered red and Mexican wolves and is presently the only facility in the United States that breeds both of these wolves for the U.S. Fish and Wildlife Service. The large, isolated enclosures at the sanctuary ensure limited human contact, so the animals are prime candidates for approved reintroduction into the wild.

WCSRC relies almost solely on memberships, gifts,

Adopt-a-Wolf and Bone Fund programs, benefits, tours, and special events for its existence.

Wolves continue to be in great need of positive action to save them from extinction. If you are interested in more information about wolves, the Sanctuary, or wish to make a donation, write to:

Carol M. Perkins
WCSRC
P.O. Box 760
Eureka, MO 63025

APPENDIX B

DOG SHOWS AND TRIALS. SCHUTZHUNDS.

When a dog shows a particular aptitude, an owner may decide to continue to work closely with it and go on to obedience or field trials, depending on the dog's abilities. Or, if the dog is an especially good example of its breed, an owner may want to enter it in shows. In each case, basic obedience serves as a foundation.

PREPARING FOR SHOWS OR TRIALS

Although it is important for dogs to be bred in order to meet the specifications required for success in shows and trials, people often go overboard in their desire to breed "the perfect dog." For instance, show dogs are often bred with too much emphasis on looks and not enough concern for temperament and practical behavior. On the other hand, working dogs are frequently bred with too much emphasis on working abilities and too little concern for conformation—beauty and looks.

When I bred German shorthaired pointers in my own breeding program I used what I like to call a triple-crown approach. I wanted my dogs to have three qualities—excellent looks/conformation; a natural ability to work in the fields; and a good temperament, so they were able to accept training well. These qualities complement each other, and, in my opinion, the "perfect dog" is a combination of these traits.

As you read about the steps and exercises a dog must go through in the shows and trials described here, it will be obvious that it must be very well trained and in complete accord with its owner or handler in order to compete successfully. If you anticipate entering your dog in any competitions, it's important to start to train it early and practice sufficiently so the dog is well prepared.

A dog that's going to compete must also be in excellent physical condition. A treadmill can be very useful to help a dog stay fit and trim, build up stamina, and learn to move better and develop the proper gait. (See Chapter 8 for how to teach a dog to use a treadmill.)

DOG SHOWS

The purpose of purebred dog shows is to recognize, improve, and continue breed standards. Shows are held under the aegis of either a breed club or kennel club. Membership in a breed club, as the name suggests, is confined to only one breed of dog. Kennel club membership is open to all pure breeds. Shows are held under American Kennel Club (AKC) rules.

The best-known dog show in this country is the Westminster Kennel Club Show, held every February in New York City's Madison Square Garden. Westminster, as it is familiarly called, was formed in 1877. Its members were fashionable society dog owners. Now participants in the show come from all walks of life and many of them are professional dog breeders. Although some dogs are trained and shown by professional handlers, owners themselves often work with and show their own dogs.

Westminster is one of only six benched shows in the United States. A benched show is one in which the dogs, grouped by breed, are on display throughout the two-day show. Visitors can walk around the huge hall and see all of the dogs and their owners or handlers. In a nonbenched show, a dog is required to be present only during its actual judging event.

In a dog show each individual animal is judged on the basis of how well it conforms to specific breed standards. Breed standards are established by the AKC and are very exact. A dog is said to Stand for Conformation in a show. To compete in a show, a dog must be intact (not spayed or castrated).

■ MATCH SHOWS ■

A match show is the first step for any dog wanting to become a champion. Match shows are actually practice shows in which dogs can prepare for point shows. They are open to beginners, and puppies often compete in them. No points are earned in match shows.

■ POINT SHOWS ■

In a point show, a dog competes first against other dogs of the same breed. If it wins in its breed, it goes on to compete against other individual breed winners in its group (for example, Working Group; see Chapter 2 for a list of AKC-recognized breeds in each group). Then the group winners compete against each other.

Each time a dog places in a point show it earns one to five points. When it has accumulated fifteen points it becomes a champion and can put "Ch." before its name.

OBEDIENCE TRIALS

Obedience trials were established by the AKC around 1910 and were patterned after the training police and army dogs received in Europe. As opposed to dog shows, in which each dog is individually compared to a breed standard, dogs in obedience trials are judged by how well they compare to other dogs when they perform the various tests.

Each exercise in an obedience trial has a practical application in dog behavior and usage. The purpose of obedience trials is to teach a dog to obey at all times, despite distractions.

To compete in an obedience trial, a dog must be at least six months old and either a purebred registered with the AKC or part of an AKC-registered litter. However, owners of non-AKC-registered dogs can apply for an Indefinite Listing Privilege (I.L.P.) to compete in obedience trials and/or tracking tests. As opposed to shows, castrated and spayed dogs *are* allowed to compete in obedience trials.

The three classes of obedience trials can be compared to grade school, high school, and college.

■ **NOVICE CLASSES** ■

There are two levels of Novice class, A and B. A dog must compete first in A before it can go on to B. A dog can earn a maximum of 200 points in the Novice class, and, in order to go on to the next level, Open class, it must win at least 170 points in three shows with three different judges. When it has accomplished this, a dog earns the title of Champion and "C.D." appears after its name.

Exercises in the Novice class include: Heel on leash, with a Figure 8; Stand for Examination off-leash; Heel off-leash; Recall; Long Sit (one minute); and Long Down (three minutes).

■ **OPEN CLASS** ■

This is the next step, in which a dog can also earn a maximum of 200 points. When this step is successfully completed a dog earns the title C.D.X. (Champion Dog Excellent). Exercises include: Heel off-leash; Drop on Recall; Retrieve on Flat (level ground); Retrieve Over High Jump; Broad Jump—over an obstacle; Long Sit (three minutes with handler out of sight); and Long Down (five minutes with handler out of sight).

■ UTILITY CLASS ■

This is the final obedience trial. To enter this level, a dog must have earned its C.D.X. Again, 200 points can be earned to get a title U.D. (Utility Dog). Exercises include: Scent Discrimination—a dog must choose a leather article with its master's scent on it; Scent Discrimination—a dog must choose a metal article with its master's scent on it; Directed Retrieve—handler signals dog from a distance which article to retrieve; Signal Exercise—dog goes through a series of exercises with commands given from a distance by hand signal only; Directed Jumping—dog is directed from a distance with hand signals only to jump a hurdle; Group Examination—dogs stand in a row together, unleashed, with owners/handlers at a distance and allow themselves to be examined by a judge.

A Tracking Degree (T.D.) follows a Utility Dog degree. To earn this, a dog must follow a scent trail laid by judges. Each dog follows the trail individually. To prepare for this trial, dogs are trained to refine their ability to differentiate between scents and to work regardless of distractions.

FIELD TRIALS

Bird dogs compete in field trials to display their field qualities. The first recorded field trial was for setters and pointers and took place near Stafford, England, in the spring of 1866. No studbooks existed then, but this competition gave birth to the setting of standards and the improvement of bird dog breeds. In the United States, the first field trial was held in Memphis, Tennessee, on October 8, 1874.

Now there are over three hundred sporting organizations and breed clubs in the United States that sponsor recognized bird dog trials annually.

There are three distinct types of bird dog.

Pointers locate game and signal the hunter. They must hold the point as the bird is flushed and shot and then retrieve the bird for the hunter. Pointing breeds include: pointers (German shorthaired, German wirehaired, wirehaired pointing griffon); setters (Irish, English, Gordon); Vizsla; Brittany spaniel; and Weimaraner.

Flushing breeds locate game and instantly flush it. They then sit or stand quietly while the game is shot and return to their owners on signal. All flushing breeds are spaniels: clumber; American and English cockers; field; Sussex; Welsh and English springers.

Retrieving breeds are all swimmers. They have webbed toes and thick, oily coats. They stand and wait while a bird is flushed and shot and then retrieve it. Kinds of retrievers are: golden, curly-coated, flat-coated, Chesapeake Bay, labrador. American and Irish water spaniels are also retrievers.

Versatile breeds perform all of the actions described above. They point, flush, and retrieve both birds and small mammals. Breeds that fit into this catagory are the wirehaired pointing griffon, German shorthaired and wirehaired pointers, Vizsla, and Weimaraner.

SCHUTZHUNDS

A Schutzhund is a dog that's trained intensively to be an expert in three areas, tracking, obedience, and protection. Schutzhund training has been practiced for many years in Europe and is now becoming very popular in the United States. This is probably a reflection of the perceived need to have family dogs that also act as protectors. Breeds most often used in Schutzhund work are working dogs—German shepherds, Belgian sheepdogs, Airedales, Bouvier des Flandres, boxers, Doberman pinschers, giant schnauzers, and rottweilers. Other breeds suitable for the work are Labrador retrievers, Weimaraners, briards, Bernese mountain dogs, collies, bull and Staffordshire terriers, and some giant dogs. The single most important desirable characteristic is a willingness to work and ability to accept obedience training.

Trials for Schutzhunds are on several difficulty levels and include tests to measure a dog's ability to track, advanced off-leash obedience, and various protection tests including search, attack, courage, and endurance tests. A dog gains points according to its performance in these tests and can win a Schutzhund I, II, III, A.D. (endurance test), or F.H. (advanced tracking degree).

OTHER TRIALS

There are several other categories in which trials are conducted and dogs can compete to earn points and titles.

Scent hounds use their superior scenting ability to track and tree small game and also to locate lost people. Recently, scent hounds have been trained to work with police to sniff out drugs, bombs, illegal goods, and so forth. In addition to the well-known scenting breeds such as bloodhounds and coonhounds, other scent hounds include beagles, basenjis, Norwegian elkhounds, and Rhodesian ridgebacks.

Sight hounds, or coursing dogs, locate their prey with a highly developed sense of sight that includes an intensified sensibility to motion. Thus, they will chase anything that moves within their range of vision. Greyhounds and whippets are the best-known sight hounds. Others are Afghans, borzois, Irish wolfhounds, salukis, and Scottish deerhounds.

Herding dogs, such as sheepdogs, Bernese mountain

dogs, briards, komondors, pulis, and so forth, have been bred to have very strong visual and auditory senses. A herding dog can respond from a distance of over a mile to a visual signal a shepherd gives with his staff, or to a high-pitched whistle command.

APPENDIX C

DOG CLUBS AND ASSOCIATIONS. SEARCH-AND-RESCUE ASSOCIATIONS. PUBLICATIONS.

DOG CLUBS AND ASSOCIATIONS

For a list of AKC-affiliated individual breed and kennel clubs in a specific geographical location, and/or 130 national clubs, write to:

AKC Library, 51 Madison Avenue, New York, NY 10010

Others, not AKC-affiliated:

American Sighthound Field Assn.
Lester Pekarski
P.O. Box 1293-N
Woodstock, GA 30188

American Working Terrier Assn.
Jean Clark
RFD 1, Box 279
Franklin, NH 03235

International Sled Dog Racing Assn.
Donna Jawley
P.O. Box 446
Norman, ID 83848-0446

International Weight Pulling Assn.
P.O. Box 994
Greeley, CO 80632

North American Flyball Assn.
Mike Randall
1342 Jeff Street
Ypsilanti, MI 48198

North American Hunting Retriever Assn.
P.O. Box 154
Swanton, VT 05488

North American Versatile Hunting Dog Assn.
John O'Brien
4302 Route 21
Marion, NY 14505

North American Working Dog Assn.
7318 Brennans Dr.
Dallas, TX 75214
(214) 821-3327

United Schutzhund Clubs of America
3704 Lemay Ferry Road
St. Louis, MO 63125
(314) 894-3431

SEARCH-AND-RESCUE DOGS

American Rescue Dog Association
P.O. Box 151
Chester, NY 10918

National Association for Search and Rescue
P.O. Box 3709
Fairfax, VA 22038

PUBLICATIONS

Many breed and kennel clubs have their own publications.

Monthly publications that cover all breeds and a listing of trials and shows are:

DOG FANCY
Fancy Publications Inc.
3 Burroughs
Irvine, CA 92718

DOG WORLD
Maclean Hunter Publishing Company
29 North Wacker Drive
Chicago, IL 60606-3298

PURE BRED DOGS/AMERICAN
KENNEL GAZETTE
American Kennel Club
51 Madison Avenue
New York, NY 10010
This also includes a monthly supplement: *Events*, a calendar of shows, trials, and tests.

INDEX